CHEMICAL ALERT! A COMMUNITY ACTION HANDBOOK

CHEMICAL ALERT!

A COMMUNITY ACTION HANDBOOK

Edited by Marvin S. Legator and Sabrina F. Strawn

 UNIVERSITY OF TEXAS PRESS, AUSTIN

Revised and expanded edition, 1993

Requests for permission to reproduce material from this work should be sent to Permissions, University of Texas Press, Box 7819, Austin, Texas 78713-7819.

∞   The paper used in this publication meets the minimum requirements of American National Standard for Information Sciences—Permanence of Paper for Printed Library Materials, ANSI Z39.48-1984.

For reasons of economy and speed this volume has been printed from computer disks furnished by the editors, who assume full responsibility for its contents.

An earlier version of this book was published as *The Health Detective's Handbook: A Guide to the Investigation of Environmental Health Hazards by Nonprofessionals*, edited by Marvin S. Legator, Barbara L. Harper, and Michael J. Scott (© 1985 by The Johns Hopkins University Press).

Library of Congress Cataloging-in-Publication Data

Chemical alert : a community action handbook / edited by Marvin S. Legator and
    Sabrina F. Strawn. — Rev. expanded ed.
        p.   cm.
    Rev. ed. of: The Health detective's handbook / edited by Marvin S. Legator, Barbara
L. Harper and Michael J. Scott.
    Includes bibliographical references and index.
    ISBN 0-292-74675-X (cloth : alk. paper). — ISBN 0-292-74676-8 (pbk. : alk. paper)
    1. Environmental health—United States—Handbooks, manuals, etc. 2. Environ-
mental protection—United States—Handbooks, manuals, etc. 3. Environmentalists—
United States—Handbooks, manuals, etc. I. Legator, Marvin S., date. II. Strawn,
Sabrina F.(Sabrina Fay), date. III. Health detective's handbook.
    [DNLM: 1. Consumer Participation—methods—handbooks. 2. Data Collection—
methods—handbooks. 3. Environmental Exposure—handbooks. 4. Epidemiologic
Methods—handbooks. WA 39 C5174] RA566.22.C35 1993
363.1—dc20
DNLM/DLC
for Library of Congress   92-25304
                                                                              CIP

CONTENTS

FIGURES

TABLES

ACKNOWLEDGMENTS

The editors wish to thank all the contributors to this handbook; our administrative staff who helped in the preparation of the manuscript — Glenda McKinney, Melinda Duroux, Pamela Bosarge, and Darnell Kea; and Jon R. Blyth of the Charles Stewart Mott Foundation, who provided financial support and much more.

INTRODUCTION

Marvin S. Legator, Sabrina F. Strawn, and Barbara L. Harper

In 1985, *The Health Detective's Handbook*, the early version of this book, was launched with much enthusiasm and optimism. We were convinced that lay persons could bring to bear the power of science in addressing their concerns: were they sicker than other communities? Could this be related to their physical environment? It was our further hope that those who could verify that a problem truly existed could use this information to spur further study by health agencies. Once a problem was recognized, governmental or legal action could be taken to mitigate the harms and risks.

Today we are even more convinced of the power of individuals, working together. Every year the list of victories grows longer. Individuals see a health threat or potential threat, join in with a group of neighbors, then fight this threat to their families, homes, and communities. Evidence that there is a problem can be helpful in the organizing effort, but the victories are based on moral arguments, not scientific ones.

EVIDENCE OF HEALTH EFFECTS

Community groups are always asked to prove harm. But the scientific tool available for use, namely traditional epidemiology, is crude and insensitive in most of these cases. In 1989, the Agency for Toxic Substances and Disease Registry sponsored a conference on epidemiology in a community setting. Papers presented were compiled as Supplement No. 1 (July 1990) of the *American Journal of Epidemiology*.

The keynote speaker, Dr. Kenneth Rothman, noted the near impossibility of finding the causes of clusters of disease from environmental exposure. Affected neighborhoods or groups often are too small to allow for "useful" epidemiological study. Reported effects and exposures are varied and tend to be low. The publicity generated by a perception of a possible effect makes unbiased gathering of information very difficult.

Another speaker, Dr. Raymond R. Neutra, claimed to be less pessimistic. Some characteristics of certain disease clusters can make them amenable to solution. These can be loosely grouped into two categories: 1) the exposure must be such that it can be identified with a particular agent and 2) the substance and illness it may be causing must have characteristics that help make the results of the study statistically significant. These too may be impossible conditions to satisfy. Exposure is most often to a variety of substances and these chemicals rarely cause unique conditions. Instead, expected effects usually are increases in background rates of common illnesses.

While epidemiology itself is a relatively insensitive tool in these cases, those wielding this tool often will have an institutional bias against finding effects. A positive study, it is feared, will lead to unpleasant political effects ranging from anger against the administration that allowed the harmful activity to demands for something to be done now. In most cases, if an agency did find positive results it would be unable to alleviate the situation. Economic effects such as depressed housing markets and lost development also may occur.

There are several techniques public health agencies can use to *not* find problems. As noted above, epidemiological studies are relatively insensitive, especially considering the small groups of exposed persons and uncertain exposures characteristic of community problems. One can further minimize the chances of finding positive results in the choice of the control group and exposed group. When differences are found, lifestyle factors, such as smoking habits are often mentioned as probable causes. (See Ozonoff and Boden, 1987.)

The U.S. Centers for Disease Control has conducted over one hundred cancer cluster investigations over two decades. None revealed any clear cause (Caldwell, 1990). There are 35 chemicals or processes that the International Agency for Research on Cancer has judged to be known human carcinogens. Only one was found through reports of cancer in a community. We also know that industry is making little effort to identify possible carcinogens. A survey of the U.S. manufacturers of 75 animal carcinogens in general commerce found only eight were the subject of completed epidemiological studies and five of ongoing studies (Karstadt and Bobal, 1982).

The Health Detective's Handbook recommended that health survey results be used to request further study by state and local agencies. For the reasons noted above, we now believe that further formal study may be counterproductive to a goal of remedial action. We now believe that more attention should be paid to organizing your community.

USING THE TOOLS AT HAND

We think it essential for the community to gather as much information as possible and practical about the problems they may face. Hence this book. If you want something done because you feel your neighborhood suffers ill health, the information you develop through techniques discussed in this book will help you make a plausible argument. This manual also can focus your efforts. For example, you may find indications that the possible source of exposure is your drinking water rather than the industrial facility nearby. The epidemiology that we are advocating may provide hints that traditional epidemiology cannot because agencies and academic institutions often do not have the interest, money, or human resources to investigate every potential problem. Epidemiology is a labor-intensive field. The motivated members of a community, who believe they may have a problem, are in the best position to ensure that the needed hours of labor are given to the project.

You are not seeking the holy grail. On the one hand, no study can provide unequivocal evidence that will immediately prompt industry, agencies, or politicians to act. On the other hand, you are not exploring an always illusive goal. A review of data on hazardous waste sites found indications of health effects in spite of the limitations of epidemiology and the few sites studied (National Research Council, 1991). Epidemiological studies reviewed provide evidence of increased rates of spontaneous abortions, birth defects, neurological impairment, and cancer in some populations living near hazardous waste sites.

There is a tradition that those who wish for change in the accustomed way of doing things bear the burden of proof for the need for change. That has meant that communities questioning industrial emissions or the siting of facilities have been asked to show that they have been or will be hurt. But unquestionable proof will never exist. That kind of evidence is almost never possible in the setting of a traditional epidemiological study. Even if it were possible, it would take years; so that while information accumulates, so does the number of victims. Many successful groups challenge the burden of proof. They point out that our society has accepted practices based on inadequate evidence. While industry has the right to operate and to seek profits, the community has the right to clean air, water, and soil. This argument will be one of your most powerful tools.

USING THIS HANDBOOK

Epidemiology is the study of the various factors determining how often, in how many people, and in which people disease occurs. This manual will guide you step by step through a descriptive study of the overall health of members of your community, geared toward environmental issues. We believe there are usually enough resources within the community itself, in terms of time, energy, common sense, and intelligence, that a high-quality general health survey can be done at the local level. You should be able to conclude either that there are no adverse health effects owing to toxic substances or that there really is an increase in diseases or conditions that could be related to toxic substances.

We have tried to write so we can be understood by an intelligent person with a high-school education or by a person who has had some college education but not in the biological sciences. We recommend using a medical dictionary, particularly for terms relating to health effects or diseases, but most actual diseases are given by name only and not by detailed description to avoid self-diagnosis by the general reader.

The need for a manual on environmental investigation for nonprofessionals has become apparent as communities have sought help to investigate perceived health problems. In some instances citizens in neighborhoods close to industrial sites, such as petrochemical plants or waste disposal areas, have become concerned about the risk these sites represent to the health of their families. In other instances members of a community have become aware that several of their neighbors were affected by the same illness. In almost all cases, the concerned citizens have been frustrated in their attempts to interest local or state agencies in assisting them. Limited budgets and lack of resources restrict the ability of government agencies to respond to such concerns.

Is there an alternative to traditional epidemiologic studies? Can a meaningful data base be generated without the costly traditional approach to community studies? We believe that such an alternative approach exists. Motivated citizens, given the proper guidance, can generate meaningful data. They can, with professional support, determine the probability that a problem is present. The goal of this manual is to provide guidelines to permit citizens to pursue such a study of their own.

CHEMICAL ALERT! A COMMUNITY ACTION HANDBOOK

ONE

YOU CAN DO IT TOO

Identification of Health Hazards
by Nonprofessionals

Marvin S. Legator

Professionals in any scientific field, whose expertise stems from years of specialized training, often give the impression that what they do and understand is unique to their calling. They write scholarly articles for journals aimed at a professional audience, they give lectures to colleagues that are intended to express and refine the complexities of their discipline, and they develop highly analytical skills in criticizing their own work and the work of others. As a consequence their techniques, and even their terminology, may seem incomprehensible to the uninitiated.

I do not wish to minimize the importance of refined and specialized knowledge. An epidemiologist, for example, must be familiar with experimental design, sampling techniques, statistical methods, and the biology of organisms. I do suggest, however, that trained professionals do not have exclusive rights to their areas of investigation and that untrained people can, in fact, perform early, simple epidemiologic studies that will be as sound as those performed by professionals and that certainly will not compromise the scientific integrity of later investigations by professionals.

In discussing the myth of exclusivity that is so pervasive in the scientific world, I am reminded of an episode that occurred while I was a branch chief with the Food and Drug Administration in Washington, D.C. Our office was involved in research on a toxic substance produced by a mold that grows on various crops, especially nuts. I thought our research would be expedited if someone from our office could learn to detect this toxin in various food products. Since analytical chemists at the Food and Drug Administration had developed a sensitive method for doing this, a chemical assay, I asked the chief chemist if they could teach the technique to a member of my staff. The chief chemist agreed to train someone, provided the trainee was a senior organic chemist who could devote at least three weeks to learning the procedure.

Unfortunately, I did not have a senior organic chemist that I could spare for three weeks, or any senior scientist who could be reassigned for

that length of time. I did, however, have an extremely intelligent laboratory helper. I had always been amazed at Mary's intelligence and was convinced that if she had the proper education she would have been an excellent scientist. So I asked Mary to put on her lab coat, go to work with
the chief FDA chemist, and do her best to learn to perform the assay.

Two weeks later the FDA chemist called to say that Mary was one of
the brightest chemists he had ever worked with and that she was qualified to perform the assay after only ten days of instruction. To this day
I have never had the courage to tell him that the senior organic chemist
who learned the assay in record time was my laboratory helper.

I have often been impressed by the speed with which a layperson can
comprehend scientific procedures and principles, and I have become
convinced that a person of average intelligence can carry on a community survey and collect epidemiologic data that will stand up to scientific scrutiny. The methods outlined in this manual are based upon this
assumption. In fact, the first investigations into the toxic effects of
many chemicals have been conducted by workers who were not epidemiologists—in many instances, not even scientists. An epidemiologist at
the National Cancer Institute has published an article that documents
the discoveries of human teratogens, carcinogens, and mutagens by nonepidemiologists (Miller 1978). The following cases demonstrate specific
methods that have been used by nonepidemiologists to investigate the
health hazards of certain chemicals.

THALIDOMIDE

Thalidomide, marketed in the early 1960s as a tranquilizer and anti-
nausea medication, is now known to produce limb reduction deformi-
ties (phocomelia) in the fetus when taken by a woman at an early stage
of pregnancy. This side effect became known when an Australian obste-
trician, Dr. McBride, observed that within a short period three of his
patients who had received the drug during early pregnancy gave birth
to infants with phocomelia. Dr. McBride, who had never before seen
this deformity in his practice, eventually attributed it to the thalidomide. Later another investigator conducted more extensive studies that
confirmed McBride's findings (Oakley 1975).

THE THALIDOMIDE LESSON

In this case, simple observation of a rare defect that occurred after exposure to a chemical prevented a far greater tragedy than did occur.
Most of the time, however, the toxic compounds we attempt to identify
do not cause rare defects, but only add to a high background rate of
specific cancers, birth defects, or other diseases and are therefore more

difficult to identify. The more common the disease, the more difficult it is to show that a specific agent increases its rate of occurrence. In most cases we have to study a population close to a suspected toxic source (a landfill or a petrochemical plant, for instance) to determine if the rate of a disease known to be caused by a toxic chemical is higher near the source than in a population not directly exposed. Thalidomide produced such an uncommon adverse effect that only a few cases sufficed to show a cause-and-effect relation. If the effect produced by a chemical is a condition that occurs often anyway, a greater number of exposed and affected people must be studied, along with a control group, before a cause-and-effect relation can be proved.

DIBROMOCHLOROPROPANE

Dibromochloropropane is used in agriculture to kill parasitic worms called nematodes. As early as 1956 its manufacturer, Shell Chemical Company, was aware of animal studies that indicated the chemical might harm the male reproductive system.

In July 1977 in Lathrop, California, two employees of the Occidental Chemical Company who handled dibromochloropropane happened to fall into discussion of their inability to father children. Further discussions with other employees revealed that many of the men working at the plant had the same problem. The employees requested an investigation, which found that the sperm count in men exposed to this chemical could decrease by a statistically significant amount in as little as two months (Legator 1979).

Thus, the revelation that dibromochloropropane could have an adverse effect on human beings originated with neither the manufacturer (who knew the chemical had caused sterility in animals) nor with the company physicians (who were, supposedly, in the best position to detect the chemical's effect upon male employees of reproductive age), but with nonprofessionals who had themselves been affected.

THE DIBROMOCHLOROPROPANE LESSON

From the facts in this case, it is apparent that people may continue to be exposed to toxic chemicals long after those chemicals have been found to produce adverse effects in animals. Moreover, even after people have been affected by exposure to a chemical, the chemical will not necessarily be implicated as the cause of the damage. Nonprofessionals should not assume that action has already been taken on data collected on a certain chemical. In fact, relevant data may not be available, or conclusions that could be drawn from the data may not have been pursued by the professionals involved.

UNION EMPLOYEE TURNED CANCER DETECTIVE

In 1981 the Detroit News announced the winners of the third annual "Michigan Citizen of the Year Award," given to people who have helped to improve the lives of the state's 92 million residents. One of the winners of the 1981 award was a thirty-seven-year-old union employee, Michael Bennett, a journeyman pipefitter at the Fisher Body Plant of General Motors in Flint, Michigan.

In 1977 Mr. Bennett began to wonder about what seemed an unusually high number of deaths from cancer among his fellow workers. For the next two years, by working with the death certificates of former employees, he compared the death rate of union workers with the national death rate for the United States population and obtained what epidemiologists call a "proportional mortality ratio." Mr. Bennett used union records to compile a master list of 225 workers who had died in a five-year period. He then examined their death certificates, developed categories for the causes of death listed there, and compared his categories with those reflected by national statistics.

Mr. Bennett made some startling discoveries. Of the 225 workers whose death certificates he examined, 82 (36.4 percent) had died of cancer; the national rate was 20 percent. Within this group of 82 workers, twice as many cases of lung cancer had occurred as would have been predicted on the basis of the national incidence. Among the white women in the group of 82, the cancer rate was three and one-half times the national rate. Although the cause of the high incidence of cancer among the employees of this plant has not been determined, the fact that a problem exists was established, and this work was performed by a person with no training in epidemiology (Howard 1981).

THE MICHAEL BENNETT LESSON

In the thalidomide example, the rarity of a condition permitted a health risk to be identified. In this example, a worker suspected a common health problem on the basis of an informed hunch and then gathered data. When the data were analyzed statistically, the hunch proved correct. In analyzing the data himself, Michael Bennett demonstrated that motivated nonscientists can conduct a valid epidemiologic study.

LOVE CANAL

The term "Love Canal" has become a symbol and rallying cry for those concerned with health problems that result from disposal of toxic waste. Since much has already been written about the case (Levin 1982), I will discuss it only briefly.

Love Canal is the name given to a rectangular sixteen-acre tract of land (which includes an abandoned canal) in the southeastern section of Niagara, New York. Hooker Electrochemical Companies, now the Hooker Chemical and Plastic Companies, admits to depositing 21,000 tons of chemical waste into the canal from 1942 to 1953. In 1953 Hooker filled the canal, covered it with dirt, and sold the land to the Niagara Board of Education for one dollar. Part of the land, a sixteen-acre tract near the abandoned canal, was sold to a real estate developer, and homes were built on it. In 1955 a school was opened near a corner of the tract.

In the late 1950s, homeowners began to complain about nauseating odors and black sludge in the area and about finding chemical burns on their children. In 1978 one homeowner, Lois Gibbs, read an article in the local newspaper about the chemicals buried at this dump site. Ms. Gibbs wanted to withdraw her son from the school adjacent to the canal, but her request was denied. She then began to ask her neighbors about their health problems and found that an unusually high percentage of the residents of Love Canal were ill in some way. With this information to enlist support, Ms. Gibbs founded the Love Canal Homeowners Association, which serves as a model for similar groups because of the outstanding success of its efforts. (In chapter 2, Ms. Gibbs provides lessons in community organizing.)

The citizens of the community were able to focus public attention on their problem. A health survey, conducted primarily by the homeowners, corroborated the informal observations of many of the citizens of Love Canal. The New York State Department of Health then conducted an epidemiologic study, which found a high incidence of miscarriages and low-birth-weight infants in the area. On 7 August 1978 President Carter declared Love Canal to be in a state of emergency and authorized "action necessary to save many lives, protect property or to avert or lessen the threat of disaster." On 22 May 1980 he declared a second state of emergency, and on 23 May 1980 relocation of Love Canal homeowners was begun.

THE LOVE CANAL LESSON

In the previous example, Michael Bennett discovered an increase in cases of cancer in a specific population by comparing the incidence of cancer in that group with the incidence in the population of the United States as a whole. Although this type of information is valuable, it is often imprecise because many factors (geographical difference, socioeconomic status, and variations in life-style) confound direct comparison of a small population with the national population. At Love Canal, however, the community organization studied the population with respect to distance from the source of contamination. This kind of study produces the most conclusive epidemiologic data for investigations of the toxic effects of chemicals, especially when chronic disorders are involved.

Although the health survey taken by the citizens of Love Canal was criticized as unscientific, the study carried out by the New York State Health Department was also criticized. In fact, a government report implied that the Homeowners Association study, carried out by Dr. Beverly Paigen, a cancer research investigator, was as valid as that performed by epidemiologists from the New York State Department of Health. The Health Department study compared the outcomes of the pregnancies of Love Canal residents not with those of a similar group, but with general statistics reported in professional journals. Such a comparison yields imprecise data, which can be misleading. No thorough, sound epidemiologic study was ever carried out at Love Canal, but the survey conducted by the citizens of the area served at least to bring its problem to the attention of various officials.

APPLICATIONS

These four examples illustrate the ways health hazards from chemical exposure can come to be recognized. The first step in any process is taken when careful observation, an informed hunch, or knowledge of the presence of toxic chemicals leads someone to believe a community health problem may exist. Rarely (as in the case of thalidomide) does the observation of an unusual health problem alone suffice to establish that a particular chemical has produced the problem. In most situations we are faced not with a rare anomaly, but with an increased occurrence of a common problem, such as cancer, birth defects, or neurological disorders. Since these problems can result from a variety of factors (numerous and diverse chemicals, personal habits, and genetic susceptibility), a cause-and-effect relation between a chemical and a health problem is difficult to establish, and further investigation must be undertaken.

In some cases comparing the rate of occurrence of a health problem in a group exposed to a chemical with the rate in the population as a whole may be enough to implicate the chemical. In most cases, however, the best approach is to compare the rate of occurrence in a population believed to be at risk with the rate in an unexposed group. Formation of a strong community organization is often a prerequisite for such a study. If community leaders know how to compose questionnaires, gather data, and interpret these data, they can then take steps to determine whether a health hazard exists. The purpose of this manual is to describe these investigative tools. If the detailed approach outlined here is followed carefully, a study performed by a community should have scientific credibility.

TWO

JOIN TOGETHER

Organizing Your Community

Lois Marie Gibbs

In the next chapter, you will learn about cause and effect relationships between diseases and toxic substances. It's useful to know this if you're doing basic research and educating yourself. But it's not very useful if you're working to *solve* problems of toxic chemicals all by yourself. The purpose of this chapter is to give you some ideas on how to get other people to share your concerns and to join with you in fighting for environmental justice. This process is called community organizing. There is little point in trying to conduct a health study or to set up a health register before you organize your community. One practical reason is that people will be reluctant to give you personal health information without knowing you or knowing why you are gathering the information. Further, even if people are willing to talk openly and honestly with you about their health problems, it's a giant, time-consuming task to take on a survey or a register project alone.

Third, unless you have an organization, what would you do with any information you collect? There are no magic facts. Even supposing you, as a private individual, overcame the barrier of mistrust and got people to talk to you and even if you overcame the physical barriers of time and expense and came up with a solid, comprehensive report that showed terrible health problems in your community, *so what*? Without an organization to follow through on demands for environmental justice (whether that's compensation or health treatment for the victims or action to stop polluters), polluting industries and government regulators will simply ignore your findings. They will assume, probably with justification, that there's no community power behind the health report, no community fighting for change.

Some people tell us they want to use a health survey as an organizing tool. They'll go door-to-door and get their neighbors to take an interest in environmental justice issues, provoked by the simple fact that they've been surveyed. This usually backfires. If you're going to do a study or a register, do a study or a register. But if you try to combine this with an organizing drive, you're more than likely going to produce a study or register that will be easy to attack and dismiss by the policy-makers you want to impress.

Public officials are rarely impressed by facts, no matter how compelling or tragic. Woburn, Massachusetts mothers collected information on childhood leukemia in their neighborhood. They documented 20 cases of the disease in their children. They believed the cause of the problem was contaminated drinking water. When they presented this information to their state health agency, the response was, "Clusters of disease happen all the time, we don't think this cluster is related to any chemicals in the drinking water." Woburn residents filed lawsuits against the polluters and, years later after burying their children, won a sizable settlement.

At Love Canal, we organized a strong community group first and collected the health information later. When the Love Canal residents discovered that 56% of their children were born with birth defects, they had a community organization in place to take action to use this information to press their demands for relocation. Each time we discovered a new pattern of health effects from toxic exposure, we plugged that information into our organizing strategy and used this to win a total federally financed relocation on October 1, 1980, three years after we started organizing.

In the following sections, we will review the process of community organizing around problems relating to toxic chemicals. We'll start from the beginning. You may already have begun organizing your community. Or, you may already have begun to do your own health survey. You may be wondering where to begin. No matter what your situation, you should review the basic steps. Even if you're on the right track, it's always smart to reflect on what you've done. And if you're not on the right track, you may find some insights that will give you ways to improve the situation. It's never too late to make a positive change.

IDENTIFYING THE PROBLEM

You think you've got a problem with toxic chemicals in your community. Usually, people express their first finds as follow:

1. "We've been seeing (or smelling) strange things." Then people will describe odd colored run-off from a site, a cloud coming from a suspected polluter, an oil slick, strange odors in the air, bad tastes in their drinking water, etc.

2. "There are a lot of illnesses in our community whenever chemical industries are operating." Then people will describe symptoms experi-

enced by themselves, their children, other family members, or even pets or livestock.

3. "We have a cluster of illnesses (or deaths)." Then people tell about the number of people in their community who have died recently, or who have become gravely ill.

These types of concerns often motivate people to believe a health study should be done. When people see pollution, they figure, "Gee, if we can prove this is hurting people, we can make the polluter stop, or at least get the regulators to take action." If they see illnesses or deaths, they feel compelled, for good reason, to try to find out why people died or became ill.

I suggest you begin by making an inventory of polluting sites in your community, rather than begin with a health study. This is more practical than trying to make a cause-and-effect link between pollution and illness, since even the best health studies don't make such positive linkages.

You can begin to discover more about local pollution sources by checking at your local planning board, city or town hall, fire department, the county health department, and in your local newspaper's library. At town or county hall (Registrar of Deed Office), for example, you can usually find out who owns the property where you suspect there might be contamination. Sometimes you can even tell from the deed how the land was used. The local planning office can tell you what licenses or zoning permits were issued for the property. The local health department might be able to tell you if any complaints were received or citations issued. It's possible your town or county might even have an official or office specifically responsible for dealing with environmental problems. You may also find information, such as complaints and permits, at your state environmental agency.

If you are concerned about plant emissions and discharges, you may want to contact your state or local emergency planning committee. They collect storage and health effects information (material safety data sheets) from industries as required under the Community Right to Know Law that was added to the federal Superfund statute in 1986, after people like you lobbied Congress for it. EPA has the discharge and disposal information, the Toxics Release Inventory, required by the law. This law is also known as SARA Title III.

Ask all of your elected representatives at the city, state, and federal levels. Your senators and representatives all have staff people whose job is constituent service, which includes helping citizens in their districts to find information like this. These officials can provide key information as well as names of other people you should contact. They can also be helpful in identifying people for you in the other relevant agencies, as well as providing the telephone number and address of your local emergency planning committee.

By contacting these elected officials you can accomplish two other things: (1) you'll often get valuable information, and (2) you'll let them know that you're concerned.

Be specific. Whenever you ask anyone to help you, be clear about what you want and establish an oral contract, reaching mutual agreement about when (two weeks, one month, etc.) you can expect action. Follow conversations with a letter saying "I'm following up on our phone conversation of [date] where I asked for [what] and you agreed you'd have a response by [when]." This way, you have a record of the conversation; you remind them of their promise; and you show them you're serious.

I've just described the informal process for getting information from government agencies. I prefer this to the formal process, which is to use either your state's open records law (nearly every state has one) or the federal Freedom of Information Act, applying to U.S. government agencies. The informal approach is usually faster. However, you shouldn't hesitate to use either state or federal laws on any agency that doesn't respond to your informal requests.

These laws give you very specific rights to information. The federal law, and most of the state laws, define what types of information you can get, what types of information you're not entitled to legally, how quickly the agency must respond, and, if the agency decides it wants to charge you (generally for copying costs), rules for reasonable charges.

Generally, you can assume you have a right to see anything other than information that violates confidentiality, trade secrets, personnel matters or on-going law enforcement investigations. Most freedom of information and open records laws require a response within 10 days. The catch is the response could be "you'll get the info when we get to it." Most of these laws allow the agencies to pass along to you all "reasonable" costs for finding, copying, and mailing the information, but also allow the agencies the discretion to waive the costs.

Many agencies and nonprofit groups can give you a standard fill-in-the-blanks form letter to use the Freedom of Information Act. These can be very handy. But, you can exercise your rights just as easily with a simple letter that says, "Dear Mr. or Ms. . . . : I am requesting under the Freedom of Information Act all correspondence; memoranda; reports; soil, air, and water tests and analyses . . . . relating to . . . ." Be sure to include your name, address and phone number on the letter.

Once you have collected enough information to feel comfortable that there's really a problem in the community, stop researching. Leave the remaining research for others joining the group later. Too often, grassroots leaders get hung up thinking, "I don't have enough information yet. I must get more facts before I can talk with my neighbors, before we start organizing, and certainly before we start to take action." Some concerned citizens never get past the fact-finding stage and become what I call "data fanatics." I know some people who have taken this mania to such an extreme that they've actually had to build additions to their homes to house all the information they've collected. Others walk around—and I'm not making this up—dragging a steamer-trunk on wheels, filled with information.

If you expect to find all the facts before you begin to act, you're never going to act. When you fight for environmental justice, you need enough information at the beginning to feel secure about your ability to discuss your concerns. As your fight goes on, there will be more information to collect and you can use the process of fact-finding as a meaningful job for new members. It builds commitment among new recruits interested in investigating the problem.

ORGANIZING YOUR COMMUNITY

Organizing a community is not as hard as you may think. Virtually everyone is affected. Their health may be at risk, their drinking water poisoned, their property worthless or business damaged. Concerns also translate into taxpayer issues. People get involved when they see a) they have a self-interest that b) they hope to address. If you are prepared to discuss pocketbook issues and nuisance problems, as well as health and environmental concerns, you should be able to appeal to everyone.

Initial Steps in Organizing

The first step to organizing is to educate the community about the problem. There are several ways to accomplish this. First, you may want to contact your local newspaper, TV, and radio stations to tell the environmental reporters what you have found. Invite the reporters over to your house and show them the documents that you have collected. This won't work in all communities, since some communities are company towns and the polluters own the media; but it is worth a try. If you can get some coverage, it will help in speaking with your neighbors. Many think if it's written in the paper or announced on TV it must be true.

The next step is to prepare a fact sheet. Remember when writing the fact sheet that you now know more than anyone else in the community. Try not to assume people already know about the problem. Keep the fact sheet as simple as possible, one page in length. You may want to include the following in your fact sheet:

- Your name, address, and telephone number;
- The location of the point of pollution;
- What chemicals people are being exposed to and at what quantity;
- What types of health effects may result from exposure to these chemicals;
  - Who owns the plant or dumpsite or who contaminated the area;
  - The effects this problem may have on property values and businesses in the area;
  - Other information you may think is useful like nuisances of noise, odors, or traffic.

The purposes of this fact sheet are to educate your neighbors as well as help them see how they are affected. If they don't think it affects them, they are unlikely to join you in your efforts for action on the problem.

It also is important to broaden the issue area to more than health problems. *Not everyone cares about health effects.* Some may care only about property values or even nuisance issues.

One interesting way to help people see how they are affected is to include a map with a bull's-eye target on it. You can either draw a rough sketch of the neighborhood or obtain a map from the city or county government. Draw circles around areas you think may be affected by health and environmental issues and also by decreases in property values, increases in traffic, or other nuisances. The center of the bull's-eye is the pollution source.

There are two approaches to distributing these fact sheets. You can either distribute them before you go door-to-door or hand them out as you speak with your neighbors. The advantage of distributing them before you speak with your neighbors is that they will have had an opportunity to think about the problem and digest the information.

If distributing the fact sheet first, it is best to distribute them a week or two before you go out to canvass the neighborhood. People have a short memory and you want to make sure they still have the issues fresh in their minds when you speak with them. You might even mention in the fact sheet that you'll be going door to door throughout the community. You could suggest that they think about questions they may have for you when you arrive.

Door-to-Door Canvassing

There is no substitute for direct contact with people. This is the basic building block to organizing. You can write all the fact sheets you want and call all the elected officials in government, but it is the face-to-face contact that will be your biggest payoff in organizing a strong community organization.

Knocking on strangers' doors is a bit frightening at first, but once you have done a few it gets easier. Thoughts going through your head are most likely not much different than for others who have gone door-to-door: "Will they slam the door in my face? Will they think that I am crazy or causing trouble?" . . . . and so on. In preparing to go canvassing there are several things you need to think about to make the first door easier.

First, what are you going to say?   You need to put together a rap to use at the door. The professionals who canvass successfully for money use one that begins with, "I am . . . ." "We are . . . ." "This is . . . ." The rap concludes with "We want your money." You can use the same approach:

- I am *your name.*
- We are *a small group concerned about . . . .*
- This is *a fact sheet [or petition] about . . . .*
- We want *you to attend a meeting [when, where] to discuss our concerns about this problem and what we can do about it together.*

Once you get your rap down, practice it in front of a mirror or on your family or friends.

As you go door-to-door you will be given a lot of information. This may be your first insight into health problems existing in the community. You will also accomplish name and face recognition by your neighbors and will begin to build trust between you and the community. When you go back to these same people to collect health information, you will not have to explain who you are.

Bring a notebook for information gathered during your door knocking.   It makes sense to carry a notebook so that as your neighbors volunteer information you can write it down. After many people, the stories all seem to run together and it can be difficult to remember who told you what.

Before going door to door, you should select a date and find a place to meet with neighbors who want to discuss the problem further.   A time and place could be put on the back side of the fact sheet you distribute through the community or you could make up new flyers for that purpose.

You may also want to circulate a petition.   You don't need a lawyer to write the petition; just write something simple: "We the undersigned residents of Our Town, USA, petition the local/state government body to . . . ." The purpose of the petition is two-fold: first, to get the name and addresses of interested people in the community and, second, to show the powers that be that there are many people — voters — concerned about this issue.

Setting up a Meeting

Now that you have gone door-to-door, put together a fact sheet, and talked with your neighbors; you're ready for the next big step, holding a community meeting.

The first two important things to think about when setting up a meeting is the location and the date. Not many people will come if the meeting is held at the same time as another big event in your town or when the highest rated TV show is on. Check with others to find out what else is happening on the date selected.

Location is important. The further you are from the people you want to attend, the smaller your attendance will be. A neighborhood school, library, church, or community center is the best choice. These institutions are also less likely to charge you for renting the space. If you are expecting a small number, you could hold the meeting in someone's home or yard.

The next step is to prepare an agenda. The agenda is very important. It helps ensure that you will cover the issues you must and will help give the meeting substance and direction. The agenda could include an introduction of yourself, background information on the problem, and general discussion and questions. After some general discussion, you need to move to the next step: "What do people want to do — set up a community group? What does the group want to accomplish?"

The Meeting

At the meeting, have a volunteer sit just outside the door to make sure people sign in before entering the room. This way you'll have a list of names for future meetings. There should also be a pile of fact sheets available for people as they walk into the meeting as well as a copy of the agenda.

Post the agenda on a large piece of paper at the front of the room. It is also helpful to have other large sheets of paper and markers available for use during the meeting. It is important to begin the meeting on time. If you begin the meeting late, people will come late. If the meetings are long, people won't come back because they have children and other commitments.

The meeting date has arrived, and here you are standing with a few new friends in front of 15, 25, or 100 people. Before you bolt from the room with fear remember these friends and neighbors share your concerns. They are there because they want to hear what you have to say.

Open the meeting by introducing yourself and others who are working with you. Explain to the group what you found out and what you are still working on. It is important to start from the assumption that people know little about the situation. In this way everyone will be brought up to the same level of understanding and will be encouraged to participate. Keep your presentation simple and short.

You may then want to open the meeting for general discussion by asking if anyone has any questions or other information. The general discussion is important because it gives people a chance to feel part of the meeting. This discussion can go on for as long as it is productive.

The next step in the meeting is to ask what people want to do about the problem. Do they want to start an organization? If so, initiate a discussion and then take a vote to establish a group.

You won't be able to fully establish an organization at the first meeting, so don't push to accomplish that task. At the end of the meeting, you might want to go over what you did accomplish, "We have all discussed the problems and now have a better understanding of the issues. We have decided to establish a group to fight for action on this site. And we have agreed to meet again at [time, date, place]. I really feel good about what we have done this evening." People will gain a sense of accomplishment and empowerment and will be encouraged to come back.

Since it is impossible to do everything at one meeting, hold several meetings. Important decisions include the following:

• What will the group call itself? A name is important for identification. A named group is more powerful than an ad hoc group of individuals.

• What are your goals? What do you want? This is probably the most important decision of a group. The goals of the group will determine not just the group's activities, but also who joins and who doesn't.

To make this decision, there is a good exercise for one of your first meetings. On a large sheet of paper list the people at the meeting and what they want. After everyone has had a chance to put their goals on the list, ask the group to rank the goals. What are our top ten goals? Top five?

Next the group decides how to handle the goals. For example, we will begin to push for the first five goals on our list and as we win the goals, we'll keep moving down the list. Ranking keeps the group focused. If goal #29 is to rid the world of caterpillars, you really don't want a committee to spend time studying the caterpillar population.

The value of this exercise is that everyone takes part in setting the organization's goal. The craziest goal will fall to the bottom without making that person feel left out. Also you will gain good insight into what people care about when formulating group activities.

The Organization's Format

Clear about what you want, you need to establish a working organization. Begin by identifying more people in the community to get involved. Getting people involved and keeping them involved is not that difficult if you set up an organization in which they feel they have a say.

There are three typical formats for community organizations. The most common organization design in communities is the pyramid. This style consists of one person at the top, usually the founder of the group. Under that person are several others (usually 5 to 10 people), who are mainly friends or a clique within the group. At the bottom of the pyramid is the rest of the community. Generally the clique and leader/founder make all the decisions, do all of the work and complain all of the time about how no one else in the community will get involved. Leaders get burned out pretty fast in this style of organization.

The second type of organization design is the consensus group, sometimes referred to as the blob. In these organizations there are no leaders and everyone must agree or reach consensus before they can go forward with activities. As a result, these groups take forever to accomplish anything. People become frustrated attending meeting after meeting where no concrete decisions are made. This is also the easiest group for your opponents to infiltrate and control. All the infiltrator has to do is disagree and no decision will be made.

The third type of organization, the wheel, takes more energy to set up but is ultimately much more effective. A round wheel, this set-up takes in the skills, talents, and interests of members of your group. It works very simply. At the center of the wheel is a hub, and from the hub comes many different spokes. Each spoke on the wheel represents a standing committee. Sample committees include outreach and education, allies, media, legal, research, health information, fund raising, action, etc. Each committee elects its own chairperson and co-chair. The committees call their own meetings and decide their course of action and present their ideas to the larger group.

The chair and co-chair of each committee then come to the hub at a set time to explain what they want to do, what they are already doing, and the results of their activities. In this way, everyone can both share and coordinate the activities of the organization. For example, if the action committee was going to do a protest, they would coordinate that with the media, allies, and education committees.

The wheel also helps to keep people involved because they can work on what they think will win, rather than having to agree on one specific approach. It gives people a diverse group to fit into. If they only want to protest then they can join the action committee or if they think protesting is a terrible and frightening thing then they can help with the education or fund-raising activities.

At the large group community meetings, the chair of each committee or spokesperson gives a brief description of what they are doing and asks for votes when necessary. They also encourage people to join in to help them and ask for other ideas.

The Organization's Targets

The next step is to identify your targets. Try list making again. There are two key questions to ask of the group: 1) Who is responsible for the situation? 2) Who can give us what we want? Under "who is responsible" you will probably have a list of names of industry polluters and the government agencies who have given them permission or what we refer to as a permit to pollute.

Under "who can give us what we want," you're more likely to have a list of government officials ranging from the local government to the President of the United States. The two lists will overlap at times but that's all right. The responsible party(ies) can also provide the solutions.

The next step in this exercise is to figure out how these people are vulnerable. What would make them do what you want them to do? One likely answer for both groups is public opinion. Industry hates bad publicity and elected officials are concerned about their image with the voters. You can also affect corporate customers and file a personal injury suit that will be seen as a pressure point for the stockholders.

Defining Your Strategies

There are three strategies commonly used in communities faced with an environmental problem. People usually fight legally, scientifically, or politically. Unfortunately few ever look at all three as complimentary strategies. However, using all three strategies together is very powerful. The following outlines their values and limitations.

Legal strategies. (See chapter 10.) Community groups who use a legal approach should have a lot of money and a lot of time. To win you must *prove* a problem. You must prove that the chemicals that you are being exposed to have harmed or will harm you in some way. When you find an attorney who is willing to assist you and file a suit two things happen. First, you lose members who now believe that the lawyers will save the day. The fight will take place in court, not in the community. Second, you will stop receiving information and testing as the other side will argue that they cannot provide that information to you because of your pending litigation.

Another problem is the possibility that through discovery your opponent will try and get all the health related data from you as part of the lawsuit. Thus all those promises you made to your neighbors about total confidentiality may be violated.

To investigate routes of exposure (how it got from the dump or plant to you) will cost several million dollars as seen in Woburn, Massachusetts. Even if you establish a route of exposure it is next to impossible to prove that your problems were not problems that would have happened by chance but are a direct result of chemical exposures.

However, the biggest limitation to the legal fight is that it is not illegal to pollute. Industry is actually given permits to pollute by state and federal governments. In the cases where there are not standards for pollution levels, such as residential exposures, the chemicals are seen as innocent and you guilty of hysteria.

The advantage of a lawsuit is that you might win compensation (dollars) for your suffering or lost property values. You may also be able to shut down an operating facility. In many cases, the lawsuit may be a stall mechanism.

Scientific strategies.   There are several advantages to using science in your fight. First, the information provided by your scientists can give your group credibility: You are not making up horrible stories. The second important result is it may give people information on health problems in the community to base personal decisions on. For example, if birth defects are high they may want prenatal testing. If children are affected, community members may send their children to relatives' homes for weekends or until the problem is resolved.

Fighting scientifically also has its limitations. There is only a small amount of scientific data useful for your purpose. The scientific material needed on exposures to low level chemicals in residential areas is only now being developed.

Fighting scientifically is essentially looking for the magic fact, the fact that just doesn't exist. In community after community, people have identified real documented health problems. In San Jose, California and in Love Canal, they found a high rate of birth defects among their children. Children born at Love Canal also experienced a high rate of other reproductive problems. In Woburn there was a high rate of childhood cancer and in Texas a cluster of children with brain cancer. None of these terrible findings alone moved the opponents of these communities into doing the right thing.

You may end up with the dueling-experts syndrome, which can confuse the community, causing the group to fall apart. Remember, without a group you have little power to effect change. When the community finds a scientist who will recognize the problem, government or industry will bring in two other Ph.D.'s who will say there is no problem and no cause for alarm. Those who don't understand the arguments or jargon, stop coming to the meetings or fall asleep in the back of the room. They have no role and no say since the battle ground is now within the circle of science.

It's quite normal to feel that if you prove there is a health problem in your community, something will be done. It's normal to feel that way, it's what we were taught in civics, but it's naive and untrue. Problems can cost millions of dollars to solve. Neither government nor industry may want to spend the sums involved.

Community scientists are often labeled as biased, liberal, or radical. They are not seen as conservative mainstream scientists, even when they do conservative work. The government's or industry's scientists (amusingly) are seen as credible, despite the fact that they are also biased. They sit on government committees and have Ph.D.'s in many different disciplines. The arguments you face here are the same arguments the legal system faces when trying to prove cause and effect.

Political strategies. Political strategies can also include legal and scientific information and tactics as support. For example, you can use the scientific information you have gathered to put pressure on the governor of the state by saying, "56% of our children have been born with birth defects. How many more will you, Governor, allow to be subjected to these poisons? How many more children must be born deformed before you act to protect them?"

Political strategies mean using your constitutional rights through democracy. This strategy involves the most people, and uses the general public for the purpose of holding public officials and corporations accountable. The strategy focuses on those holding elected positions. Proof becomes much less of a burden because you are trying to change public opinion rather than proving your case beyond the shadow of a doubt. The ability to reach an elected representative or corporate executive is much more achievable. Public officials have local offices or homes somewhere in your state. The cost of these fights are much less compared to the legal approach or paying for scientific experts.

History shows us that evacuating a community, cleaning up a dumpsite, and/or forcing an existing industry to clean up its discharges are political decisions.

For example, Love Canal was evacuated because Governor Carey was running for re-election and was pressured by the Love Canal neighbors. The Love Canal residents followed him everywhere he went including to black-tie fund-raisers. They carried signs and distributed fact sheets and press statements at all of the governor's events. The residents held the governor personally responsible for the Love Canal situation.

Times Beach, Missouri was evacuated when EPA was in trouble over Rita Lavelle and Ann Gorsuch. EPA needed something big to draw attention so they would look good to the public during the height of these scandals. So, they evacuated the residents of Times Beach.

Using the political strategy has historically proven to be successful. In order for the strategy to work you must include some tactics or actions to get attention and raise the public's awareness.

What is a Plan of Action?

There are many options open to an organization that wants to apply pressure, educate the public, or relieve tension within a community. However, you must be careful not to overuse or burn out the membership through too many activities. Each action must be carefully calculated: What do we want to accomplish with this action? Who is our target? Should we take this action or wait for a better opportunity?

Plan your activities carefully for a time when you can accomplish something. If your action is successful people are likely to come out for the next one. They'll feel good about the group and about themselves.

An action is useless if nobody knows about it.   Media coverage is also important for an action to be successful. Notify them in advance, with a news advisory, and have someone call the day of the action. If you use signs, make them large enough so that the cameras can capture the message. Be sure to keep your signs simple and your statements concise. Talk and write in everyday terms that anyone can understand.

There are many techniques for calling attention to your organization or cause. Although your group can learn from those successes, it is beneficial to be creative and develop your own tactics. Some of the actions and tactics used across the country are listed below.

• Rally. This one day event brings attention to your issue, educates new people about the problem, and motivates people in the fight for justice. This is also a good forum for bringing large numbers of people together, especially if you use a speaker or entertainment or something else that will attract a crowd. You could also use this opportunity to allow the elected officials who support you to speak.

• Walk of Concern. This can be done with religious leaders or the cub scouts, for example. Walk to an elected official's office or the plant gates or around the site. A news conference and a presentation of some sort is a good idea.

• Symbolic Coffin/Motorcade. You can have a funeral march to your target presenting him/her with a symbolic coffin as a symbol of the dead and dying in your community. If you do it by motorcade, consider rush hour to alert (but irritate) a lot of people.

• Picketing. This form of protest is used by almost every organization. You might want to get a permit for this action although most people don't. Generally, if you keep moving, even if it's in a circle, you won't get in trouble with the law. The advantage of picketing is that it can be used any where: City Hall, around the dump, at the plant site, at the steps of the capitol, or even at the home of the president of the corporation. Having fact sheets available for passing cars and pedestrians will be generally helpful.

• Prayer Vigil. This can be done at a church near the site. This is a good action for the seniors and others who physically cannot participate in some of the other activities or feel safer doing this.

• Talking Outhouse or Dog House. This is very useful for both public education and media attention. Build an outhouse frame or dog house and place a speaker inside. You also need someone with a wireless microphone nearby who can provide the voice for the house. When people walk by, have the house talk to them about your issue. For example, the house could say to a passerby, "did you know Governor ____ is in the dog house? He is allowing the people in OUR TOWN to be exposed to poisons and die. I, although made of nothing more than wood, am asking you for help. Could you take the flyer from the person behind you and call the governor's office and ask him/her to help our community? His number is on the flyer." People actually carry on conversations with these houses. They at first think it is a candid camera type show, later they are just amused.

Use your imagination when thinking about actions to do. One thing the grassroots groups seem to have plenty of is creativity.

Fund Raising is Necessary

Part of organizing and maintaining a community group is raising money. You can do a lot with little or no money but you will need to pay the phone bill and printing costs out of the organization's funds at some time. Most people pay for these expenses out of their own pocket at the early development stages of the group. This adds up and stresses the family budget. It is also unnecessary. If you really have a community organization then you should be able to raise enough money to cover your costs.

There are many ways to raise money. Here are some ideas on raising money both from inside and outside the community.

• Pass the hat at your meetings. Churches do this every week and people don't complain.

• You could have a 50/50 drawing. This means you sell tickets at the door for maybe $1. At the end of the meeting you have a drawing. Whoever wins, splits the money collected 50/50 with the organization.

• The group could sell T-shirts with the group's name and message on them. You can make a small profit and you can get your message out through the design. Actions also look great when everyone is wearing the same shirt with the same message. It clearly says we are united in this struggle.

• Your local businesses may be willing to give a donation of money or goods. If a supermarket wants to give your group a side of beef, TV, or something else, you could raffle that donated gift. Raffles can raise a few thousand dollars for the group.

• A fund-raising dinner/dance is another idea. You make the most on these when the hall and food are donated. Otherwise it can be a low profit event but good for morale. It would also be a great opportunity to give awards or certificates of appreciation to your hardest working people.

Once again, use your imagination when thinking about fund raisers. Talk with other groups in the community and ask them how they raise their funds. It doesn't take a professional to raise funds for a group. Just keep in mind these three ingredients: it should be fun, cost the group little, and be simple.

The ideas, learning, and strategies described in this chapter have been successful in organizing citizens at the community level to get action in addressing hazardous wastes and public health risk issues. Many of these approaches have also been used by other public interest groups to stop unnecessary highway construction, improve public transportation, and challenge discriminatory practices. The value of community organizing around any problem or issue should never be overlooked. It is the power of citizens to organize and directly assert their influence that is the ultimate defense policy for protecting our families, property, and our environment.

HEALTH STUDIES FROM THE COMMUNITY PERSPECTIVE

We have talked about how to organize your community to form an effective group to fight for justice. Now let's look at the actual tasks and issues you need to think about when doing a health study or setting up a health registry.

Collecting health information in a community is not an easy task. It takes a tremendous amount of time, energy, and hard work to be successful. Before beginning, your group should decide if at the present time you can afford to give the level of attention that is needed to carry out this type of project. Remember a health study or registry should never be used as an organizing tool. Some leaders may think, "A health study is a great way to build awareness of our issues." While this is true to an extent, there are enough things that could go wrong with a health project that you should look to better, more tried-and-true techniques mentioned at the beginning of this chapter.

One of the most critical parts of a successful health study or registry is the percentage of cooperation you receive from the community. You must be able to interview the majority of families living in the defined neighborhood. Some scientists have expressed a need for 80% of the population to participate, while others believe that only 60% is necessary. In any case, an unorganized unconvinced community will probably only yield a 40% to 50% participation. (See chapters 5 and 8 for a discussion of statistical issues.)

Once you have thought through the question of time and labor, there are several other issues to consider.

Why do you want to do a health survey or registry?   Do you think there is an increase of a certain disease in the neighborhood? Do you want to find out for sure what the neighborhood's health status is? Have several of your neighbors reported to you or to your organization similar health problems? Or do you want to prove that you're not crazy like all your opponents say you are?

What do you hope to accomplish in conducting this survey?   Do you want to convince your neighbors or your elected officials there is a problem? Are you planning to use the result (if positive) to pressure the health authorities to conduct a detailed scientific study? Or do you want to use the results to put pressure on the powers that be to evacuate or clean up the point of pollution? Does your attorney plan on using the information in a lawsuit?

It is important to define your major goals in advance to know how to determine if a health survey is appropriate for your situation. If it is appropriate, then you need to decide, step-by-step, how best to use it to achieve that goal.

After answering those questions you now must think through whether you want to do a health study or health registry. There is a big difference between the two and based on your goals one may not work for you.

The size of the community is important.   The next question you need to ask yourselves is whether your community is large enough for either a study or a registry. If the community is really small it may not be worth your while to invest the time and resources in doing a health survey. The size is important because there are a certain number of diseases expected in every population. A health survey must have a high enough number of participants to show that your results are valid, or in other words, that a disease is happening more often than could be expected in a normal population.

What if the Health Study Shows an Effect?

It is important to think about the situation you may be creating if a positive effect is found. People hearing of a real health problem may be fearful and anxious. Families living in the community will want to know what they can or should do to protect their families. Questions will surface: Should I leave everything I've worked for all my life and move out to protect my family? We have waited five years to have a baby; do we put if off even longer? Will the unborn child I'm carrying be okay?

You must be prepared to handle potential emotional problems. Take into consideration the repercussions of the survey results and provide some mechanism to assist the concerned residents. Your group might think about bringing in a supportive family doctor to answer questions or give advice on preventive tests people might want to include in their yearly check ups. You might want to arrange to have the local crisis center establish a hotline for your community. Or you could establish your own support center within your organization.

Legal Issues

There are two major legal issues to resolve before you start: statutes of limitations and loss of privacy through legal discovery. The statute of limitation laws define a specific period of time during which a person who has suffered can file a lawsuit to recover damages. In most states, the laws say that within X number of years following awareness that you have suffered an injury, you must file suit against whomever caused that injury. In some states, the period allowed is as short as one year.

Your survey could cause the statute of limitations clock to start. You bear some responsibility for helping people to protect their legal rights.

This need not be a problem, if you act responsibly. Find out, from a friendly lawyer or your local legal aid center or bar association, what your statute of limitations laws are and how they might apply to the situation in your community. Inform people of their rights, especially if your research reveals that your survey will, indeed, start the clock. You may want to suggest that people who discover injury through your survey contact a lawyer. You could set up a referral plan, but keep in mind that this creates even more responsibility, as you should be able to vouch for these lawyers.

The second concern, privacy, has far-reaching effects. Your opponents, the responsible party(ies) in any legal action, could through the legal discovery process have the court order all of the health information and identification documents you have collected be given to them. You would be providing the other side with everything you have about people's personal health problems and histories. The opponents of course will use all of that information to build their case against your neighbors. Furthermore, you would have broken your promise to the community that when participating in your survey they would not be identified. It will certainly raise doubts the next time you make promises. Even if it is not your fault, that will be lost in the anger and violation people feel.

At Love Canal, Occidental Petroleum tried desperately to obtain such information from the Love Canal Homeowners Association. They never got it at Love Canal, but it was close. At Stringfellow Acid Pits in California, the opponents were successful in getting the health information. In this case it was not the community's information they won but the California State Department of Health's survey documents.

So it's not too early for you to think about this issue and protect yourselves against it. You can protect yourselves in part by removing the names from the questionnaires and destroying the identifying page. Or maybe just not do the survey at all. In any case, thought should go into this issue or your lawyers will have no surprises to present in court nor will your opponent need to ask very many questions.

There are many questions and issues a community must think about before deciding to do a health survey. Health surveys should not be taken lightly. A survey or registry is a tool to help you to understand what is going on in your community, or part of your strategy to win justice for the victims. The results can be far reaching in affecting the families themselves, lawsuits, and overall goals of the group. Such studies take a lot of people and resources and could physically drain the group.

If your organization chooses to undertake such a project, step carefully through the maze. Think through each step, where your group is going, and how you plan to get there. The problems and obstacles can be overcome when you seriously work through them.

An Alternative—the Health Registry

A health registry is conducted the same way you would do a health study. You would circulate a questionnaire and review the data to determine if any disease patterns exist. But you don't need a control population, although you can still use one if you like. A registry can also be an on-going activity of the group. With a study you look at a certain period of time, then stop. With a registry you can continue to keep a record of changes in the health of the people who live in your neighborhood.

However, one of the biggest advantages of a registry over a study is that if there is no increase in disease, you won't be hurt as a result. If you did a study and found no increased health problem, then your group could look very foolish. Your opponents will be the first to jump on you, to verify what they have been saying about your organization right along. You were falsely creating hysteria in the community over nothing.

This has actually happened in two community groups and literally tore the groups apart. In one community their site was even put at the bottom of this list for immediate action since "they proved themselves" that there was no problem.

A registry on the other hand is an on-going monitoring device for communities. If there is no increased disease that's alright. The purpose of a registry is to monitor health to see what happens over a period of time. In certain diseases like cancer, for example, you don't expect to see an increase for 10 to 20 years after exposure.

You could still collect the same information and if a problem was indicated, you could use that information in the same way. For example, you could explain that you found an increase in childhood cancer and you want . . . (whatever your goals are). You could even take it a step further to say you want a full scientific health study done in your community. Argue that although you identified this result, it is probably an underestimate of the true problems. After all, you're not scientists. The next chapter, however, will provide an understanding of environmental health problems.

THREE

DO YOU SUSPECT A PROBLEM?

Known Exposures, Known Effects

Barbara L. Harper

Although many environmental health problems are caused by temporary exposures and the overt effects decline after exposure stops, this chapter stresses chronic or permanent effects (cancer, mutation, and birth defects) because these are traumatic events and because there is a definite possibility that some of these effects can be transmitted to offspring (i.e., are inherited conditions). We know that we are not yet able to detect all these effects, and we do not know the effects of long-term or low-dose effects even of chemicals known to be human carcinogens at high doses. We have all read about instances where residents are assured that a contaminated neighborhood is safe to raise children in, yet officials who come into their backyards to collect samples for analysis wear protective outfits resembling space suits. Since it is wiser to err on the side of caution, this manual lists known human carcinogens (causing cancer) and teratogens (causing birth defects and other adverse birth outcomes).

Although acute and often reversible symptoms are generally viewed as less serious, they are often easier to measure and are much more common. Children, however, while often the most susceptible to hazardous substances, are the hardest to assess because a parent must observe the child's behavior and interpret it. A good study should reveal other high-risk or more susceptible subgroups. Many such groups we already know of: the unborn, children, the elderly, and persons with pre-existing conditions who may develop environmentally triggered symptoms in whatever organ system is already affected. This idea is the basis for the concept of multiple contributory causes: many things (chemicals, infection, structural damage, and so on) contribute to the appearance of both acute and chronic disease.

While acute (and reversible) symptoms may have a theoretical threshold below which every single toxic molecule is detoxified and no overt symptoms are caused, this threshold, if it really exists, obviously can differ greatly for different people and for different organs within an individual. However, for agents such as carcinogens and mutagens that can in theory cause permanent damage if only one molecule gets to the right place in the cell, there is no threshold of safety. Additionally, there are many instances in which a toxic substance is retained in the body, accumulating until some recognizable condition (poisoning, neurological deficit, etc.) occurs. In other instances small amounts of damage remain unrepaired even after the substance is gone, so that with recurrent exposure effects may accumulate until they are noticeable. One more reason to justify expending the effort needed to conduct a good health survey is the multitude of effects toxic substances have on people. Some chemicals cause acute symptoms but have never shown to cause cancer. Some carcinogens are relatively nontoxic, so lengthy or large exposures can be physically tolerated. Last, some substances obviously cause different symptoms in different people, so that one person may experience only acute symptoms while another may develop a chronic condition.

There are two situations in which we hope this manual will be of assistance: (1) if you live near a source of real or potential chemical or radioactive contamination or suspect there are harmful chemicals in your air or water but do not know whether they are having an adverse health effect on health; (2) if you suspect that the incidence of specific diseases or general ill health in your area is too high (relative to other communities) but do not know whether the effect is "real," or statistically significant. This manual is meant to enable your community organization to conduct a systematic environmental health survey of sufficient quality either to convince yourselves that there really is no excess of health problems relative to other communities or to your area of the country, or to convince state or national officials that there probably is a real problem and that they should give priority to a more careful study of your community.

The information given here is not primarily aimed at finding specific causes of health problems, nor is it absolutely necessary that you know the specific chemicals involved, their source, or the particular way you are exposed. It is the responsibility of state agencies to identify the pollutant and to eliminate its source; but it will be much easier for them to respond to a well-organized community group that has good-quality data on health effects than to a few individuals who have collected some anecdotes.

This chapter will acquaint you in a general way with some human health outcomes influenced by exposure to toxic substances: cancer, birth defects, mutation, and acute and chronic toxicity. We will review known environmental sources of toxic chemical and radiation exposure, along with some professional surveys (epidemiologic studies) conducted around pollution point sources.

KNOWN HEALTH EFFECTS OF TOXIC SUBSTANCES

Almost every day popular articles appear in newspapers and magazines telling of some newly discovered exposure to hazardous substances. For example, the National Clean Air Coalition reports that plants in Akron, Ohio, are legally emitting almost 600,000 pounds of the carcinogen acrylonitrile per year. The same group listed 312 carcinogen-emitting chemical plants, oil refineries, and coke ovens; Texas has more than twice as many plants (53 in all) as any other state. *Discover* magazine (March 1982) described the underground spreading of toxic chemicals into Atlantic City's public water supply. Also in March 1982, residents of the island of Oahu learned that their milk was being recalled because a routine check revealed contamination with the carcinogenic pesticide heptachlor. In December 1980 chlordane was detected in the water supply of several suburbs of Pittsburgh; chlordane is difficult to remove, but the "continuous flushing action of normal water flow will eventually eliminate" residual contamination (*Morbidity and Mortality Weekly* Report 30, 46 [1981]:571). *Mechanics Illustrated* (September 1980, p. 54) listed the "dirty dozen" worst pollutants with respect to the amount of human exposure and in terms of relative toxicity. These pollutants include arsenic, benzene, cadmium, carbon tetrachloride, chlordane, chromium, dioxin, lead, manganese, mercury, polychlorinated biphenyls (PCBs), and trichloroethylene (TCE). A significant amount of the produce in our grocery stores, particularly imported produce, has measurable levels of a variety of pesticide residues, some of which are "allowable" and some of which exceed permissible levels. In the mid-1980's, the U.S. Congress passed a law requiring manufacturers to report annually to the U.S. Environmental Protection Agency and to the states the amounts of some 300 toxic chemicals they release into air, water, or land. Over six billion pounds of releases and transfers were reported for 1988 (EPA 1990).

How can we possibly be aware of all our potentially hazardous chemical exposures? Obviously we are notified of only a small fraction of the hazards we are exposed to. A brief reflection will bring to mind many exposures similar to the ones listed above. Additionally, we constantly expose ourselves by choice to a multitude of potentially hazardous chemicals in cigarette smoke, insect sprays, paint strippers, weed killers, and so on, with little consideration for their poisonous nature as long as there is no immediate effect.

Every person in this country carries in body fat an average level of the pesticide DDT of ten parts per million (range 5–20 ppm; Roberts 1982; Wolff, Anderson and Selikoff 1982), 0.1–0.6 ppm each of dieldrin and benzene hexachloride, and lesser amounts of other toxic substances (reviewed by Hayes 1975). In one study, DDT values increased from 0.0015 ppm (the national average for blood-serum DDT) to 0.0076 ppm in the population of a town downstream from a defunct DDT plant, and the amount of DDT stored in body fat increased linearly with the age of the individual. In other studies, DDT levels reached 1,000 ppm in body fat of DDT formulators (Hayes 1975). Finally, certain regions of this country have been exposed to individual agents (such as PBBs, polybrominated biphenyls), and almost all of the local or regional populations there may have measurable levels of the contaminants in their tissues (Wolff, Anderson, and Selikoff 1982).

What are the effects of these chronic multiple exposures? We are aware of only the most obvious adverse health effects of some chemicals. In some cases we are aware that particular groups of people may be especially sensitive to certain compounds ("high-risk groups"). For example, the fetus is especially vulnerable to many things that may have no observable effect on the mother. Similarly, asthmatics are particularly sensitive to permissible levels of sulfur dioxide present in smog (*Science* 212:1251). Biochemical and physiological processes contributing to the general maintenance of good health are very complex. Chemicals or drugs may act at a multitude of biochemical or physical sites, disrupting or subtly altering the delicately balanced and interlocked processes that allow us to function optimally. Some chemicals are toxic in the sense that they interfere with the balance of these processes and thereby produce vague symptoms that can best be described as just not feeling well. Some chemicals interfere with specific reactions and may therefore cause specific or intense symptoms that are more easily recognized. Still other chemicals we know to specifically cause cancer or birth defects.

Since we evolved with exposure to low-level or "background" exposures to X radiation, ultraviolet light, carcinogens occurring naturally in plants, other natural toxins, and so on, we have developed the capacity to detoxify (to render harmless by biochemical processes) many natural compounds as well as toxic waste products generated as natural byproducts of metabolism and to repair most spontaneously occurring lesions. Thus we can also detoxify many modern foreign compounds, but the levels of specific enzymes that catalyze these reactions vary from person to person and depend on the genetic makeup of the individual.

That we can metabolize foreign compounds has two consequences. (1) Some of these biochemical reactions increase toxicity before the compound can be attached to other molecules and rendered inert so it can be eliminated from the body. During the short period that the chemical (or drug) is bioactive, it can attach to the large molecules in the cell, such as proteins or DNA, which in turn can cause cell damage or mutation in certain circumstances. (2) With compounds whose only effects are acute toxicity (i.e., those that do not cause mutations), a low level of the compound may be tolerated without adverse effect because the cells can detoxify a certain amount of it. The level of the compound below which no adverse effect is seen is termed the "threshold" level. The more toxic a chemical is, the lower its threshold, or the less can be tolerated. In addition, not every person can tolerate the same amount of a particular chemical, so the threshold level of effect may vary from person to person. The most sensitive individuals, then, are those at highest risk for developing symptoms.

Although we may be able to detoxify low levels of some toxic chemicals, there is no concrete evidence that we can safely tolerate even small amounts of carcinogens below some theoretical "threshold" of detoxification. Most damage is repaired by normal repair mechanisms, but it may take only one molecule not detoxified or one lesion not repaired to begin the process of transforming a normal cell into a malignant one. As an analogy, driving at thirty miles per hour is safer than eighty, but not as safe as 20, and the only way to be completely safe from the particular risk of driving is not to drive at all.

Human Carcinogens

> *Carcinogen* — an agent that causes new, uncontrolled, and progressive growth (cancer).

Recent analyses indicate that overall cancer rates in persons under sixty-five years of age are not increasing (Doll and Peto 1981). However, other recent articles have shown that some kinds of cancer, particularly those associated with smoking and occupational exposures, are increasing, particularly in the older age groups (Davis, Bridboard, and Schneiderman 1982; Gittelsohn 1982; American Cancer Society, 1990). Whether cancer rates are increasing or decreasing is a controversial topic, complicated by arguments such as whether to examine cancer occurrence (incidence) as opposed to cancer-related deaths (mortality), what age groups to examine, whether improved treatment of cancer in younger age groups offsets increased mortality in older age groups, whether a shallower rate of increase in lung cancer is following decreased incidence of smoking or use of low-tar cigarettes, and so on. It is definite, however, that several human-made chemicals cause cancer in the workplace and, by logical extension, in the general population.

Table 3.1. Occupation and Cancer: New Findings

Occupation or Industry	Site or Type of Cancer
Rubber and tire workers	Prostate, lymphatic leukemia
Paint and coating manufacture	Bowel, rectum
Petroleum industries, petrochemicals	Stomach, brain, leukemia, multiple myeloma
Welders and metal workers	Respiratory
Pressroom workers	Buccal, pharyngeal
Farmers, pesticide applicators	Soft-tissue sarcoma
Hospital workers (ethylene oxide)	Stomach, leukemia
Aluminum reduction workers	Lymphoma, lung, pancreas
Plumbers, pipefitters	Respiratory, lymphatic
Laundry, dry cleaning	Kidney, genitals
Leather workers	Bladder
Spray painters (zinc, chromates)	Lung
Automotive manufacture (casting, plating)	Lung

Source: Modified from Davis, Bridboard, and Schneiderman (1982).

Certain occupations have long been known to be associated with increased cancer risks (Hunter 1978), and other associations are still being discovered or confirmed (Davis, Bridboard, and Schneiderman 1982; Table 3.1). Increased cancer rates generally parallel national chemical production patterns (David, Bridboard and Schneiderman 1981), but though some industrial processes associated with increased risk of cancer can be linked to specific chemical exposures, in others the agents have not been identified. Many industries use a variety of known carcinogens, and several popular books have documented this sort of exposure.

There are many other occupations, some with obvious and some with not-so-obvious exposures to known human carcinogens, that should also be considered. Workers in such occupations include pesticide formulators and applicators, farmers or ranchers who apply their own fertilizers and pesticides or work heavily treated land, and persons who handle carcinogenic drugs (pharmacists, veterinarians, nurses). Few occupations are totally free of at least sporadic or trace exposure to carcinogens.

The compounds and processes that have been identified as established or probable carcinogens for humans on the basis of sufficient evidence from epidemiological studies are shown in Table 3.2. For example, EPA also lists some nickel compounds, creosote, trichloroethylene and (TCE), and both the International Agency for Research on Cancer (IARC) and EPA list a number of polyaromatic hydrocarbons such as benzo(a)- pyrene. Carcinogens cause cancer within multiple organs, but substances for which we have evidence of human carcinogenicity are usually potent and site specific, causing cancer largely within a single organ. For example, a very specific kind of cancer (mesothelioma) is caused by asbestos, although asbestos also causes cancer in the lung. The list of human carcinogens does not include some of the most important, such as cigarette smoke, since these have not yet been evaluated in the IARC program. Many other chemicals probably contribute to human cancer but have not been detected as such because their use is more limited, because they are less potent, or because they increase overall cancer levels rather than cancer at a specific site. On the other hand, not everything causes cancer, and most chemicals that have been examined in human populations have no observable effect. The drawback to this argument, however, is that relatively few chemicals have been extensively examined, and in point of fact we do not really know whether they are completely safe. We can never guarantee with complete certainty that a chemical is safe for everyone; we might have found an effect had we looked at a few more people.

A detailed discussion of the causes of cancer is too technical for this manual, and such causation is currently a topic of heated debate. Briefly, however, the development of neoplastic disease involves lesion(s) in the genetic material of the cell (the material that contains all the coded information needed to make a new human being and all the types of cells), abnormal promotion of the growth of the cell, interaction between host defense systems and the abnormal cell, and progression of the cell and its progeny through various stages of malignancy as the tumor becomes independent of normal limits on growth (Figure 3.1). Thus, multiple factors contribute to the development of cancer, many arising outside the body. There are five categories of cancer-causing factors, and though the exact contribution of each to the cancer process as a whole is very controversial, they may eventually prove to be of roughly equal importance. These categories are (1) smoking; (2) chemicals (both industrial and environmental), radiation, noise, and heat; (3) life-style, including alcohol intake, dietary fat and fiber, stress, vitamins, urban effects (such as smog), personality type, and general health habits; (4) genetics of the individual, including predisposition, first-degree relatives with cancer, repair of genetic damage, and other biochemical factors beyond our control; (5) other factors such as other exposure to drugs, pesticides, and household or hobby chemicals and interactions and synergisms between them, certain infections, background radiation, and random chance. Thus it is not unreasonable to say that most of the causes of cancer we know about are within our power to modify, or that most cancer is preventable. It will be many years before we can say why one person develops cancer while another person does not, but we are slowly beginning to understand some of the

Table 3.2. Chemicals, Industrial Processes, and Industries Established as Carcinogenic or Probably Carcinogenic to Humans by the International Agency for Research on Cancer

Acetaldehyde (2B)
Acetamide (2B)
Acrylamide (2B)
Acrylonitrile (2A)
Actinomycin D (2B)
Adriamycin (2B)
Aflatoxins (1)
4-Aminobiphenyl (1)
Amitrole (2B)
Analgesic mixtures containing
  phenacetin (1)
Arsenic and certain arsenic
  compounds (1)
Asbestos (1)
Auramine, manufacture of (1)
Auramine, technical grade (2B)
Azathioprine (1)
Benzene (1)
Benzidine (1)
Benzo(a)pyrene (2A)
Benzotrichloride (2B)
Beryllium and beryllium
  compounds (2A)
Bis(chloroethyl)nitrosourea (BCNU)
  (2B)
Bis(chloromethyl)ether (1)
Boot and shoe manufacture and
  repair (certain operations) (1)
1,3-Butadiene (2B)
1,4-Butanediol dimethanesulfonate
  (Myleran) (1)
Cadmium and cadmium
  compounds (2B)
Carbon tetrachloride (2B)
Chemotherapy for lymphomas
  (certain combinations including
  MOPP) (1)
Chlorambucil (1)
Chloramphenicol (2B)
Chlordecone (Kepone) (2B)
Chlornaphazine (1)

Chloroethyl cyclohexylnitrosourea
  (CCNU) (2B)
Chloroform (2B)
Chloromethyl methyl ether,
  technical grade (1)
Chlorophenols (2B)
Chlorophenoxy herbicides (2B)
Chromium and hexavalent
  chromium compounds (1)
Cisplatin (2B)
Coal-tar pitches (1)
Coal-tars (1)
Coke production (1)
Conjugated estrogens (1)
Cyclophosphamide (1)
DDT (2B)
Dacarbazine (2B)
1,2-Dibromo-3-chloropropane
  (DBCP) (2B)
3,3'-Dichlorobenzidine (2B)
1,2-Dichloroethane (2B)
Dichloromethane (methylene
  chloride) (2B)
Dienestrol (2B)
Diethylstilbestrol (DES) (1)
Diethyl sulfate (2A)
3,3'-Dimethoxybenzidine (2B)
Dimethylcarbamoyl chloride (2B)
Dimethyl sulfate (2A)
1,4-Dioxane (2B)
Direct black 38, technical grade (2B)
Direct blue 6, technical grade (2B)
Direct brown 95, technical grade
  (2B)
Epichlorohydrin (2B)
Estradiol (2B)
Estrone (2B)
Ethinylestradiol (2B)
Ethylene dibromide (EDB) (2B)
Ethylene oxide (2A)
Ethylene thiourea (2B)

Table 3.2. (*continued*)

Formaldehyde (2A)
Furniture manufacture (1)
Hematite mining, underground
  (radon) (1)
Hexachlorobenzene (2B)
Hexachlorocyclohexanes (2B)
Hydrazine (2B)
Isopropyl alcohol manufacture
  (strong-acid process) (1)
Isopropyl oils (1)
Lead and lead compounds (2B)
Magenta manufacture (2A)
Melphalan (1)
Mestranol (2B)
Methoxsalen with ultraviolet A
  therapy (PUVA) (1)
Metronidazole (2B)
Mirex (2B)
Mustard gas (1)
2-Naphthylamine (1)
Nickel and certain nickel
  compounds (2A)
Nickel refining (1)
Nitrogen mustard (2A)
Norethisterone (2B)
Oral contraceptives, combined (2A)
Oral contraceptives, sequential
  (2B)
Oxymetholone (2A)

Phenacetin (2A)
Phenazopyridine (2B)
Phenoxyacetic herbicides
  (occupational exposure to) (2B)
Phenytoin (2B)
Polychlorinated biphenyls (PCB)
  (2A)
Procarbazine (2A)
Progesterone (2B)
Propylene oxide (2A)
Propylthiouracil (2B)
Rubber industry (certain operations)
  (1)
Soots, tars, and oils (1)
Styrene (2B)
Tetrachlorodibenzo-p-dioxin
  (TCDD) (2B)
Tetrachloroethylene (2B)
ThioTEPA (2B)
Tobacco products, smokeless (1)
Tobacco smoke (1)
Toluene diisocyanates (2B)
o-Toluidine (2A)
Treosulfan (1)
Triaziquone (2B)
2,4,6-Trichlorophenol (2B)
Uracil mustard (2B)
Urethane (2B)
Vinyl chloride monomer (1)

Note: IARC classification scheme

Group 1: Carcinogenic to humans; sufficient evidence of a causal association in humans.

Group 2A: Probably carcinogenic to humans; usually, limited evidence of carcinogenicity to humans but sufficient evidence of carcinogenicity to experimental animals.

Group 2B: Probably carcinogenic to humans; limited or, usually, inadequate evidence of carcinogenicity to humans, and, usually, sufficient or limited evidence of carcinogenicity to experimental animals.

This classification scheme is based on strength of evidence of carcinogenicity.

Exposure to carcinogens, continuous or intermittent, or exposure to multiple agents that can initiate and/or promote carcinogenic processes

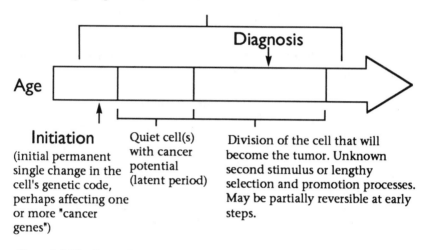

Figure 3.1 The Cancer Process

causes of cancer, and therefore ways to prevent it. It may be a by-product of this manual that additional causes of environmentally related cancer may be identified, or that we may come to understand the relative contributions of some of the factors mentioned above.

Humans are usually not exposed to high doses of individual chemicals, except in some occupational situations, so it is often difficult to pinpoint a chemical culprit or establish causation, and it is not really necessary to do so in the context of this manual. As we mentioned before, we are exposed to multiple agents that may influence each other's metabolism and effects. Other factors that we can control by choice (smoking, in particular) have been used as the legal defense of "contributory negligence" — in other words, the victim contributes by choice to his own disease. This defense has been used to unfair advantage by industry in individual cases, but large-scale epidemiologic studies are clarifying such contributory factors not on an individual basis, but according to population. Practically speaking, however, one can appreciate how difficult it is to prove that but for exposure to chemical X, this chain smoker would not have developed lung cancer or bladder cancer. Legal questions like this are discussed further in chapter 10.

One point we wish to emphasize strongly is that there are few individual causes of specific types of cancer, but many factors that contribute to cancer. This is equally true of most environmental disease conditions. Though specific "cancer genes" have recently been identified, the disease process, which we know to be very complex, can be said to result from cumulative insults to the host's genetic material and to other biochemical processes. In a simple analogy, we can regard the body as a tray full of bottles, each labeled with the name of a disease or health condition. Each bottle is filled little by little until one overflows and that particular disease develops. These "bottles" represent almost any sort of adverse health condition, such as brain cancer, leukemia, neurotoxicity, pneumonia, chemical allergy, or birth defects. Notice that they include acute toxicity as well as diseases that take a long time to develop, and also diseases commonly thought of as having a single specific cause. What fills these bottles and therefore results in specific adverse health conditions? If people have certain genetic conditions (first-degree relatives with cancer, or known genetic repair deficiencies, for example), they can be thought of as starting with their cancer bottles partially full. A fetus may have the bottle labeled liver disease half filled or three-quarters filled owing to undeveloped detoxification pathways. A chain smoker may fill the lung cancer bottle by smoking. The pneumonia bottle may be filled by the presence of the infecting organism supplemented by underlying lung damage plus an impaired immune response. The allergy-prone person, the child, the elderly person, the asthmatic, and others may all have bottles partially filled, not necessarily for a cancer outcome, but for other disease states as well. Thus environmental factors may hasten the onset of a condition that would inevitably have developed in that person. Some chemicals cause quite specific symptoms or diseases (asbestos is associated with a particular form of cancer and vinyl chloride monomer with an otherwise rare liver tumor, for example), but even in these situations we should not say that exposure A was the only cause of condition X. There are at least four reasons why this should be obvious: (1) even the rarest tumors sometimes occur without known exposure to the chemical or agent in question; (2) not all of the most heavily exposed persons develop that condition (100 percent incidence is seen only with some very potent poisons), so there must be other factors at work in the disease process; (3) although there may be key symptoms or conditions for a particular agent or chemical, no symptom is unique to a particular chemical (the closest thing to an exception is chloracne seen in chlorinated polyaromatic hydrocarbon exposures); and (4) a chemical or agent may cause different symptoms in different people, depending to some extent on the "physiological reserve" or resilience in particular organs or tissues.

As we stated earlier, many chemicals can be detoxified, or rendered harmless, before they do any damage. At low exposure levels, a chemical (or radiation) may not damage enough molecules to cause the death of a cell, or may not kill enough cells to affect the function of an organ enough to be clinically evident. In addition, much of this type of tox-icity is reversible; the damaged cell may eventually be replaced in or-gans that have this kind of repair capacity. In terms of the bottle anal-ogy, this "no observable effect level" would not be exceeded or detected clinically until a bottle overflows. It should be apparent, however, that smaller, but quite real effects may be occurring that eventually add up to a significant body burden.

We also know of several instances where the effect is synergistic: in simple terms, if chemical 1 produces X amount of effect and chemical 2 produces Y amount of the same effect, the amount "X and Y" is an additive effect and the amount "X times Y" is a synergistic effect. We know of several instances of synergistic effects of multiple factors, most notably smoking and radiation, smoking with asbestos exposure, and polychemotherapy (treatment with several drugs) in cancer therapy. The reason for synergistic effects lies in the multiple effects of a single chemical or, as in smoking, for example, the effects of thousands of chemicals. Research in this area is only beginning, but it is clear that chronic exposure to low levels of multiple chemicals is a cause for concern.

There are a number of general problems with studies of human car-cinogenicity, and if one of your community health problems is cancer you should be aware of them. As we have mentioned, we are exposed to a multitude of chemicals and to a multitude of factors that influence development of cancer, so it is very difficult to determine the contribu-tion of a particular chemical. The average latency for cancer (the period between the initial exposure to the carcinogen and the development of cancer) is about five to forty years (less for some leukemias), which means it is very difficult to assess exposures so long after the fact. These and some statistical arguments that have not yet been resolved make the entire field of quantitative risk assessment difficult in human pop-ulations and almost impossible with respect to individuals. Bear in mind, however, that these arguments have no effect at all on the va-lidity of your data; regardless of what contributed to it, the cancer inci-dence you find is real and is easily confirmed. The scarcity of good hu-man data and the unfortunate burden you or the state will face in proving you have been harmed by particular chemicals are scientific and legal questions that will not arise until much later and that will be the responsibility of professionals in those fields. This is addressed fur-ther in chapters 9 and 10.

Animal Carcinogens

Given the unlikelihood of detecting human carcinogens by epidemio-logical studies, can we rely on animal studies to indicate human cancer potential? We can examine the overlap between human and animal carcinogens. The human data on animal carcinogens are mostly incomplete and difficult to obtain (Karstadt, Bobal, and Selikoff 1981). We do not know how many animal carcinogens are also human carcinogens, but only one human carcinogen (arsenic) has not been conclusively shown to cause animal cancer, and even arsenic causes other genetic damage closely involved in the carcinogenic process. Therefore all animal carcinogens should be viewed as potential human carcinogens. Since the degree of evidence that particular substances cause cancer and the quality of experiments is highly variable, a complete list of animal carcinogens is not included here (it would include at least three hundred chemicals); this technical information can be obtained through your resource professionals. We have, however, included animal carcinogens that are probably human carcinogens, as judged by IARC (Table 3.2).

There are many problems in trying to quantify human risks through animal studies. Animal bioassays are usually conducted using high exposures of a single chemical throughout the two-year average lifetime of mice and rats. This design maximizes the probability of detecting a positive effect within a manageable number of animals, but even so, for conservative statistical reasons only the most potent carcinogens are detected. Most animal studies are not designed to pick up an overall increase in nonspecific cancer, to detect early development of tumors that normally develop later in life in a particular strain of rat or mouse, to detect agents influencing growth of the tumors, or to measure changes in host resistance to the tumors. Unfortunately, people do not live in controlled environments like experimental animals, which drink pure water, breathe filtered air, eat balanced diets, do not smoke, drink, or have underlying disease, are not exposed to multiple chemicals and drugs, and are carefully bred so that we know exactly what their inherited makeup is.

For some of the more potent chemicals that cause cancer in both humans and animals, we can find similarities and differences in metabolism of the chemical, the site where the tumor occurs, and its incidence. Thus a weak human bladder carcinogen may be detected in mice as a potent liver carcinogen. Owing to specific differences in the enzymes present in various rodents used for cancer studies, a chemical may be carcinogenic in one species but totally negative in another. Other biological factors also influence the accuracy of extrapolation: latency (the time between exposure and disease), sensitivity or threshold (whether or not below certain low levels a carcinogen will cause detectable disease), and so on. Nevertheless, we should not assume that animal carcinogens are safer than known human carcinogens. If a chemical has been shown to be an animal carcinogen, we must assume it is a possible human carcinogen.

Mutagens

> *Mutagen*—an agent that causes a permanent, transmissible change in the genetic material (DNA) or that causes visible damage in the genetic material.

Most carcinogens are mutagenic, and most mutagens, when studied extensively enough, have proved to be animal carcinogens. Structure-activity studies have given us a fairly clear picture of why some types of carcinogens are not detected in standard mutagenicity assays (Rinkus and Legator, 1980). For instance, these carcinogens may act at other stages in the complex processes leading to cancer that mutagenicity assays are not designed to detect. However, once we know that a chemical is a mutagen, we can examine the role of mutation in biological processes.

Figure 3.2 shows potential effects of mutations. Some of these are well established, and for some (aging, neural dysfunction) we have suggestive but less concrete evidence at this time. Most of a chemical may be detoxified before it can cause genetic damage, most of the damage may be repaired, and most mutations, if fixed, probably have no effect. However, we have identified many of the mutational defects that cause inherited inborn errors of metabolism and other genetic diseases (Bloom et al., 1989). We can also calculate how many of these cases represent new mutations (in the case of dominant inheritance), as well as how many defective genes we each carry that would be lethal if the same defect were inherited from both parents (recessive inheritance). The presence of defective genes that are not harmful as long as the paired gene is normal is called "genetic load." Thousands of diseases or conditions have clear genetic (or heritable) components and can be inherited in a relatively straightforward manner. Many others have less direct connection to individual genes and are termed multifactorial (many genes contributing to the appearance and severity of the condition). Some of these conditions tend to run in families but do not follow a simple and predictable pattern of expression. A few examples include hypertension, coronary artery disease, peptic ulcer, enteritis and colitis, breast cancer, schizophrenia and manic depression, diabetes mellitus, and diseases that cluster around certain human immune response antigens (HLA), such as rheumatoid arthritis, ankylosing spondylitis, and several others. Intelligence and neurological/behavioral conditions have genetic components. The reason for reviewing genetic disease is that any gene is theoretically susceptible to mutation, and many of these mutations may be deleterious. It is thus clear that mutation probably contributes to inherited conditions even though the effect may not become apparent until the genes responsible for them accumulate in

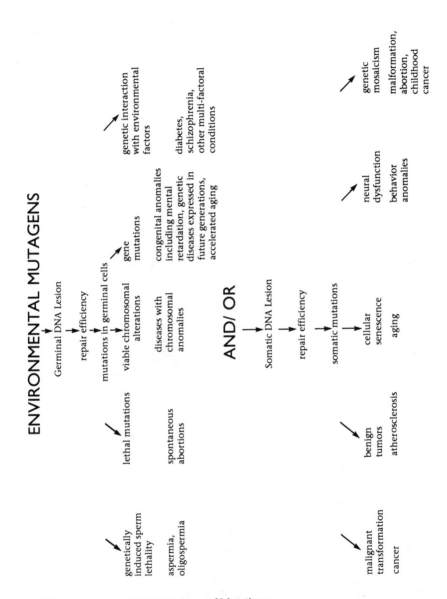

Figure 3.2 Suspected Manifestations of Mutations

future generations. If the mutation occurs in a cell not passed on to offspring (somatic mutation), there may be other outcomes that we are just beginning to understand and that by definition are limited to the person in which they occur. Given the multiple potential adverse effects of mutation, we should be concerned about excessive exposure to any known mutagen.

Teratogens

> *Teratogen* — an agent or factor that produces physical defects in the developing embryo or that otherwise causes an adverse outcome at birth.

Many agents have been identified as teratogens; these include both agents that act directly at the DNA level (many carcinogens or mutagens are in this category) and others that interfere at particular stages of development (thalidomide, viral infections). As with carcinogens, only the most potent and site-specific human teratogens have been identified. Other agents, particularly drugs, may be site-specific teratogens but owing to their limited exposures, may have been associated with only a few cases of birth defects, not enough to be definitely implicated. Even if a teratogen doubles the effect of an early recognized defect that has a normal incidence of one in a thousand births, 23,000 infants known to be exposed to that agent during the first trimester would need to be studied for that teratogen to be detected. And detecting agents that cause less easily recognized syndromes requires extremely large studies. An example of this is fetal alcohol syndrome, which has been identified only recently, even though humans have been consuming alcohol for thousands of years. Most human teratogen studies have been relatively large; only when a specific defect appeared, as with thalidomide, could the effect be noted in a smaller population; some of these problems are discussed by Kallen and Winberg (1979). One particular case they discuss involved the report of a slight increase in a small area of a particular defect (myelomeningocele) that first appeared in the local newspaper. An extensive study was done, but only cigarette smoking could be linked to the defect; no evidence implicated phenoxy acids, locally regarded as the obvious cause of the birth defects. This scenario has been replicated in many communities many times.

Low birth weight and prematurity are also categorized as adverse birth outcomes, as are altered sex ratios (ratio of males to females at birth), spontaneous abortions, late fetal death, and neonatal death. Known human teratogens are shown in Table 3.3. Note that smoking is also

Table 3.3. Human Teratogens

Drugs (not a complete list)

Sex hormones (different types of DD), ovulation stimulators, hormonal pregnancy tests, androgens (cause masculinization), progesterones (heart defects), DES (adenosis, cancer)
Anticonvulsants plus the underlying disease cause a variety of effects, especially cleft lip and heart defects
Antimetabolites: folate antagonists (methotrexate, aminopterin), alkylating agents cause DD
Tranquilizers (thalidomide, diazepam, possible others) cause DD
Salicylates: LFD, ND, LBW/P, DD (conflicting data)
Warfarin: LFD, DD ("warfarin syndrome")
Heroin: SA

Alcohol-many possible effects, including fetal alcohol syndrome

Smoking-LBW/P, possibly other effects

Radiation-many effects, including cancer

Anesthetics-SA

Chemicals and trace elements (not a complete list)
　Vinyl chloride monomer (DD)
　Mercury (DD)
　Lead (DD, growth retardation)
　PCB (LBW/P, DD probably)
　TCDD (DD)
　Carbon Disulfide
　Glycol ethers
　Thallium
　Fluorine (teeth)
　Lithium (probable)
　Copper, cadmium, nickel, manganese (possible), magnesium, arsenic = animal data only

Note: SA = spontaneous abortion; LFD = late fetal death; ND = neonatal death; DD = developmental disability; LBW = low birth weight; P = prematurity.
Source: Adapted from A.D. Bloom, (1981).

included owing to the low birth weight and prematurity (and other adverse outcomes) that have been associated with it. Low birth weight and prematurity are in turn associated with problems such as poor oxygenation, intracranial hemorrhage, and a number of other medical events, so the developing brain is particularly at risk after premature births. The most common adverse birth outcomes detected in the Love Canal studies were low birth weight and spontaneous abortion.

Other fetal deaths and neonatal deaths are often associated with visible chromosomal effects. In turn, severe mental retardation has a large chromosomal component (about one-third) and an overall genetic component of one-half (i.e., one-half the cases of severe mental retardation are thought to be of genetic origin, including both visible chromosomal defects and mutations at the DNA level). One-third of the cases of mild mental retardation are thought to be of genetic origin (Blomquist, Gustavson, and Holmgren 1981). Note that "mild mental retardation" indicates an IQ of 50–69; any lesser reduction of IQ (closer to the average of 100) cannot be reliably measured in small populations. Minor neurological dysfunction of children is very complex and cannot be measured very well in animals. However, behavioral toxicology in mice or rats after parental exposure to known mutagens or teratogens is contributing some useful information in this regard.

Although largely unrecognized, perhaps the most common "birth defect," mild mental retardation (and possibly minimal brain dysfunction and behavioral or learning deficits), may also be affected by in utero exposure or perhaps even by parental exposure before pregnancy. We may never be able to measure these types of effects—not only do we not know the true incidence of these conditions, we have no true control groups, since it is so hard to determine that anyone is not exposed to many of these things. Furthermore, postnatal conditions ("nurture") also influence these conditions. We wish to emphasize the exceptional vulnerability of the developing nervous system to toxic substances.

Some professionals in this field also consider childhood malignancy, genetic diseases that manifest themselves in adolescence or adulthood, and inborn errors of metabolism to belong to the general category of birth defects. In this sense we could also expand our definition to include any deleterious mutation occurring in germinal cells and present at birth, even though their effects may be too subtle to measure. This might include any of the outcomes shown in Figure 3.2 as well as defects in enzymes that repair mutational events, factors that predispose us to cancer or other diseases, premature aging of the types that are seen to run in families, and many other possibilities.

On the other hand, some birth defects are not due primarily or entirely to mutation. A survey of historical associations of congenital malformations (Wynn and Wynn 1981) has correlated birth defects appearing after World War II with malnutrition; this supports earlier reports of the same conclusion and again emphasizes the vulnerability of the developing fetus. The thalidomide epidemic is well known; one of the lessons we learned from subsequent laboratory studies was that well-fed rats showed no effect of thalidomide whereas vitamin-deficient rats were affected. The special sensitivity of the fetus to acute toxins is discussed in more detail later.

There are other effects on reproduction besides adverse birth outcomes, such as impotence, decreased fertility, and so on. Some recent examples: the nematocide dibromochloropropane (DBCP) is a strong sterilant: up to 100 percent of workers handling DBCP may be sterile. The flame retardant Tris (tris[dibromopropyl]phosphate) has been linked to decreased sperm counts and has been detected in the urine of children wearing treated sleepwear as well as in the semen of men sleeping on treated mattresses. Many drugs also have side effects of impotence and sterility.

Paternal exposures may also be involved in adverse birth outcomes, particularly in decreased fertility. Anticancer agents, alcohol, radiation, kepone, lead, DBCP, and other chemicals have all been implicated as causing damage in offspring without direct maternal or fetal exposure. Research in the area of paternal exposure is still new, but such exposure may eventually be proved to add significantly to the number of adverse birth outcomes.

Special Susceptibility of the Fetus, Children, and the Elderly

Periods of susceptibility in the fetus and in children can be understood by examining what happens at different stages of development. During the first half of pregnancy organ systems are developing, and during the second half organ functions are developing. Throughout pregnancy and during the birth process, substances given to the mother essentially move freely back and forth across the placenta (Levy 1981). Major physiological changes occur in the fetus and neonate as the child's metabolism moves toward self-sufficiency. Many organ functions are not fully developed at birth (especially the detoxification processes of the liver), and of course the brain undergoes tremendous growth during gestation and early childhood. At puberty, sex hormones start to function. Finally, organ function declines after middle age, so that the elderly are in many respects metabolically similar to infants (Lowe 1974). The developing nervous system is especially vulnerable to toxic substances, both before and after birth (Suzuki 1980), and all the neurotoxins and central nervous system depressants discussed later should be considered especially hazardous during this period. For example, assuming that the fully developed human brain contains on the order of 100 billion neurons and that no new neurons are added after birth, these neurons must be generated in the developing brain at an average rate of 250,000 per minute (Cowan 1979).

The National Research Council Subcommittee on Reproductive and Neurodevelopmental Toxicology published a recent review (NRC, 1989) on the use of biologic markers as screening tools. New research on neurodevelopment and on the interactions between the nervous, immune, and endocrine systems will help clinicians recognize the more subtle effects of chemical exposures. The recent report on long term effects of low doses of lead on learning and behavior is an alarming case in point (Needleman et al., 1990).

Some of the effects in offspring may be very long term. Development of cervical cancer in daughters of mothers treated with DES (diethylstilbestrol) is a well-known example. Another example is the more subtle effect of prenatal X-ray exposure: survivors of in utero exposure to atomic bomb blasts have shown significant stunting of growth and mental retardation (Meyer and Tonascia 1981).

Other Adverse Effects

Most of the adverse health effects detected will not be cancer or birth defects but will result from other mechanisms of toxicity. We cannot hope to catalog all the chronic and often subtle adverse effects of toxic substances. Acute effects of high doses of chemicals received on the job are the realm of occupational medicine. There are several excellent medical texts on this subject, such as Hunter (1978), Proctor and Hughes (1978), and Key et al. (1977). Since many industrial chemicals are legally or illegally released into the environment, occupational medicine is not necessarily limited to the workplace. It is often difficult to recognize and diagnose occupational disease, but recognizing symptoms of the "mildly intoxicated patient" is even harder.

Diagnosis of chemically caused conditions is a nebulous area, and the vagueness of the symptoms leads them to be often misdiagnosed. Pesticide poisoning, for example, may mimic brain hemorrhage, heat exhaustion, hypoglycemia, heatstroke, gastroenteritis, asthma, or pneumonia. Symptoms may include headache, irritability, nervousness, anxiety, sleeplessness, fatigue, mood changes, loss of appetite, nausea, vomiting, cramps, and so on. Finding a physician who recognizes the features that distinguish pesticide poisoning from other conditions can be a frustrating task.

Another set of conditions that are probably more widespread and even more often misdiagnosed are allergies or multiple chemical sensitivity. This includes not only contact dermatitis, but also other manifestations diagnosed as ITP (idiopathic thrombocytopenic purpura), vasculitis, thrombophlebitis, and similar entities, which have in common symptoms of blood-vessel inflammation, coagulation disorders, and impaired immune response. Symptoms may include swelling, susceptibility to infection, recurrent spontaneous bruising or small red spots, recurrent nasal stuffiness, headache, fatigue, and a number of other things (Rea et al. 1981). There is a growing concern about low exposures and chemical hypersensitivity, such as the "sick building syndrome" and other multiple chemical sensitivities. While symptoms may involve multiple organ systems, they may be attributed to "malingering workers, hysterical housewives, and workers experiencing mass psychogenic illness" (quoted from the New Jersey Department of Health).

Clearly, symptoms of chemical sensitivity or chemical poisoning and those of a number of other diseases overlap, and the physician must be careful not to routinely exclude chemicals as a cause. Symptoms of chronic toxicity are still a major concern to the patient, though they may not be regarded as seriously as cancer or birth defects in terms of workdays lost, medical care required, or impaired quality of life in general. We wish to emphasize that not all extra headaches or miscellaneous aches and pains are due to chemical exposure, yet the problem is obviously underrecognized and underdiagnosed.

An excellent chapter on occupational symptoms by James P. Hughes (Proctor, Hughes, and Fischman, 1988) lists effects (by organ system) and agents known to act in different ways. Table 3.4 lists a few representative agents causing specific symptoms and the total number of chemicals listed as causing each symptom in Hughes's original tables. We also summarize symptoms involving some of the organ systems most likely to be involved in nonoccupational exposures (Table 3.5).

As we can see by the number of agents causing vague effects, it is often difficult to prove causality. Furthermore, we are continually exposed to hundreds of chemicals from environmental, occupational, and household sources. Nevertheless, in most situations carefully conducted and well-controlled studies can detect an excess of a particular symptom or set of symptoms over the incidence in the control group. Again, this may be done without knowing if there is a particular chemical exposure.

The point here is that even though proving cause and effect in a medical or biochemical sense may require more rigorous methods than this manual is intended to provide, you should still be able to prove whether an unusual health problem exists in your community.

Table 3.4. Selected Agents Causing Specific Symptoms

Mild Irritants (eyes, mucous membranes) (a total of 164 agents)

Alcohols	Formaldehyde
Phthalates	Ketones
Many solvents	Petroleum distillates
Chlorobenzene	Phenol
Cyclohexane	Styrene
Epoxy resins	Tri- and tetrachloroethylenes

Severe Pulmonary Irritants (67 agents)

Acrolein	Isocyanates
Ammonia	Acid fumes
Chlorine	Anhydrides
Ethylene oxide	Higher fluorides

Pulmonary Sensitizers (16 agents)

Cobalt	Wood dust
Enzymatic detergents	Polyvinyl chloride fumes
Grain dust	Some compounds that are
Nickel	also irritants

Methemoglobin Formers (17 agents plus isomers)

Aniline and aniline derivatives
Nitrobenzene and related chemicals

Cholinesterase Inhibitors (13 agents)

Insecticides: carbaryl, malathion, parathion, dichlorvos, others

Central Nervous System Depressants (114 agents)

Acetates, alcohols, other solvents
Benzene and substituted benzenes (cresols, xylene, styrene, toluene)
Cyclohexane and related compounds
Ethers
Ketones
Ethylene compounds
Hydrocarbons (octane, heptane, pentane, etc.)
Cleaning fluids (chloro- and fluoroethane, -ethylene, -methane, -propane)
Carbon tetrachloride
Naphtha, petroleum distillates
Oxides (ethylene, propylene)

Convulsants (33 agents)

Pesticides (aldrin, dieldrin, DDT, 2,4-D, endrin, heptachlor, lindane, toxaphene, etc.)

Camphor	Nicotine
Hydrazine	Nitromethane
Methyl iodide, bromide, chloride	Ethyl and methyl leads
Phenol	

Table 3.4. (continued)

Neurotoxins Producing Peripheral Neuropathy (15 agents)

Acrylamide	Lead compounds
Arsenic compounds	Mercury
Hexane	Methyl bromide
Trinitrotoluene	Methylbutylketone

Primary Chemical Irritants of the Skin (over 230 agents plus isomers, salts)

Hemolytic and Bone Marrow Depressants (9 agents)

Benzene	Dinitrophenol
Naphthalene	Trinitrophenol

Skin Sensitizers (39 agents)

Acids, anhydrides, ethers, isocyanates, metal dust, fumes (beryllium, cobalt, chromium, nickel, platinum, copper)

Epoxy resins	Naphthalene
Formaldehyde	Chloro-, nitrobenzenes
Diamines	Pyrethrum
Cresols	

Liver Toxins (25 agents)

Carbon tetrachloride	Chlorinated napthalenes
Polychlorinated biphenyls	Kepones
Chloroform	Chlorinated ethane, ethylene

Source: Adapted from Proctor, Hughes and Fischman (1988).

EPIDEMIOLOGIC STUDIES OF POLLUTION POINT SOURCES

Many authors have documented the extent of chemical exposures and environmental pollution. EPA has listed over 1,000 dump sites that are top priority because they are near large population centers. There are thousands more dump sites of comparable toxicity that are not near large population centers and at least an equal number not yet officially cataloged by the EPA.

If this manual serves its purpose, you may be performing an epidemiologic survey similar to many found in the technical literature. For this reason, we will briefly describe some of the more recent epidemiologic studies of environmental problems occurring around sources of environmental pollution.

Low-level Radiation

These reports include both nuclear test sites and areas around uranium mines. Nuclear exposure at the Nevada Test Site has been blamed for

Table 3.5. Symptoms of Chemical Poisoning
(Selected Organ Systems)

Nervous System
  Severe headache-carbon monoxide, nitrites, alcohols, lead compounds,
    methemoglobin formers.
  Drowsiness, vertigo-central nervous system depressants
  Irritability, convulsions-convulsants
  Behavioral changes-CNS depressants, convulsants, carbon monoxide, lead,
    manganese, mercury, methyl chloride
  Tremors, weakness-manganese, carbon disulfide, lead, tin, mercury, DDT,
    methylene chloride
  Peripheral neuropathy-neurotoxins

Pulmonary
  Pneumonitis-ammonia, chlorine, oxides, dusts, fumes
  Asthma-pulmonary sensitizers
  Tracheobronchitis-severe irritants

Digestive
  Nausea-many chemicals, CNS depressants, cholinesterase inhibitors,
    irritants

Skin
  Generalized dermatitis or dermatitis limited to exposed areas-irritants,
    sensitizers, many other chemicals

Immunologic
  Allergic reactions (asthma, hay fever, abdominal cramps, allergic
    dermatitis, vascular inflammations)
  Diminished response (susceptibility to infection, decreased clotting ability,
    selective decreases in particular components of the immune system
    causing imbalances)

Source: Adapted from Proctor, Hughes and Fischman (1988).

sheep deaths and allegedly high cancer rates (*Science* 290 (1980):1097;
Stebbings and Voelz 1981), and the cases are still not settled. The Four
Corners area is also experiencing adverse birth outcomes (birth defects,
a difference in the male/female sex ratio at birth) that seem to be associated with the use of mine tailings * in residential construction (Wiese
1981), as well as a variety of other health problems of unclear cause.
Some problems with general population studies conducted around nuclear facilities are discussed by Tokuhata and Smith (1981). Since these
studies, many more have been published, some purporting an increased
incidence of a variety of adverse health effects around nuclear facilities,

* Tailings are the solid wastes left after ore extraction.

and other studies that not only criticized the former, but even claimed that small amounts of radiation were actually beneficial (hormesis).

Radon may be a "sleeper" exposure — it is the second most common cause of lung cancer after smoking. New findings indicate that the risk of developing cancer from exposure to low-level radiation is higher than previously estimated (National Research Council — BEIR V). Several national and international agencies are arguing heatedly about the implications of these findings with respect to health standards. While the public continues to view the potential of a catastrophic nuclear accident (which has a minuscule chance of actually happening) with horror, the much more significant problem of "natural" radon in basements is almost ignored.

Smelters

An extensive study of children living near twenty-one smelters was conducted by Landrigan and Baker (1981). Increased lead levels in blood was noted near a lead smelter, increased arsenic in urine near a copper smelter, and elevated cadmium levels in blood near a zinc smelter. There are many other examples of studies done around smelters and similar point sources.

Other Point Sources

Much of the environmental exposure from factories is due to release of occupational and industrial chemicals. The EPA listed twenty-one types of industries cited for excess of toxic chemicals (Sittig 1980; Table 3.6); identifying such industries locally may help you decide if you are looking at a point source of pollution or a more uniform exposure. Additionally, there is a well-documented "urban effect," or slightly increased cancer incidence in cities (for example, Melton, Brian, and Williams 1980). An extensive study in an industrial area of Baltimore was reported by Matanoski et al. (1981) in which data were compiled from the 1960 and 1970 census records for census tracts around a chemical plant (with particular reference to arsenic production). Death certificates from residents in those tracts (with the reporting drawbacks inherent to death certificates) were correlated with soil samples and with crude and adjusted mortalities after hospital validation of cause of death. An increase in lung cancer was seen in males but not in females. This study points out some of the difficulties in a retrospective study but is also a good example of how these problems can be handled.

The methodology of epidemiologic studies around point sources of pollution (chemical plants, smelters, power plants, mines, and so on) is

Table 3.6. Industries Cited by the Environmental Protection Agency as Often Discharging Hazardous Chemicals

Timber products processing
Steam electric power plants
Leather tanning and finishing
Iron and steel manufacturing
Petroleum refining
Inorganic chemicals manufacturing
Organic chemicals manufacturing
Nonferrous metals manufacturing
Paving and roofing materials
Paint and ink formulation and printing
Plastic and synthetic materials manufacturing
Pulp and paperboard mills, converted paper products
Ore mining and dressing
Coal mining
Textile mills
Car washes and laundries
Soap and detergent manufacturing
Rubber processing
Miscellaneous chemicals
Machinery and mechanical products manufacturing of any sort
Electroplating

Source: Adapted from Sittig (1980).

discussed in a series of papers that appeared in 1981 (Stebbings 1981; Gifford 1981; Lyon et al., 1981; Stinnett, Buffler, and Eifler 1981). Problems include estimating ground-level exposures, choosing between case controls and cohort control (discussed in later chapters), and deciding what health outcome to measure. Since point sources often lead to air pollution and therefore inhalation exposure, respiratory indicators may be used (Lebowitz 1981), although surveillance for lung cancer clustering (Lyon et al. 1981), liver cancer clustering (Stinnett, Buffler, and Eifler 1981), or a general health effect (Stebbings 1981) may be in order. Other "markers" should also be considered, such as embryonic and fetal deaths, or environmental clues (Hook 1981). Most of these professional studies were undertaken because of political pressure generated by local public concern, "even though the study could not qualify as research" and thus constituted mainly a public service (Stebbings 1981).

Although many cancer clusters occur in industrialized areas, it is almost impossible to prove causation by specific chemicals. Large epidemiological studies have been done around hazardous waste sites, showing some slight increases in some cancers, as well as increases in the usual symptoms (headache, rashes, stomachache). Even these, however, do not prove specific causality, but they do indicate potential problems (Griffith et al., 1989; chapters in Andelman and Underhill, 1987).

In other health surveys, it is often the case that while increased incidences of non-cancer symptoms are found, many or most of these are discounted as being self-reported, unconfirmed by physicians, clinically "insignificant," or without obvious environmental cause. Nevertheless, they may be sufficient to warrant further surveys and medical monitoring.

One last well-documented phenomenon is the existence of known regional cancer "hot spots" often including wider areas that have a high density of oil refineries, chemical plants, or other sources. Occasionally a unique local phenomenon has been found, such as the pickling process linked to esophageal cancer in northern China. Because of regional variations in the incidence of cancer, birth defects, and other conditions, you must either have a local control group or, failing that, must compare your results with the most localized incidence rates you can obtain (discussed in later chapters). Remember, you are probably most concerned with a community incidence greater than that in surrounding communities and less concerned with factors contributing to your regional or state rates.

INDOOR POLLUTION

This discussion would not be complete without mention of the hazards recently recognized in new airtight, highly insulated homes. It is common sense that the less exchange there is between inside and outside air, the more slowly the indoor pollutants will be eliminated. There are many sources of indoor pollution besides the obvious one of cigarette smoking: gas space heaters (ozone and carbon monoxide) insulation (formaldehyde or asbestos), furniture and plywood (formaldehyde), concrete (radon daughters), household products (cleaning fluids, pesticides, and many other chemicals), and crafts and hobbies (paints, paint strippers, glues and many other things). Several instances of contamination have even occurred from heavy application of insecticides for termites on the ground before a foundation is poured; the fumes then slowly seep up through the slab. The last item to be mentioned here is the extremely hazardous chemicals released in even the smallest of fires; this of course may be a source of occupational exposure to firefighters.

CHEMICALS IDENTIFIED IN DRINKING WATER

Many chemicals have been identified in water; some are the result of "rare" accidents, and some are present more frequently. The EPA has listed 129 toxic pollutants considered hazardous enough to warrant limits on discharge into water systems from the twenty-one particular industries mentioned above (Sittig 1980; Table 3.6).

The presence of organic compounds in water may be either natural or due to contamination. Natural gas or small hydrocarbons produced by fermentative bacteria may be present. Organics from sewage may inadvertently enter the water system, and street, garden, and farm run-off is an important source of particular chemicals such as pesticides or heavy metals. Other well-known instances of contamination arise from landfills, injection wells for chemical waste, illegal dumping, and so on. Many of these compounds have some toxicity by themselves, but chlorination of water greatly increases their toxicity. Adding chlorine and bromine atoms to these molecules may cause them to accumulate in nonpolar tissues (lipids, or fatty tissue), where they may persist for a lifetime. The most prominent of the identified chlorinated hydrocarbons are the trihalomethanes (THMs), including chloroform, dibromochloromethane, and dichlorobromomethane. At higher doses these compounds cause the usual set of vague symptoms: headache, dizziness, lassitude, fatigue, irritation of eyes, lungs, and skin, confusion, nervousness or irritability, insomnia or somnolence, nausea, loss of appetite, polyneuritis, and effects on other organs.

LIFE-STYLE

The last source of exposure we will discuss includes not only some factors with the most impact on our total exposure, but also the ones we can most easily do something about. While we tend to get more upset when we are exposed to agents beyond our control, we forget just how much we expose ourselves by choice. If we are really concerned about our own and our children's overall health, each of these factors is important in itself.

Smoking

Bioassays in laboratory animals have identified tumor initiators, tumor promoters, and organ-specific carcinogens in tobacco and its smoke (U.S. Department of Health and Human Services 1982). Smoking also contributes to premature birth and low birth weight and also to heart disease. Its effect may be synergistic with other causes of cancer (especially asbestos). It may also be causing an increasing amount of cancer in nonsmokers by "passive" or "side-stream" exposures (Shephard 1982). Lung damage from smoking places the lung at increased risk to chemicals that can affect it.

Alcohol

Besides acute and chronic effects on the central nervous system and liver, alcohol also causes fetal alcohol syndrome and is associated with some cancers (oral cavity, esophagus), as would be expected. By causing liver damage, it places the liver, the major site of metabolism and detoxification, at increased risk to chemicals.

Dietary and Social Factors

There is no doubt that good nutrition is a deterrent to cancer and many other diseases. In particular, vitamins have come under particular attention as protecting against cancer; conversely, diets low in fiber may be associated with colon cancer. High ratios of certain dietary fats may contribute to heart disease. Obesity is correlated with many adverse effects as is lack of regular exercise. There are other components of lifestyle not discussed here (personality type, intactness of family units, and other psychosocial and behavioral factors) that also have some influence on the development of disease, but they are probably less important than individual genetic and environmental factors. Recent arguments that natural carcinogens far outweigh the "trivial" risk from pesticide residues are misleading, and generally ignore the role of natural anti-carcinogens. A list of "nature's pesticides" would include aflatoxin, penicillin, streptomycin, caffeine, nicotine, cycasin, several chemotherapeutic agents, quinine, cocaine, ipecac ethanol, and so on. Obviously, some of these we use to our medical advantage, and some we abuse. One could add to this list several minerals and vitamins, some of which are essential in low doses but toxic in high doses. The notion that we are swimming in such a large sea of natural carcinogens and natural pesticides that a few synthetic pesticides won't be noticed is not valid, and the public does not tolerate the deliberate addition of incremental risk, no matter how small.

ENVIRONMENTAL CLUES

Careful observation of wildlife or vegetation in your area may provide some clues to extent or type of contamination. Most of this evidence comes from common sense, but it should be carefully documented. The excellent book by Waldbott (1978) contains a chapter on this topic.

Vegetation

When evergreens are damaged on the side facing the prevailing winds, especially downwind from an industrial establishment, pollution must be suspected. Some plants are particularly susceptible to certain air pollutants. Care must be taken here to minimize observable effects due to different fertilization patterns, temperatures, winds, sunlight, water, infectious agents, and so on before reaching a conclusion. It might also be helpful to document farm yields, size of fruits, or stunting of growth compared with previous years in order to minimize the influence of variation in growth conditions. In addition to the effects of identified air pollutants, vegetation damage from herbicides should be readily apparent and may result from deliberate spraying or from application drift. County agricultural agents should be able to provide much of this information.

Animals

We are all aware that honeybees are very sensitive to certain insecticides. Check with beekeepers or with farmers who keep hives to pollinate their crops. Veterinarians should be able to identify acute poisonings of farm animals, and zoo veterinarians may be the first to note effects in sensitive zoo animals. However, it may take quite a bit of detective work to trace the source of contamination when livestock (and later humans) are affected.

Contamination of wildlife has occurred many times. In some areas bird populations were greatly reduced by DDT, although they have now largely recovered. Wild ducks may have high levels of lead from lead shot and from endrin or other chemicals sprayed on remote feeding areas. Numerous reports of fish kills and damage to aquatic life have appeared in the press; regional EPA officials or fish and game officers should be of help in this regard. In one study, although about two-thirds of fish kill mortality was un known, municipal waste accounted for about one-fourth and industrial and agricultural applications accounted for about 7 percent each (Waldbott 1978, p. 56). However, these figures do not reflect the size of individual fish kills or areas of occurrence; more detailed information may be obtained from EPA regional offices (see chapter 11). Other individual instances of poisoning continue to occur, for instance, when frustrated farmers or backyard gardeners declare all-out war on bugs.

THE TOXIC CHEMICAL RELEASE INVENTORY (TRI)

Mandated by Title III of the Superfund Amendments and Reauthorization Act (SARA) of 1986, TRI contains provisions for reporting by industry on releases of over 300 toxic chemicals into the air, water, and land. Data submitted to EPA (with duplicates to each state) include names and addresses of facilities which process, manufacture or otherwise use these chemicals in certain amounts, as well as amounts released to land, water, injection wells, air, public owned sewer treatment works, and amounts transferred for disposal off-site. EPA collects this data annually. Various national groups have prepared reports ranking states and counties on the basis of environmental releases, selected carcinogens, releases to air, and so on. Several state agencies, such as the Pennsylvania Department of Environmental Resources and the New York State Department of Environmental Conservation, are preparing reports. Local groups have used the data in negotiations for reduced releases.

Access to this information is provided in several ways. The data is available at federal depository libraries — on microfiche, and/or computer diskette. EPA publishes annual summary reports. Call the toll-free EPCRA Hotline at 800-535-0202 for library addresses or for information on purchasing the data. In addition, the TRI database can be accessed on-line through the National Library of Medicine. (See chapter 11 for the NLM address and for groups active in right-to-know issues.)

The annual data is based on estimates of releases rather than on actual monitoring and therefore is of limited use in predicting actual health impacts, but TRI is still extremely useful for assessing the general magnitude and type of releases. It is also very useful for identifying individual chemicals released by individual facilities, or identifying all releases (or specific chemicals released) to each medium for a particular state, county, city, or zip code.

WHAT ARE APPROPRIATE TESTS?

Enhancing Health Care

Marvin S. Legator

Citizens residing in an area of possible exposure to toxic substances have a justifiable concern for adverse health effects attributable to these chemicals. This concern usually is accompanied by a need to seek assistance from health professionals. Probably no single decision facing individuals or community organizations is as critical as deciding which health professionals to enlist. Also of great importance are which diagnostic or other tests should be used to help characterize chemically induced adverse health effects. All too often, invasive procedures are performed that predictably cannot provide useful information.

SELECTING A PHYSICIAN

Our system of medical care is such that almost all disease possibly attributable to low dose exposure to toxic chemicals will not be detected. We've discussed elsewhere (see especially the introduction to this edition) how difficult detection is even when you are looking for a relationship between exposure and disease. With little or no training in toxicology and confronted with one patient complaining of a common illness, most physicians would not draw a link with toxic exposures. To increase the opportunity for detecting associations between chemical exposure and health outcomes, the community group should identify one physician to be the treating or consulting physician for members of the group.

Since most of the health problems associated with toxic substances are seldom unique, but instead add to the existing background of common afflictions, it is essential that a single knowledgeable physician evaluate all members of the exposed population. It is far less likely that if different physicians see patients from an exposed community an association between chemical and health effects will be perceived because each will be seeing a significantly smaller population. In addition, most health professionals have not received training in toxicology and are frequently not aware of the problems posed by chemical pollutants. For example, a physician may notice several patients complaining of non-specific effects such as fatigue or weakness. This physician may tell his patients that a virus is going around, causing illness in many of his patients. Only the rare physician would associate a generally non-specific feeling of fatigue or weakness with exposure to trichloroethylene or some other contaminant in the water supply.

The community needs to take the time to identify sympathetic health professionals familiar with the toxic effects of chemicals. Granted, identifying a knowledgeable physician or health professional will not be easy. While most physicians are not trained to detect health effects of chemicals, still others are reluctant to make connections with toxic chemicals (and important local economic entities) for fear of litigation.

You have an opportunity not only to identify a physician to help you, but also to educate your health care community. For example, your group could issue periodic bulletins to physicians listing the signs and symptoms related to exposure to environmental toxins and listing the predominant toxins in your area. Make the proper identifications of chemicals "the standard of care in the community." Press the local medical society to invite speakers, send out bulletins on health hazards, and otherwise inform the community about these issues.

The ideal physician to assist the affected individuals in your group would be a primary care physician (internist or specialist in family medicine) who has an understanding of the toxic properties of chemicals. The primary physician would, I hope, refer, if necessary, his patients to equally knowledgeable specialists. Contact community leaders who may know of appropriate professionals. Also query national or regional organizations such as the Citizen's Clearinghouse for Hazardous Wastes, the National Toxics Campaign, or the Environmental Health Network for assistance. Suggested physicians may not be geographically close, but may know of colleagues who are nearby. Scientists who have characterized the adverse effects of specific chemicals may be an excellent source for medical referrals. You should search medical and scientific literature for scientists currently conducting research in the chemical(s) you're interested in. Ask for the assistance of a reference librarian to get you started.

Depending upon who referred you to a particular physician, you may need to do some more investigatory work. Although you may not be contemplating any legal action, be aware that many physicians offer their services as experts in legal cases. Their general philosophies may be reflected in their choice of clients.

Do not be overly influenced by the numbers or type of degrees a physician or other health professional displays. For example, medical toxicologists are well trained and knowledgeable. It would seem that this specialty would be the primary source for evaluating you or your family's health problems. If you find, however, that you have access to one of these highly trained physicians in your area, but that this particular physician primarily testifies for or consults with toxic waste generators, you may wish not to engage his or her services.

You may wish to have an initial meeting with the physician. Think of the meeting as essentially a job interview for the post of primary physician for your family and community. You can use the meeting to alert the physician of others in your community who may wish to make appointments, and to ask about the diagnostic tests the physician might want to use. In sum, your initial task is to mobilize your neighbors (who have experienced similar exposure to toxic chemicals). Next, identify a qualified physician. Let us now consider what procedures are likely to generate useful results and, more importantly, to consider those procedures usually not worth doing.

EVALUATING PROCEDURES

Do not agree to a medical procedure or community study without knowing the significance of the test or study and how results may be used. It would be unfortunate to be victimized again by expensive, worthless studies.

Figure 3.2, in the previous chapter, shows the various steps from chemical exposure to final clinical disease. For exposures occurring years in the past, there are a few limited techniques used to associate exposure with various steps in the disease process. If exposure is current, health effects may not appear for years and, therefore, also will be difficult to detect. The greater the time from exposure to final disease outcome (either looking backward from disease to chemical or forward from exposure to potential health outcome), the more difficult it becomes to make a valid association. Nevertheless, a failure of current methodology to detect a response does not mean a cause-and-effect relationship did not exist.

Described below are the commonly used procedures and their usefulness in characterizing present chemically induced health effects or potential health effects.

Determination of Specific Chemicals in Body Fluids or Tissue

It is naive, but seductively common, to think that, suspecting chemical exposure, you can go to the doctor who will then run a single blood or urine test to immediately confirm your exposure. Unfortunately, there is no single analytical procedure that will detect all chemicals. Different analytical procedures are required to detect different chemicals.

It is therefore necessary to have a hypothesis about your exposure before any analytical testing. For example, it is worthless to test for metal exposure if you are exposed to volatile organic chemicals. You must have, or discover, information about the type of chemical and the source and frequency of exposure.

If your exposure is to a chemical that remains in the body only for a brief period (for example, the biological half life of many volatile organic chemicals is hours), you should *not* consider chemical analysis unless your exposure still occurs regularly each day.

Not only must physicians look for the chemical using only appropriate tools that could detect it, but they also must search in suitable tissues or fluids. Another consideration, therefore, is the distribution of the chemical in the body. For example, formaldehyde is usually confined to the respiratory tract if the exposure is by inhalation. In this case, an analysis of body fluids may not be informative.

In general, if you have been exposed to metals, chemical analysis is justifiable, especially if exposure is current. If not current, certain procedures, depending upon the metal, still may be justifiable. Analysis of children's baby teeth can indicate past exposure to lead, even when lead cannot be detected in the blood. With the possible exception of the determination of arsenic levels, hair analysis is of questionable value.

Certain insecticides, such as DDT, dieldrin/aldrin, chlordane, and heptachlor (and other chlorinated hydrocarbons such as PCBs), which are highly lipophilic or fat-loving, can persist for years or even decades in fatty tissue. It appears, however, that lipophilic chemicals and metabolites are mobilized out of fatty tissue under rapid weight reduction or stressful conditions. Absence of levels of these chemicals in fat or plasma, therefore, cannot establish lack of exposure. Moreover, while high levels of DDT, for example, indicate a high exposure, normal levels do not preclude adverse health effects.

This raises the question, "what constitutes high levels?" All of us still have DDT and its metabolites in our fatty tissue, although these levels have been decreasing since DDT was removed from the U.S. market. It is not sufficient to find a chemical in body fluid or tissues and conclude that there is an association with a given adverse health outcome. The concentration of a substance detected in these tests must be related to known background levels or to similar tests run on individuals who reside near the exposed population. Suitable controls are frequently required for a meaningful interpretation of results.

An interesting approach for detecting chemicals in tissue or body fluids is to consider the individual as his or her own control. Let us examine a situation where volatile organic solvents have contaminated a water supply. These chemicals have a short half life in the body and are often present in drinking water. To decide if an individual is exposed to these chemicals through his/her water supply, blood samples are taken during the day, within 30 minutes of drinking water. The individual is given bottled water for one week and then retested. The individual therefore serves as the control. The concentration of volatile organic chemicals found in the system after the initial sampling can be attributed to the drinking water. If the chemical(s) are in the water supply and have a short half life (lives), then the blood levels will decrease after switching to bottled water. There could be variations of this approach, such as having a sample taken when on vacation.

Finally, another aspect to consider is the laboratory doing the actual testing. Generally, your physician will not do the testing; instead, the doctor will draw the sample and then send it out to be tested. Make sure that the laboratory conducting the test is certified by a professional organization and has experience in the collection techniques and analytical procedures required. Also inquire about the manner in which the results will be generated. Frequently laboratories will furnish the physician or the patient with raw data in the expectation that the patient or physician can interpret the results. For results to be meaningful, however, the laboratory should provide information as to the type and sensitivity of the procedure used, as well as a comparison of the results with historical control data on tests performed by the laboratory.

Biomarkers, a Biological Response to Chemical Exposure

The process from exposure to potential disease is a continuing one. If the time from exposure to adverse health outcomes is relatively short (in cases of respiratory or skin irritation, allergies, and specific effects on the central nervous system, for example) intermediate steps cannot be determined. Other effects may take weeks or months from exposure to disease (e.g., abnormal liver biochemistry before specific liver disease). Years or decades may pass before cancer or transmissible genetic damage attributable to chemical exposure appear. In the latter two cases, when the body's response is delayed, several procedures are available to indicate the potential for future problems.

Several procedures indicate stages in the disease process but are not associated with a final disease outcome. Liver enzyme and kidney function tests are often used in cases of chemical exposure. Though frequently used, these non-specific tests may be better suited for population studies than for individual diagnostic purposes. The normal range for these tests is very broad and rarely does an elevation in a specific enzyme relate to a specific chemical. I can relate the ambiguity of these tests best from an example of a study we conducted of workers exposed to chloroprene. Results of liver enzyme tests in the exposed population were within the normal range. But when we plotted the results of the test, in which we compared exposed workers to controls, we saw that all of the exposed workers fell into the high normal range while the control workers were all in the low part of the normal range. There was little doubt about the effect of the chemical on liver enzyme induction, which could indicate future problems.

The above example illustrates the advantage of a population-based rather than individual analysis. It also indicates how a test may be interpreted as not significant when it reflects an abnormality. The need to evaluate studies of biomarkers, where the final disease outcome is not measured, must be carefully considered. If you cannot have studies done on a population, consider joining several neighbors in undergoing evaluation, with the same physician, during the same time period. A group study will increase the opportunity for obtaining useful information.

MEASUREMENTS OF DISEASE OUTCOME

A disease outcome can be definitive ("Your tremors result from damage to your peripheral or central nervous system") or it may be more conjectural ("You are tired or can't remember things because of damage to the central nervous system"). In either situation, we are identifying an outcome and questioning if an association exists with chemical exposure. The more obvious the disease is and the closer in time to chemical exposure, the easier it becomes to associate the affliction with the toxic chemical. If, however, the health effect occurs years removed from exposure, even an obvious outcome such as cancer can be associated with exposure only with great difficulty.

I will briefly mention neurotoxicity, respiratory effects, immunotoxicity, developmental effects, and carcinogenicity as examples of frequently encountered disease outcomes resulting from exposure to toxic substances.

Neurotoxicity*

These effects are usually seen soon after or during exposure and removal from exposure will usually diminish symptoms. Although most effects are transient and occur during exposure, if exposure is prolonged or at

* The author wishes to acknowledge the assistance of Thomas J. Callender, M.D. for the section on neurotoxicity.

high levels, then permanent progressive effects occur that vary from mild to severely debilitating. One of the most potent neurotoxins is lead. Children are especially sensitive to this metal. Even extremely low levels of lead exposure can lead to mental impairment in children and this effect may not reverse with time. Whether it is reversible or not will depend on when and for how long exposure occurred and what was the dose. In addition to lead, many other metals, organic solvents, hydrogen sulfide, cyanide compounds, and other chemical groups have been associated with various neurotoxic effects. Even household products such as floor cleaners and wax products (with phorbol esters) and spray cans (with methylene chloride) contain neurotoxins.

The mechanisms by which these poisons work largely are not understood, although in general neurotoxins are poisons that have the ability to penetrate nervous tissue. Many diverse chemicals with apparently different chemistry produce similar effects. This complex of symptoms includes loss of taste and/or smell, convulsions, tremors, changes in personality, ataxia, imbalance, intellectual deficits, fatigue, intolerance of heat or strong odors, unexplained chronic pain such as headaches, depression, anxiety, numbness, muscle weakness, memory loss and insomnia. Specific effects will vary with the neurotoxin, the sensitivity of the individual, means of exposure, length of exposure, and the concentration and amount of substance to which the victim was exposed. Due to the fact that these symptoms are not unique to environmental toxicity, several factors must be considered when attempting to establish cause and effect. Solvents, in particular, are associated with a disease cluster called "neurasthenic syndrome" including such non-specific symptoms as lethargy, weakness, inability to concentrate, memory impairment, etc.

The cause may be identified by assessing the development of symptoms and/or physical problems over time relative to the exposure, i.e., the relative lack of problems of the same degree and frequency prior to exposure as compared to during or after exposure. Tests for chemicals are rarely helpful. However, in some cases where the chemicals have long half lives in the body, such as inorganic heavy metals and some halogenated hydrocarbons, chemical testing can be helpful but seldom will predict the clinical status of the patient. Most chemicals such as organic metal compounds and most organic solvents are short lived and it is unlikely that one can measure metabolites in the urine or blood. Even persistent chemicals or metabolites may be stored in areas of fatty tissues (e.g., the brain) that cannot be easily sampled.

Although neurotoxins with long-lasting effects are illusive, they may have left a footprint in the nervous system that can be found with the proper battery of tests. These tests include measurements of overall mental capacity, i.e., neuropsychological function and measurement of the functional capacity of several neural circuits. These measurements include nerve conduction function testing (nerve conduction velocity, current perception threshold, evoked somatosensory potentials, and endogenous evoked potentials), vestibular function, fine color and odor discrimination, visual field mapping, blink reflex, reaction time, etc. If the symptoms or findings are severe enough, Positron Emission Tomography (PET) brain scans in combination with Magnetic Resonance Imaging (MRI) or Computer Assisted Tomography (CT or CAT) are useful in demonstrating the degree and distribution of central nervous system dysfunction. If these tests reveal widespread nervous system dysfunction, then a systemic or widespread cause is apparent. By ruling out systemic diseases such as diabetes mellitus or thyroid disease or other pre-existing neurologic disease, we then can reach the conclusion that an exogenous toxin was the most likely culprit.

If the above considerations can be applied to a population with similar exposures, then epidemiologic methods can be applied. This method can have considerable power even with low numbers of subjects due to the fact that it is unlikely for many of these independent measurements to be abnormal at the same time in a small group whose common denominator is a neurotoxic exposure.

Evaluation of Respiratory Function

If inhaled, many chemicals irritate the respiratory tract and may alter lung function. Results occur at time of exposure. The severity of symptoms as well as their persistence will depend on concentration, length of exposure, sensitivity of individual, and potency of the chemical. In order to determine whether your community suffers excessively from respiratory system impairment, it is necessary to first establish from questionnaires that the rates of various respiratory problems are higher than for a control community (say about 5 miles distant from the apparent source of exposure). For example, inquiry needs to be made about complaints such as frequency of colds, sinus problems, bronchitis, emphysema, bronchial asthma, difficulty in breathing, etc. It is extremely important to be aware of age, sex, cigarette smoking status (including passive smoking exposure) for each individual and any occupational exposures (asbestos, etc.) of both the presumably exposed as well as control populations. Before having community members undergo expensive pulmonary function tests, it would be useful to establish that the complaints indicated above have a rate equal to or greater (when age and frequency of cigarette smoking is matched) than for a control population. Assuming that such is the case, pulmonary function testing, or spirometry, could be done on a selected sample, matched for age, sex and cigarette smoking status, in exposed and control groups.

The parameters that are usually determined are forced expiratory volume per second (FEV) and forced vital capacity (FVC). Based on values normalized for age, it can be determined whether each individual is "normal" or has a "restrictive" (relating to a fibrosis as in silicosis or asbestosis) or "obstructive" (as in byssinosis or toluene diisocyanate asthma) impairment or a mixed impairment. Whether an individual has impaired breathing naturally is important to that individual but may not have much bearing on whether the community is exposed since that individual may have congenital problems or impairment due to previous pneumonia, influenza, allergies, smoking, occupational exposures, etc. However, if the community has a high rate of impairment of a similar type compared to the control, this may be significant.

Immunotoxicity

Our immune systems are highly complex, involving interaction of several types of cells, cell products, tissues, and organs. Studies of animals, chemicals in the workplace, and of community exposure to specific pollutants have indicated effects on the immune system. Many agents that cause cancer also alter immune function. Immune system injuries can lead to serious health consequences, including increased rates of infection and allergy (immunologic hypersensitivity). Autoimmunity, which occurs when the immune system considers natural components of the body as foreign and attacks them, can be crippling or even lethal. A battery of tests can be employed to measure immune system components or function. Although I have included this type of toxicity as an example of final disease outcome, the effects of chemically induced immunosuppression may lead to other adverse health outcomes. Although chemical effects on the immune system usually occur at the time or soon after exposure, effects (susceptibility to infection, for example) may not be immediately obvious.

Consider methods to determine effects on the immune system, realizing that many of the procedures are difficult to interpret as to their significance. It is important to select a physician who is knowledgeable as to the effect of chemical pollutants on the immune system. As with most of the human investigations, population studies have a greater potential to detect an association with chemical exposure than studies in individuals.

Developmental Toxicity

This toxic manifestation of chemical exposure includes spontaneous abortions, congenital anomalies, and functional alterations. The various outcomes may occur from chemical exposure of either parent (mother or father) prior to conception (transmissible genetic damage), exposure during prenatal development, or postnatal exposure to the time of sexual maturation. The adverse developmental outcomes can be manifested anytime during a lifetime. Low birth weight is a frequent indicator of developmental problems that may occur later in life, such as mental retardation. The correlation between developmental effects in humans and animals is excellent. This correlation is realized when all indices of developmental errors in animals (early fetal death, intrauterine growth retardation, congenital anomalies, and functional modification) are considered. Although animal studies are excellent for identifying developmental anomalies, specific effects will often differ between animals and humans. With notable exceptions, however, developmental effects attributable to chemicals are derived from animal studies, rather than relying on epidemiological evidence.

Carcinogenicity

The dangers of cancer from chemical exposure remain as the major concern of communities. The occurrence of cancer, following exposure to toxins, is also the most difficult health outcome to authenticate. Epidemiological studies in a community setting will invariably prove to be ineffectual. The long latency period, the marked age and health differences found in communities, the restricted number of exposed individuals, and the difficulty in establishing a suitable control population are a few of the many reasons that argue against the chances of finding meaningful results. Of special concern is the strategy of initiating a preliminary feasibility study followed, if warranted, by a time-consuming classical epidemiological study. Invariably the results of the feasibility study will indicate reason for a definitive epidemiological study. Almost without exception the results of definitive study, for the reasons already described, will be ambiguous. The study, in all likelihood, will not detect cancer resulting from chemical exposure. It should be emphasized that the failure of epidemiology to detect cancer is not because the chemicals did not cause cancer in your community, but because of the insensitivity of epidemiology to identify cancer causing agents in a community setting. The failure to detect a statistically significant effect will often be used as proof that there was no effect. The best advice to communities where a cancer epidemiology study is being considered often can be simply not to cooperate.

There are a series of non-invasive tests that can establish exposure to cancer causing agents and identify the initial stages in the multi-stage process that leads to cancer. These assays can be grouped under the general heading of "genetic monitoring." In genetic monitoring, a small number of exposed persons and controls (50–100) are evaluated for effects of chemical exposure on DNA.

Based on the knowledge that the initial step in cancer is alteration of DNA, the tests are non-invasive and carried out from blood samples of the test subject. Results are available in months and these procedures cost only a fraction of conventional cancer epidemiological studies. Unfortunately, these procedures have not been used extensively in communities; however, experience in the workplace indicates they are meaningful and sensitive. Genetic monitoring is not to be confused with cytogenetic testing used to detect genetic defects (for example, testing for Down's syndrome). Genetic monitoring procedures are informative only when used on a population basis, where an increase over a reference population is evaluated.

Cancer occurs when daughter cells produced by the cell with the DNA change proliferate and become the dominant cell form in specific tissues or organs. In blood samples we can detect the initial reaction of the chemical with DNA (adduct formation) and consequences of genetic damage such as gene mutations and chromosome alterations. Any one of these tests alone is much less likely to detect effects; therefore, a battery of these procedures should be used. If the correct criteria are established, these techniques are powerful tools for identifying exposure to carcinogens and indicate the initial step in the process that leads to cancer. Genetic monitoring overcomes many of the difficulties of conventional cancer epidemiology and should be used in future community-based studies.

It is generally agreed by the majority of scientists within government and academia that there are severe limitations in community cancer epidemiology. They therefore consider animal studies the definitive tool in characterizing a chemical as a carcinogen. All known human carcinogens were identified or could have been found in appropriate animal cancer bioassays. As to acceptable levels of exposure to carcinogens, there is no known safe level. Even the smallest concentration of exposure to a chemical carcinogen will incrementally increase the risk of acquiring cancer.

In summary,

• "say no" to a community based cancer epidemiologic study;
• realize that genetic monitoring, under the proper circumstances, can be an appropriate tool for determining exposure and initial biological effects of chemical carcinogens; and
  • understand that animal studies establish a chemical as a carcinogen and even the smallest concentration of a carcinogen can increase the risk for developing cancer.

SUMMARY

Selecting a single knowledgeable physician is important when trying to determine chemically induced adverse health outcomes. As to diagnostic procedures, few are specific for chemical exposure. Before agreeing to medical studies, make sure that the results can be interpreted and are meaningful. Neurotoxicity, respiratory effects, immunotoxicity, developmental effects, and cancer are some of the outcomes frequently associated with chemical exposure. There are procedures, such as genetic monitoring, that may be useful in characterizing exposure to cancer causing agents. Conventional community epidemiologic studies, however, will almost never indicate exposure to carcinogens and should not be considered in the case of chronic exposures and latent effects such as cancer. A chemical should be considered as cancer causing if it is positive in animal bioassay. Exposure to small quantities increase the likelihood of developing cancer.

There is no substitute for common sense, thorough research, and the utilization of knowledgeable experts when attempting to characterize the effect of toxins in a community.

FIVE

WHAT YOU NEED TO KNOW BEFORE YOU START

Introduction to Experimental Design

Michael J. Scott

Before designing your survey you need to formulate exactly what you wish to know, so that you can choose whom to survey and what to ask them. Since you cannot survey every member of a large community, you must use some selection process that lets you survey a representative smaller group of people. You may suspect that everyone in your community is exposed equally (to evenly spread air or water pollution, for example), in which case a random sample would be appropriate. If you know of a "point source" such as a dump site, you must collect information from groups of people living progressively farther and farther away from the source. There are certain rules to ensure that the people you survey are representative of the entire group to be assessed. Since many of the health effects you wish to measure are not "reportable" and so no state or national studies have been done to determine how frequently they normally occur, selecting an unexposed community or group with which to compare the results for your own community is extremely important if you are to conclude whether a health problem exists.

This chapter is intended to give you the background information needed to understand the scope of the work you plan to undertake. When you begin a "scientific" study, you are attempting to approach a problem in a methodical way and from as many angles as possible, in order to eliminate any bias you may have brought into the study (even unknowingly). The researcher looks for the heart of the truth and tries to understand what is really happening. This process has a few universal components, so this chapter will serve as a general introduction to experimental design.

THE EXPERIMENTAL PROCESS

Science, as an art and a discipline, came into its own with the acceptance of four elements — classically considered to be hypothesis, methods, results, and conclusions — as the constituents of a sound inquiry. These elements, arranged in that order, provide the framework for a community health survey. Contemporary research adds another component, "analysis," which is done after the results have been obtained. Each of these elements depends on the success achieved in performing the previous one.

Hypothesis

The hypothesis is a statement of what you believe is going on, and from that stems the purpose of demonstrating that the hypothesis is correct. The hypothesis of your study needs to be stated clearly to serve as a starting point. Since you have already begun the study process with this book, you probably already have in mind a hypothesis and a purpose.

You may believe, for example, that living near a chemical dump site is causing adverse health effects in your own children. The purpose of your study, therefore, would be to determine whether the children of your community, as a whole, living near this dump site, experience a greater number of adverse health conditions than would normally be expected. Your purpose might span a wide range of possibilities — from a study limited to certain occupations to one that surveyed whole townships; from a study of a specific disease, such as brain tumor, to one as general as a search for any detectable change in health status.

Although these ranges are possible, a concept of cause and effect at the outset will guide you to select the group of people to include in the study and will indicate the nature of the problems you can expect to encounter. An axiom of epidemiologic research is that the more specific the proposed cause-and-effect relation, the easier it is to prove it exists. A paradox about hypothesis formation is that, once you have refined what you believe is happening, you actually set out to disprove the opposite. It is very difficult to "prove" a hypothesis. If you believe that living near a dump site is affecting your health, you do not try to prove that. Instead, you state that living near the dump site has no effect on your health and then set out to disprove this statement. This "no effect," or "null," hypothesis is the basis of the statistical analysis that will be taken up in chapter 8.

Methods

Methods are the ways you will execute the study. Most of this book is directed at presenting methods and tools to use in your work. Remember that these methods need to be directly useful in accomplishing your purpose. For example, a study that tries to determine the health status of a group of employees by counting the sick days they used in a month may be seriously flawed. Many factors contribute to workers' use of sick time, so the study may well be measuring factors other than physical health: for example, psychological health, employer/employee loyalty, workers' sense of "being needed" on the job, and so forth. Compatibility between what you wish to study and how you study it may be difficult to achieve. Try to appreciate the particular strengths of each of the methods and how they can contribute to achieving your purpose.

Results

Results are the body of information you obtain — a collection of data. Viewed carefully, they can begin to tell you something about the problem in your community. They may tell you that in a "normal" community one-third of the children have allergies, but in your community almost all the children do. From your results, you will draw conclusions about local health hazards.

Analysis

Sometimes results are not easy to interpret, and mathematical interpretation, or analysis, may be necessary. Chapter 8 will deal more thoroughly with analysis of data, but a simple example will illustrate why analysis may be necessary. If you were to flip a coin ten times and count the number of heads you got, would you expect to see five heads and five tails? How often would you expect to see ten flips of the coin yield five heads and five tails? Statistical analysis shows that only once out of every four sets of ten flips would you get five heads and five tails. Therefore, although you expect, "on the average," five heads from ten flips, in fact, at any one set of ten flips it is unlikely that you will see five heads.

Community health surveys are similar to this example in that you might expect, on the average, to see twelve cases of a certain type of tumor in your community but in fact see fifteen. Techniques of analysis can help you decide how "real" the difference between twelve and fifteen is — whether fifteen is well within the normal, expected range of tumor incidence for your community.

Conclusions

Conclusions come from pulling together all the information gathered during your study. They tend to support or disprove the original hypothesis. Since *definitive* proof or disproof, however, is difficult to achieve without a much more sophisticated type of effort, your conclusions will simply indicate an effect or suggest a correlation between an environmental or life-style factor and a particular disease or effect.

THE STUDY DESIGN

A community health survey must be built within the framework of classical experimental design. You must define the population of people you wish to study and determine how you wish to study it. You must, by some means, compare this population with a concept of a normal group, and from this comparison you must infer the possible influence of an environmental factor on the health of the population.

Populations

The term *population* will be used to refer to the group of people being studied in a health survey. A population is simply a collection of people, though not just of the people you would like to use in the study. It is not, at least in the beginning, just your next-door neighbor or the couple down the street. Rather, it is a group selected on the basis of a specific set of conditions. If you are concerned about living near a chemical plant, then your population may be *all* the families living within two miles of the plant's perimeter. It must be all the families, not just those you happen to know. You can be more specific in your selection criteria so that your population includes only the group of people you are specifically interested in. Therefore your population might be limited to children, eight to thirteen years of age who moved into the community in the past three years and who now reside within two miles of a specific chemical plant. Since these selection criteria will determine who is in your population, they must be carefully formulated. Once you have arrived at your criteria, you must find all the children who satisfy them. If your child and the next-door neighbor's child fall into the population, they do so through a valid study design. They are part of the population because they meet the criteria you used for establishing it.

Your population, therefore, has some commonality. The people were chosen for a reason, and that reason should be pertinent to the purpose of your study. Every time you add a selection criterion for your population, you should be able to say why you feel it is important. Haphazard selection criteria can severely damage a study, either by encompassing people who are at very little risk from the suspected environmental insult or by excluding its chief victims. You should begin with the widest possible definition of the population, then add selection criteria one at a time until the final population is a reasonable and complete group of the people you expect to be affected by the environmental insult. Remember that the source of exposure and the suspected effects (such as skin allergies in children, pulmonary disease or heart attacks in older persons) are your two chief selection criteria.

Selection criteria generally fall into two areas: those that identify the exposed population and those you suspect of modifying the effect of the exposure. In selecting the criteria to identify the exposed population, you must consider three main factors: (1) Is the suspected exposure related to occupation or workplace? If so, what workers have been exposed? (2) Is the exposure geographical in nature? (That is, did the subjects live near a chemical plant or dump site? Did their residences use a certain water source? Was the community near heavily sprayed crops or woods?) (3) Is the exposure measurable in time? Events like chemical accidents or seasonal spraying might produce effects that are clearly related to time. If you understand the nature of the exposure itself, the people exposed will be easier to define.

The effect of an exposure can be expressed in many ways, so you must be alert to observe which segments of the population demonstrate extreme sensitivity to the exposure. Although the entire population may experience an exposure, for example, only people working in a particular occupation may be noticeably affected. Personal factors such as age may also tend to modify the effect of an exposure. Children, for example, are generally outdoors more and in direct contact with soil or water; in addition, they may be more sensitive to the irritating effects of contact with environmental contaminants. They may therefore be the first and most obvious group to study for adverse effects from chemical exposure.

At the other end of the spectrum, aged members of a community may be especially susceptible to lung irritants or other forms of chemical pollution. The researcher may choose to look at only these special groups or may maintain a broad definition of the population of interest and then look within it, at the end of the study, for especially susceptible subpopulations.

Other personal factors to consider would be sex, race or ethnic group, smoking, and possibly socioeconomic factors. Their possible role should be considered, though they should be incorporated into the study design only if there is good reason to believe they are influencing the expression of an adverse health effect.

Once this population is described, you will begin surveying it to determine whether some adverse health effect is present. In some circumstances this defined population may prove fairly small—because the original base of the population was small, or because the selection criteria were so specific that most of the community was excluded. On the other hand, you may well find yourself with a population that is potentially massive. Your selection criteria may not have been fine enough to identify a population of manageable size for your study, or there may be few factors other than exposure to use in defining your population. In this case you have two basic options: sampling the larger population or adding a final selection criterion.

An example of adding a final criterion to refine a study population may be found in a hypothetical situation. If you live in a community of 25,000 amid a great variety of potential environmental polluters, such as chemical plants, and you think something is amiss with the general health of the community, you probably cannot be sure which of the several possible sources of exposure is responsible: air pollution, contaminated water, or occupational factors. The general health of the community seems poor, but no single age group or sex seems more susceptible than any other. Where do you go from here? It would be almost impossible to survey 25,000 people. Aside from sampling (which will be discussed later), the only thing to do is apply selection criteria to define your population further.

Using occupation as a basis for selection should probably be ruled out quickly unless there is strong reason to suspect it is the source of exposure. Occupational exposures are usually plant specific (or unit specific), and the initial alert to a health problem will identify the probable source. Next, although the water source is a good candidate for the route of dissemination, exposure to it is fairly uniform throughout the community. Therefore the selection of any population will also take into account the possibility of contaminated water.

Exposure to chemical plants, on the other hand, is not equal throughout the community, although wind conditions could ensure that all residents receive *some* exposure. Combined with varying susceptibility, a community-wide effect might seem to result from pollutants released at a limited source point. A proximity rule could be used in defining the population. Since the actual source of the exposure is unknown, the group of people who experience the greatest *potential* exposure should be considered, such as those who live between plants. If one area appears to be a hot spot of health problems, it can be used to guide you to the source of exposure. If you study the group with the greatest potential for exposure, you can hope to have defined the population that is receiving the chemical exposure responsible for adverse health effects.

What if this group is still too large for you to work with, say 3,000 people? If you are convinced that these 3,000 all have an equivalent risk of exposure (and thus of adverse health effects), then you can limit the group further simply by arbitrarily making it smaller. You can use boundaries such as those of census tracts, election precincts, or postal regions and by this means precisely define a smaller population to study.

Using predefined boundaries to limit the size of a population has a few disadvantages: for one, it might suggest bias in the study. The possibilities for defined boundaries are generally limited, and if a rare disease is under study, the area within the boundary will generally contain a greater proportion of the disease than occurs in the entire community. This is almost impossible to correct because the choice of boundary cannot be random. The perception that an outbreak of a disease has begun, especially a rare disease, almost precludes the use of boundary techniques to limit the study population.

Another problem with boundaries involves the reason a population is selected in the first place. You choose the population because you want to make some inference, by means of your study, regarding their health status. By reducing the population size (with this boundary technique), you reduce the population base about which the inference can be made. This means you artificially focus attention on your limited population when in fact a much larger community is affected. By thoroughly understanding the study design and communicating its significance to interested parties, however, you can use a boundary-defined population as a "red flag" for a larger community.

In general, be cautious about overselecting your population, which may create a lot of work without significantly improving the study.

Subdividing a Population

Populations are usually not uniform in their makeup and may not be uniform in their susceptibility to adverse influences on health. Individuals in a population may have different degrees of exposure to a suspected environmental pollutant or may be uniquely sensitive to it. For these reasons, we will present two additional approaches for handling populations. (These are not techniques for defining a population, which you will have already done. Rather, they are ways of handling a defined population to ensure that you will get maximum information from it.)

Generally a population is heterogeneous in character. However, in certain cases you may suspect that one segment (aged persons, for example) is more susceptible to an environmental contaminant, yet you are also concerned about the other members of the population (children, pregnant women, or families as a whole). We have already discussed how to define a population based on the group suspected of greatest susceptibility. It is possible, however, to define the whole spectrum of the community as the population, then to subdivide it—to develop subpopulations based on factors suspected of modifying a person's response to the environmental insult (age, sex, pregnancy, and so on). You can then determine who in the population as a whole experiences adverse health effects and whether certain subpopulations are more (or less) susceptible. This technique permits you to look at various correlations that might result from interaction of population characteristics with the specific environmental pollutant to yield an effect different from that in the population as a whole.

The second common technique for subdividing a population is stratification, which means partitioning a population into subgroups (each expected to be different). Stratification is especially useful if the suspected source of exposure is limited geographically (such as a chemical plant or chemical dump). The group closest to an exposure source is probably receiving the greatest exposure and should be found to have the health problems. Love Canal was a classic example of this effect: the people with homes closest to the dump site experienced the greatest problems. By dividing the population into strata, you can demonstrate the source of the problem more easily and can point to a strong association between community health status and the contaminating source. A ring system of stratification, like that used at Love Canal, is an effective technique. In this manner even a mild effect may be clearly evident among the group with highest exposure (zone 1), whereas it might not be apparent if the general population were looked at as a whole.

The choice of ring size and boundaries should be dictated by the nature of the exposure. Airborne contamination may have a blanketing effect, so that only a few (maybe two) fairly large rings would be appropriate, whereas chemicals leaching from a dump site might have a confined effect, so that the first ring would enclose the houses situated on top of a dump, the second, the houses one or two blocks away, and the third, those three or more blocks from the dump. The key to determining the size of the rings would be where you suspect you will find major changes in the degree of exposure.

Once again, stratification and developing subpopulations are not methods of defining a population but are modifications of design to take into account the specific variations in your population. These techniques should be used when you suspect that some characteristic of the population is significantly affecting the measurement of health used in the survey.

SAMPLING

Sampling is used to estimate various characteristics of a population without counting each member individually. It can significantly cut down the work required and still obtain an accurate measure of the characteristics of interest. You can sample a population of 2,000 people by studying only 500 of them, with the expectation that those 500 will be representative of the 2,000 as a whole. If these 500 are not a good representation of the population, however, then the conclusions you draw regarding the population as a whole are invalid. Therefore, the method you use to select the sample is important.

We can use this population of 2,000 as an example and say that your interest is recent changes in their overall health. If you send out 2,000 postcards asking these people to participate in the study and you take the first 500 acceptances, are these 500 respondents representative of the population as a whole? Not at all. First, they agreed to participate. They might have done so because they have a problem or fear that one exists. Also, the first 500 might be those who feel a sense of urgency, so they might represent the extreme cases. Although in some cases selecting people in this manner may produce a group that is *almost* representative, even the slightest bias will seriously impair the validity of your work and waste the effort invested in the study.

When sampling is properly done, each member of the population has an equal chance of being included in the study. The researcher samples the population; the members of the population may not modify the outcome of the sampling process once it is completed. If the subject of your investigation is skin allergies among children, for example, and you use a sampling technique, you cannot add or remove anyone, even if the two worst cases you know of were not selected in the sample. Further, only a breakdown in the sampling procedure that makes you suspect it was inappropriately done or biased would give you a reason to resample. This is an extremely rare problem, however, so you should not be critical of a sampling simply because certain individuals are not included.

You may have an intuitive problem with randomly sampling a population for a disease that we have already said does not occur randomly; however, the underlying factors contributing to adverse health effects will be randomly distributed in both the exposed and unexposed groups, so the nonrandomness of the disease process itself should not play a role in the distribution of the disease.

The Sampling Procedure

Sampling is done by obtaining a list of the members of the population and then randomly picking those to be surveyed. Each person has an equal chance of being picked and, once chosen, must be included in the study. The first step of this process is often the most difficult: obtaining a complete list, a roster, of the population you have defined.

A roster of 2,000 names, as in our example, may be almost impossible to obtain. If you were investigating problems related to occupation, local unions might be able to provide membership lists; for elementary school children, school registration lists might be available through the schools or school board. There is no guarantee that these lists are absolutely correct, but they may be accurate enough that they will not introduce significant bias to the study. Two keys to building a roster are the type of list you are putting together and your ingenuity in obtaining material for it. (Some additional techniques will be introduced later about how to use other sources of materials.)

One technique that will greatly ease your work is to modify your roster — convert your population into another unit of measure. Instead of a head count of individuals, you might consider listing households. Instead of defining your population as all individuals within two miles of a chemical plant, you would then define it as all households, and you would thus reduce your roster to both a more manageable number and a more obtainable unit. (Street addresses are easier to obtain than names of individuals in a community.) You can still ask questions about individuals in households and look at confounding factors and correlations within each household (age, sex, smoking, etc.), and you can still stratify according to exposure, but you will be considering exposure to the household. Such a population roster is easier to obtain and the individuals in it can be approached in a more manageable way, yet the wide spectrum of individual differences characteristic of any community will still be taken into consideration.

As we stated at the beginning of this section, sampling of your roster (people, household, residential phone numbers, or whatever your population unit) is done randomly. You must choose some of these units to represent your population as a whole. A simple random sample is like drawing names out of a hat, but with a large roster that becomes impractical. Random sampling can also be done by various other devices. They may sometimes look like a game, but they serve the purpose of achieving an unbiased selection of units from the population as a whole.

Random Number Table

Selecting units by means of a random number table is a paper-and-pencil method that achieves the same result as picking names out of a hat. It is done by applying numbers to a list of your population arranged in an arbitrary but orderly manner — here, alphabetically. The list can consist of individuals, families, or houses, etc., but the technique is equally applicable to any population unit.

We can allow a random number table to dictate which names to choose from the population list. A random number table is simply a list of numbers, 00 to 99, arranged in columns and rows in random order. You could prepare your own random number table, but we have provided one that you can apply in your study (Table 5.1).

Sequential Sampling

Sequential sampling can be done by selecting from a roster at arbitrary intervals. A procedure as simple as taking every fourth unit could give you your sample of 500 from a population of 2,000. This is an easy method, and with a list of individuals, it is probably as random a sampling as you will ever need. If you were dealing with something like home addresses, however, this might not be satisfactory. Sequential sampling of a list of households by street and house number might produce a sample that included only houses on the same side of the street because of an odd/even street numbering system. This may not affect your study, but if the study is around a chemical dump, for example, excluding one side of the street may introduce bias.

Other Techniques

Dice rolls and coin flips are both simple examples of random processes that can easily be used in sampling. If you wanted your sample to include about one out of six people, you would simply roll one of the dice for each name on the list and then include only the names for which you rolled sixes.

One final sampling technique that may be of use is cluster sampling. A cluster sample assumes that the population is generally homogeneous and that any group of people or households you select will be representative of the population as a whole. So, instead of selecting individuals one by one, you choose small groups, or clusters. If your population is based on households, for example, you could use city blocks as the basis of your sampling.

Surveying all the people on any one block is much easier than tracking down the same number of individual residences scattered throughout town. The key to using this method, however, is that the population must look very much the same over all, so that selecting one block over another does not influence the outcome of the survey. If major differences in social or socioeconomic character are found in the area, then cluster sampling is not appropriate.

If these techniques are ranked by effectiveness, a random number table is best if it is available. Other than that, a sequential technique is good if there is no reason it should be biased. Finally, a simple process

Table 5.1. Use of a Table of Random Numbers

How to randomly select 20 names from a list of 80.

25	19	64	82	84	62	74	29	92	24
23	02	41	46	04	44	31	52	43	07
55	85	66	96	28	28	30	62	58	83
68	45	19	69	59	35	14	82	56	80
69	31	46	29	85	18	88	26	95	54

1. Assign a number from 1 to 80 to each of the 80 names.

37	31	62	28	98	94	61	47	03	10
66	42	19	24	94	13	13	38	69	96
33	65	78	12	35	91	59	11	38	44

2. From the table of numbers (see right), pick any column.

76	32	06	19	35	22	95	30	19	29
43	33	42	02	59	20	39	84	95	61

3. Cover your eyes, then pick a number in that column. This is your starting number.

28	31	93	43	94	87	73	19	38	47
97	19	21	63	34	69	33	17	03	02
82	80	37	14	20	56	39	59	89	63
03	68	03	13	60	64	13	09	37	11

4. Match this number to one of your (now numbered) names.

65	16	58	11	01	98	78	80	63	23
24	65	58	57	04	18	62	85	28	24

5. If the number you have picked from the table does not have a corresponding name (if, for example you picked the number 94), simply proceed to the next number in the column.

02	72	64	07	75	85	66	48	38	73
79	16	78	63	99	43	61	00	66	42
04	75	14	93	39	68	52	16	83	34
40	64	64	57	60	97	00	12	91	33
06	27	07	34	26	01	52	48	69	57
62	40	03	87	10	96	88	22	46	04

6. Continue down the column, selecting a total of twenty random numbers and matching these numbers to your names. If you reach the end of one column, continue at the top of the next column.

00	98	48	18	97	91	51	63	27	00
50	64	19	18	91	98	55	83	46	09
38	54	52	25	78	01	98	00	89	85
46	86	80	97	78	65	12	64	64	70
90	72	92	93	10	09	12	81	93	00
66	21	42	77	60	99	35	72	61	22

7. Maintain a list, in numerical order, of the numbers you have used from the table.

87	05	46	52	76	89	96	34	22	37
46	90	61	03	06	89	85	33	22	80
11	88	53	06	09	81	83	33	98	29

8. Since you can use a number only once, skip to the next random number listed if any number repeats.

11	05	92	06	97	68	82	34	08	83
33	94	24	20	28	62	42	07	12	63
24	89	74	75	61	61	02	73	36	85
15	19	74	67	23	61	38	93	73	68
05	64	12	70	88	80	58	35	06	88
57	49	36	44	06	74	93	55	39	26
77	82	96	96	97	60	42	17	18	48
24	10	70	06	61	59	62	37	95	42
50	00	07	78	23	49	54	36	85	14

Source: Adapted from Bahn (1972).

such as rolling dice or flipping coins can be used to select people randomly for your study. Cluster sampling should be reserved for very homogeneous populations. If such a situation exists, then cluster sampling is a powerful and effective tool.

Sample Size

Since sampling is used when you are trying to reduce your work yet still arrive at some answers, you must decide how much work you can perform adequately (or wish to) and how difficult it will be to prove that a problem exists. As a guideline, if you can mobilize enough people to survey the entire population in a reasonable amount of time (say three months, though the time involved is really your decision), then try to do so. Nothing is as convincing as results based upon a survey of the entire population. You should not settle for surveying fewer than 200 people unless your entire population is smaller (as in small communities, occupationally related exposure, and other situations of confined exposure or effects).

The sample size will be a function of the type of information you are collecting. The rarer the disease or the more subtle the effect, the more people you will need to survey to demonstrate the presence of a health problem. If you are looking for an increase in skin allergies, for example (normally 10 percent of the population might be affected), and this increase seems to be a major one (three to five times greater than normal), then the 200 people suggested earlier should be sufficient to show that a problem does exist. If you were trying to demonstrate a doubling in the rate of brain tumors, however, you might have to survey a population of 10,000 to 15,000. Chapter 8, on data analysis, will explain the requirements for population size more fully and will help you determine how large a sample you need to have a reasonable chance of proving an effect. You must realize that some of these adverse health effects are going to be difficult to demonstrate, and so the more people you can possibly study the better.

STANDARDS OF COMPARISON

Selecting and surveying a population is not, alone, enough to prove that a community health hazard exists. You will need a standard of comparison, some measure of what is normal, against which to compare your findings. If you determine that the rate of cancer in your community is 34 percent this finding by itself does not permit you to draw any inference. But if you determine that it would be expected to be 25 percent on the basis of some known standard (or one you have developed), then the inference of an increased risk of cancer in your community is supportable. Three basic types of standards may be used: official health statistics, an actual comparison group of people, or the stratification technique mentioned earlier.

Health Statistics

The easiest way to gather baseline health data is from government statistics. All levels of government collect health data, which then are available to the public. The data are usually well analyzed for major causes of death or illness and are characterized with regard to contributing factors. Four main pitfalls may affect your use of health statistics: they may be taken from a population (state, county, etc.) that is entirely different in makeup from the population you are studying; the data may be significantly out of date; factors you might wish to take into account (such as age, sex, pregnancy) may not be reflected; and rarer types of disease or illness factors may not be listed or may be inadequately reported, which makes the health statistics useless to you.

Comparison Populations

Another baseline can be set up by putting together a comparison population (control group), a group of people that resembles your population in every way except for the factor you suspect represents an environmental hazard. This comparison population should have the same age and sex distribution and socioeconomic makeup as your study population; jobs should reflect the same types of work environments, and the social structure should be closely similar. What you hope to find is what the health status of your study population "should be." Any discrepancy between that and what you have observed may indicate an adverse environmental influence. Such a group may be hard to find and difficult to survey, but the strength a comparison population adds to your study is tremendous.

Stratification

Stratification separates your population into subsections arranged according to decreasing levels of exposure to the suspected pollutant. The group with the lowest level of exposure can serve to represent the normal background levels of certain disease states. It is not uncommon for such a subsection to be the most appropriate group obtainable for comparison as well as the one most easily defined.

Certain factors must be considered, however, when you plan to use stratification to obtain your baseline population: stratification assumes that the exposure source identified is actually the one at fault; good stratification implies that you have a clear grasp of what type of exposure is affecting the population and that you know the health effect of interest is significantly influenced by exposure to it. And proper stratification means that only the one pollutant is being considered and that no other pollutant is accidentally affecting the stratification.

The key to using stratification as your comparison technique is guessing right (by educated guesses or otherwise). If no differences can be found between the groups that are related to stratum (that is, level of exposure), you will have to seek other methods of comparison. Stratification is generally used to reinforce your suspicions about the exposure source (the closer the source, the worse the health effects). A second comparison technique (such as health statistics) should then be used on the study population as a whole.

HYPOTHETICAL STUDY

The following scenario demonstrates some ways you can approach a problem.

Our hypothetical couple, the Wilsons, live in the town of Jackson. Their second child has recently been in the hospital for minor problems associated with neurological disorders: occasional dizziness, nausea, blurred vision, and so on — just six weeks after a sibling was similarly affected. A casual remark by the clinic nurse that "something must be going around" caught Mrs. Wilson's attention. Though their first child had complained of similar problems, no medical problem had been identified, and the symptoms continued to follow a pattern of recurrence and resolution over the subsequent weeks. Mrs. Wilson observed that bed rest seemed to eliminate the problems but that when the child was up and about, visiting friends and playing outdoors, the symptoms returned. The child also had apparently become aware of this, because for the past week or more he had chosen to remain indoors, content to play with toys and ask friends to come over.

Mrs. Wilson then made inquiries among friends, and uncovered two similar accounts from parents in the same neighborhood as well as an observation that some elderly people had recently begun to develop respiratory problems. Over the next two weeks the series of stories began to infuse Mrs. Wilson with a sense of urgency, since the more she learned the more she was convinced that the poor health of her community was excessive.

Jackson is a community of 38,000 that has two major chemical production plants as well as seven or eight smaller chemical production units. The great majority of local employment is in some aspect of these chemical industries, and the overall socioeconomic pattern of the community is fairly uniform except for one region where the employees of higher rank live (manager, unit supervisor, and so on). The plants themselves are clustered along the river and form a fairly consolidated industrial complex.

The more Mrs. Wilson thought about the community health problems, the more she came to believe they were associated in some way with the chemical plants, though she had no way of knowing which plant was responsible. When she shared her concerns with other residents, however, she met a fair amount of cynicism, though she was able to recruit a few concerned individuals. The Jackson Citizens for Community Health, as Mrs. Wilson's group called themselves, was formed and began studying the health status of the residents of Jackson. This is how the group approached the task.

Step 1. Defining the Problems

Problem 1. To determine if the health status of the Jackson community is poorer than it should be.

Problem 2. If the health status is indeed poorer, to determine whether this effect is associated with the chemical plants in the area.

Step 2. Developing an Approach

One option was to try to draw attention to their suspicions through the local and regional media. This method is usually ineffective, however, and tends not to solve anything. The other choice was to try to demonstrate that the health problem was real and that the chemical plants might have something to do with it. Though public services might assist in many cases, as they did with Mrs. Wilson, community members must start the process themselves.

Step 3. Generating a Health Survey

With the help of various resource materials and individual input, a study to survey the community's health was pieced together.

Step 4. Formulating a Hypothesis

Mrs. Wilson's group formulated a hypothesis:

• The community suffers adverse health conditions at a higher rate than expected.

• These adverse health conditions are directly related to chemical exposure from the chemical plants in the industrial complex.

• The frequency of adverse effects in various measures of health is directly related to proximity of residences to the chemical plants.

Mrs. Wilson's group ruled out occupation as a possible source of chemical exposure because it was not immediately obvious. They took advantage of a concept of dosage, however, by proposing that the effect was related to proximity to the chemical plants. They also proposed that the community of Jackson was different, in general, from normal communities so that the lack of a demonstrable adverse effect from the chemical plants would not nullify the possibility that Jackson might have a serious health problem.

Step 5. Defining the Population

The first step Mrs. Wilson took was to define the population as all residents of the town of Jackson (excluding the upper-middle-class to upper-class area at the east edge of town). Patterns of illness can sometimes follow socioeconomic patterns, and for the sake of homogeneity in the study population this small sector of the community was excluded. Impoverished neighborhoods were also excluded because they pose a similar problem. This is not to say that these groups did not have health problems or that the citizens' group was not concerned about these areas. It was simply that in Jackson most people were of the same basic socioeconomic group, and concentrating on a large, homogeneous population would result in an easier, more significant study. Concentrating on small, unique groups may be more difficult because of confounding factors, and a comparison population is not easy to obtain. If the study population is shown to have an abnormal health status, however, concern should be voiced for the health status of the other two groups.

Using the individual as the basis of the population causes various problems: in generating a roster, if one chooses to sample; in locating subjects, if one chooses to stratify the population; and in obtaining responses, if minors or infants are part of the population. As a consequence, Mrs. Wilson's group chose to define the population by households, keeping the same constraints as before. Using a detailed city map, they identified the areas in Jackson that were to be used as the basis of the population. According to available census data, these areas now encompassed 32,000 people in about 9,000 households.

Step 6. Stratifying the Population

Because Mrs. Wilson believed the health problems were associated in some way with the chemical plants, she decided to divide the population into three groups based on how close they lived to the chemical complex: within a mile and a half of the plants; between a mile and a half and three miles of the plants; and three miles or more away. These were called zones 1, 2, and 3. Zone 1 contained 2,880 people in 810 households; zone 2 had 6,400 people in 1,800 households; and zone 3 had 22,720 people in 6,390 households.

Step 7. Defining the Control Population

The built-in control group. If an adverse health effect indeed proves to be related to living near the chemical plants, then the stratification process described in step 6 will result in a built-in control group and will also indicate that the chemical plants are at fault.

The outside comparison group. Since the health effects observed up to this point could indicate a number of illnesses, compiled health statistics could not readily be used as a basis of comparison. What Mrs. Wilson did was to identify another community, Franklin — eight miles from Jackson and with 18,000 people — that was of essentially the same socioeconomic level but whose economy was based on a heavy machine assembly plant. She applied the same selection criteria to this group that she used in Jackson and came up with about 4,200 households that could serve as an appropriate comparison group for her study.

Step 8. Sample Size

The general rule of at least 200 households per study group is probably a good starting point for sample size. Mrs. Wilson needed to sample approximately 200 households from each stratum as well as at least 200 households from the comparison group in Franklin. Because the comparison group is so important in establishing the baseline health status, the statistics generated for it need to be even more precise than those for the study population. Mrs. Wilson finally decided to sample 200 households in each of zones 1 and 2 in Jackson and 300 households each in zone 3 and in the comparison population of Franklin.

Step 9. Sampling Technique

Using detailed city maps of both towns, Mrs. Wilson established residential blocks either by using streets or by introducing artificial boundaries where courts or circles disturbed the traditional concept of a residential block. Once all the blocks were identified, they were labeled and rosters were generated for each zone and for the town of

Franklin as well. A block averaged twelve households. Using cluster sampling, seventeen blocks were randomly chosen out of each of zones 1 and 2, and twenty-five blocks were selected from zone 3 and from Franklin. These households constituted the people who would be surveyed.

Since Mrs. Wilson occasionally found that one of the blocks sampled turned out to be commercial, she specified that when a block proved to have more than 25 percent business enterprises or fewer than six homes it would be excluded and a new block selected.

Step 10. Surveying the Population

This step will be covered in succeeding chapters. Once you have reached this point, you have completed the major part of the study design. During analysis, you can concentrate on specific subpopulations that you find of interest.

One problem you may encounter is how to motivate the comparison population to participate in the study. You could do this by emphasizing how the study might benefit them by revealing health problems that might be beginning in their neighborhoods. We will address the question of promoting subject participation later.

You may also find that the comparison population is a good distance away and requires a large amount of work to survey. Planning and organization can make this process easier to execute. As we mentioned before, although comparison populations are difficult to deal with, they are definitely the most desirable way to establish baseline health statistics.

WHAT INFORMATION DO YOU NEED?

Questionnaire Design, Administration, and Limitations

Barbara L. Harper, Mary C. Lowery

The purpose of the health survey is twofold: to let you conclude with some degree of certainty that a health problem does or does not exist in your community and, if it appears that one does exist, to provide enough information to convince state or federal officials that this is true. You will first need historical, physical, and demographic (characteristics describing the residents) information. You will also need to approach resource individuals and groups. The conduct of the survey itself will depend on the preliminary information you collect, how much you know about the suspected problem, and the number of volunteers available to administer the survey. As a first step, a series of nonrandom interviews of some of the most severely affected people, using your entire questionnaire, will tell you many things: how many people are being affected, what the most prevalent symptoms are and how severely and frequently they occur, and so on. Since the questionnaire we provide (chapter 7) was designed to be applicable to diverse situations, certain questions may not be needed in particular cases, and certain sections (occupational, for instance) are not applicable to certain individuals (nonworking mothers and children). However, it is usually better to have too much information than too little, so proceed cautiously if you decide to shorten the questionnaire. For a community-organized health survey, it will probably be most convenient to make contact with the households to be surveyed, deliver the questionnaire in person, let the members of the household fill it in at their convenience, then retrieve the questionnaire in person and answer any questions that have arisen. You must consider how you can ensure that individual answers will be kept confidential, while still being able to pinpoint symptoms on a map. You must also be aware of the limitations of any kind of health survey. First, the people who do not return the questionnaire are not a representative sample of your community. Second, knowing that your community may be exposed to something often leads to a more careful survey than is done in the unexposed group. Third, the conditions reported in the survey will probably not be verified by physician or hospital records, so you will be relying on lay individuals to report symptoms and on other lay individuals to code the answers. Finally, as you collect information, certain questions will be raised and inferences made that you will have to answer. These largely arise from the attempt to extrapolate the results you obtain for your entire community (probably expressed as an average for the neighborhood or community) to individual cases. Since there are certain natural background rates for each condition, you will not be able to say with 100 percent certainty that a particular case was directly caused by chemical X. By preparing your answers to these kinds of questions, you should be able to alleviate some of the trauma that inevitably arises when you conclude that an adverse environmental health effect exists.

This chapter will acquaint you with methods for collecting needed information, both health related and community related. The next chapter includes a questionnaire that can be used as a preliminary health survey and that, if necessary, can be shortened for a larger survey once you are sure which medical conditions are most prevalent in your community. Specific instructions for administering the questionnaire are given, and limitations of health surveys are discussed. Remember, your purpose in conducting this survey will be to document the incidence of some of the most prevalent conditions of concern in your community, not the exact incidence of every symptom. Your group owes it to itself and to the community to do a good job, and we firmly believe this is within the capability of intelligent citizens.

At this point you will have formed a community organization and begun to focus on specific issues. Before actually beginning to collect your data, however, some preliminary research is in order, if you have not already done this. Take advantage of city services to collect information on whichever of the following items are pertinent to your situation.

The Chamber of Commerce and other offices in city hall can provide information on the economic and tax bases of your town and on the major employers, and they should be able to give you a breakdown of employers by type of industry and tell you whether they have filed permits to emit or discharge waste and so on. The archives of your library can supply old city directories and other material on local history — this will tell you what industries existed in the past (and where), the approximate age of housing (when water lines were put in), and similar items. A detailed city map combined with census tract figures (obtainable in the reference section of your local library) will help you define your population sample groups and may suggest additional factors to consider in your survey. Also match the map to terrain: elevation, drainage patterns, wind patterns, vegetation, and natural and human-made bodies of water. Note land-use patterns (farming, mining) and compare them with earlier patterns (for example, an earlier industrial site may now be residential, a landfill may be a school playground). Your library will have a wealth of information of this sort and can guide you to local historical groups or knowledgeable individuals who may prove to be valuable resources and save you a lot of time. City (and state) planners will also have similar information used for forecasting, but they may not be enthusiastic about sharing it if it appears to them that you are trying to prove it is hazardous to live in their town. Use common sense and remain carefully neutral and objective when asking for help from someone who might have something to lose, tangible or otherwise.

Another resource you may approach with more or less success is local health professionals (family physicians, pediatricians, general practitioners, paramedics), who may have already noticed something and may even discuss particular symptoms you should include in the questionnaire. Local health officials may also be willing to help. Not only is it common courtesy to advise these groups in advance that you will be conducting an environmental health survey, but it will also increase the likelihood of their later support and cooperation should you find that a problem exists. These groups tend to be cautious and conservative, but they should react favorably to an objective, high-quality survey even if it is conducted by a nonmedical group.

During these initial stages you will begin focusing on just what questions you hope to answer. Two general situations might arise: (1) you know there is a (potential) source of pollution but don't know if it has caused any adverse health effects; (2) you suspect too high an incidence of illness but don't know if it is real or don't know of any reason for it. Often the actual situation is a combination of the two: you think there is a problem and have already assigned the blame to a particular source (a trap you should be careful to avoid in the interest of objectivity, especially since your assumptions may eventually be disproved).

The actual conduct of the survey, and your sample sizes in particular, will depend on your particular situation. We cannot hope to address every possibility that may arise, but we will give examples and guidelines so that you should be able to proceed without difficulty. A number of community situations are possible:

• You are absolutely sure you have collected every case of a major or usually rare disease in your community (such as childhood leukemia) and know your total population size and age distribution. In this case you can quickly calculate an incidence rate, as described in chapter 8.

• Your community or division numbers fewer than 250 households, and you have enough volunteers to survey every household. You will need to find a comparable control (unexposed) group, as described in the previous chapter.

• Your community is too large for you to survey everyone, but you suspect that everyone is equally exposed. You will need to survey a cross section by random selection to be sure that the incidence of disease accurately represents the incidence in the community as a whole.

• Your community is not evenly exposed: (a) You have a point source of pollution, and the farther away the residence, the less exposure there is. The previous chapter described how to "stratify," or assess the effect of distance from the source on incidence of health problems. (b) You have a point source of pollution with unequal exposures in different directions, usually characteristic of air pollution or pollution of a river or stream. In this case you will have to "stratify" differently in different directions (upwind or downwind, or by quadrant).

• You do not know how the community is exposed, or whether health effects, if any, are evenly distributed, or whether the pollution occurs evenly or unevenly. Pinpointing cases on a map will be one of your tools in this case.

At this point you will probably want to conduct a small series of "open" or "unfocused" interviews. This "discovery" procedure will alert you to particular facets of your situation (symptoms, environmental clues, the history and scope of the problem, etc.). A medically skilled interviewer is beneficial here to relate symptoms to organ systems and exposures, and also because open interviews like this depend on recall. You will be collecting a lot of hearsay anecdotes, which do have limited use as an overview even though they are not scientific or admissible in court. If you have no one skilled in any sort of interviewing, your task force or steering committee will need to use the entire questionnaire as is, and you will probably want to do some background reading from the various references in this manual. If you need to use a large sample and are short on volunteers, you may wish to consider using this questionnaire as a preliminary survey of twenty-five or so most affected people to collect all symptoms that are appearing. From this you can formulate a short version concentrating primarily on a few key conditions. Don't be in too great a hurry to eliminate seemingly irrelevant questions, however, since a chemical can affect different people in different ways. A complete preliminary survey should nevertheless be sufficient to uncover the most common symptoms (which will be enough for you to prove your point). If you are sure that you are concerned only with one or a few specific conditions, you may even condense the questionnaire into a page or two, short enough to fill out by telephone, as described later. Use your common sense in choosing what questions to ask: an air pollution route of exposure means you may find respiratory symptoms and certain environmental clues that you would not find in waterborne exposures, while waterborne contaminants may lead to intestinal symptoms and fish kills. Again, however, just because you know of the presence of one airborne chemical you must not assume that chemical is necessarily the only cause of the problems; they may actually be caused in part by another, entirely unrelated waterborne chemical, for example.

QUESTIONNAIRE DESIGN

We have compiled our questionnaire using material from a number of large, well-tested questionnaires and have added some environmental questions. That most of the questions have been field tested means we will not have to summarize the entire area of questionnaire design, itself the subject of many professional books. Some of these texts are listed as references for those who wish further information.

We have tried to design the questionnaire to be as widely applicable as possible, and therefore we have had to make some assumptions both about the exposed group and about what kind of data you will want to collect. First, both acute and chronic conditions are included; this concept is very important with respect to the end points you are measuring. Symptoms of chronic exposure may resemble, in a milder form, symptoms of acute poisoning by the same agent. Some symptoms may be slowly progressive so that their onset cannot be pinpointed. Adverse birth outcomes obviously have more or less a nine-month waiting period. Cancer, however, has a variable latency, with few or no symptoms appearing in the interim. Since it may take five to forty years for some cancers to develop, there are many problems in obtaining estimates of exposures that occurred far in the past. Occupational histories should therefore extend back as far as possible; we have allowed space for a complete occupational history since age sixteen plus detailed questions for more acute (past five years) exposures.

Finally, the length of the questionnaire is less important than question content; though it may seem long, you still have the option of adding questions based on your own open interviews.

ADMINISTRATION

The major question to be decided at this point is whether the questionnaire will be administered by an interviewer or will be self-administered. Several studies comparing the two have found that self-administered questionnaires are generally just as valid, and a little more valid on sensitive questions (Siemiatycki 1979). Optimal response will probably be generated by making initial contact by mail or telephone, then mailing (or hand delivering) the questionnaire and using an interviewer only for persistent nonresponders. You may be criticized for not using an interviewer for every questionnaire or for using several different interviewers (if your sample size is small enough to allow you to interview everyone). Probably the major problem of your entire project will be how to ensure high-quality data when laypeople report their symptoms to nonmedical interviewers or scorers. Untrained interviewers may also be biased, especially in a local setting where they know about exposures and what symptoms might be expected. For those reasons, unless you are overwhelmed with skilled volunteer interviewers, the questionnaire should probably be self-administered. The questionnaire can thus be filled in at the convenience of the household, will not need to be completed in one sitting, and will allow respondents time to look up personal medical records. You may choose to limit contact to the initial telephone call and have subjects mail the questionnaire back in, or you may prefer to pick up the questionnaires and at the same time answer any questions there might be. Even better, you may hand deliver the questionnaires and review them with the respondents, who will then fill in the appropriate sections at their convenience.

The first step in the health survey itself will be to verify addresses and send a "preletter." The letter should look as professional as possible, depending on funds. Perhaps a printing business would donate paper and print a letterhead, the letter itself, or the questionnaire; if any businesses or groups have agreed to be sponsors, include them somewhere in the letterhead. The preletter not only is a courtesy, it increases the response rate. This letter will describe the group and its history, tell subjects they will be receiving the questionnaire, explain its purpose, and tell why your group is conducting the survey, why people should participate, how they were chosen and of which groups they are members, how individual responses will be kept confidential, how the results will be used, and whether respondents can expect any benefits. Offer to send a summary report (at the end of the questionnaire you may ask whether respondents would like a summary of the results).

A short time after the initial letter is sent, you may want to telephone each household to ask if the letter has arrived, explain how important it is that they participate, and ask if they are willing. Have a phone number and references ready.

At this point you will already realize that nonparticipants are proving to be a problem. Every epidemiologic study is plagued with nonparticipants. They present a particular difficulty when they are part of a random sample that must accurately represent your entire community.

Strictly speaking, once subjects have been chosen as part of a random sample, they must remain part of that sample. The nonparticipants should not be replaced by another randomly selected person. The reason for this derives from the reasons people do not want to participate: they do not have a problem, they do not perceive that anyone else has a real problem, they have a health problem but do not want to admit it, they perceive the survey as an attack on their employer and therefore on their job security, and so on. In other words, the nonparticipants may have a different makeup than the rest of your community, and their nonparticipation may cause inaccuracies in your calculations. By repeatedly approaching these people as your study progresses, perhaps you will succeed in convincing them to participate. The few who absolutely refuse may at that point be replaced from your list of alternates, also chosen randomly. Remember, however, that if you are concerned about a sensitive condition (sterility, for example), your nonparticipants may include proportionally more affected people than you would expect based on the rate you establish for the rest of the community. Another important point: if your random selection includes people who have recently moved away because of health effects and you cannot reach them, you may miss some of the most severely affected cases.

You are now ready to deliver the questionnaire. Attached to the front of each questionnaire will be a cover letter, which should be neat, official looking, short, and to the point. It will review the nature of the study and tell how the data will be used, and it will include particular instructions. Ask that it be returned as soon as possible rather than by a firm deadline; this will avoid having people think it is to late to turn it in at all. If the questionnaire is delivered and returned by mail, enclose an addressed return envelope (stamped, not metered). An actual sample cover letter is not supplied with the questionnaire because details will vary with each survey. General instructions are supplied at the front of the questionnaire.

There are two additional points to consider before the questionnaires are sent. First is the possibility of including an unannounced "incentive" with the questionnaire, which creates a sense of obligation to fill it out. If your funds will not permit enclosing money, perhaps businesses will donate discount coupons, certificates for free hamburgers, or something else people are likely to appreciate.

The second point that will need careful consideration is the issue of confidentiality and anonymity. True anonymity (in which case you really do not know who has answered and who has not) will probably not be applicable to most environmental situations, though large random-sample surveys usually adhere to it. You will need to know the exact or approximate address of each household (at least which block and perhaps which side of the block) so that residence and symptoms can be correlated. There are a number of ways to handle this. First, you can ask for name and address and assure the people of confidentiality. Second, you can assign each household a number (being careful that the right code number goes into each envelope) and keep the code numbers and matched names and addresses in a locked safe, safe-deposit box, or other secure place. Third, you can keep names and addresses separate so that you can map symptoms without connecting them to names and faces.

Three to five days after mailing the questionnaire, mail postcards thanking subjects for participating (and reminding them to fill them in if they have not). Obviously you will have to know who has returned the questionnaire and who hasn't in order to follow up non respondents. At this point don't be afraid to be persistent (but not obnoxious), since these reminders are a very effective technique for improving response rate. Let nonrespondents know that their response is really needed. You may need to hand deliver another questionnaire or have an interviewer administer it. Follow-ups may be humorous postcards or telephone calls. Remember these are your data and it is important to your efforts and those of numerous volunteers.

LIMITATIONS

Let us briefly discuss some of the drawbacks pertaining to the quality of data obtained by using this particular questionnaire. The first major criticism you may encounter will be for the lack of interviewers (if you have not used interviewers at all) or for using untrained or semitrained interviewers (if you have). As we discussed above, the only way to counter this objection with limited local resources is to make every effort to remain nonbiased, to avoid asking leading questions or digging for symptoms just because you know a person has been exposed, and to write down everything you plan to say ahead of time so it will always be the same. This weakness will remain a point of contention, but with common sense and close supervision it can be minimized.

The second weakness will be lack of verification by a physician of either symptoms or conditions. The survey information will be collected from laypeople by other laypeople, and furthermore it relies largely on recall. Accuracy is proportional to overall self-awareness of current symptoms and also to people's ability to remember names of major diseases. Whether a medical interviewer would improve data quality or not, however, is in doubt: medical doctors classify fewer patients as having priority health problems than do the patients themselves (Bennett and Richie 1975), and local doctors are often not the ones who first recognize a general health problem.

Other limitations are inherent in any questionnaire. Reasons for not responding to a questionnaire include language barriers and racial, cultural, and literacy factors. On the other hand, a person may have good health and not perceive a problem or any need to determine if there is a problem for others. Bad health may physically interfere with answering. Those who do not bother to take care of their general health may not want to answer a health-related questionnaire. People also tend to report better or more socially desirable habits than they have, so recreational drug use, smoking, drinking, and so on will be underreported to some degree. Some types of questions, especially on reproduction, are usually answered less accurately, as are certain conditions that may still carry a social stigma. In occupational histories, lower job satisfaction is correlated with overreporting of symptoms. Length of residence itself is a variable in that affected persons move away first and less sensitive ones stay, and the same thing pertains to occupations (sensitive people self-select themselves out of uncomfortable jobs). People may also move out of the area at retirement or if they become disabled.

One final factor that will probably remain with you throughout your investigation is the bias introduced as soon as a person knows he may be exposed to something. He may find out through the local newspaper, from your initial contact, or from his neighbors. Your group should discuss this from the outset and agree on answers that will not cause undue alarm yet will be as accurate as possible. People in the control group will want to know if they are exposed (answer: not to the factors that you are studying, as far as you are aware). Exposed or potentially exposed people will want to know about the exposure (to what, how much, how often). You probably will not have had a water or air analysis done, but, if you have, can you reasonably withhold this from them? In terms of statistical validity, knowing which group they are in instantly biases people's answers. There is usually underreporting of symptoms in controls and overreporting in exposed subjects unless the condition is so clear-cut that this is not a factor (you either have cancer or you don't). When people know they have been exposed, poorer health is not only acceptable but almost expected. Known exposure can also be a built-in excuse for poor health or poor health habits. Questions are bound to arise during the course of your study, such as: Why are you asking about my hobbies? Did this cause my baby's birth defect? Did my husband bring home poisonous chemicals on his clothes? and so on. You will be asked how you can link one chemical to its particular health effects in individuals if you cannot say one way or another what caused a particular birth defect. The answer is a statistical one: the degree of increase of a particular condition that a certain exposure is "likely" to produce in a population is not really applicable to individual cases. Remember the analogy of contributory factors filling up a person's bottles until one overflows and a disease develops. (See chapter 3.)

To give some perspective on this issue, we will use an imaginary example: Suppose that in the air of a suburb of a large city a known animal carcinogen has been identified. Of the 20,000 people in that suburb, 18,000 "feel fine." (This is hypothetical, of course, since it is not practical to ascertain the health status of all 20,000 residents.) Of the 2,000 who feel less than fine, the symptoms of 1,950 can be attributed to "natural" causes (old age, infections, etc.) and occur with the same frequency as in the unexposed control group. Of the fifty whose health problems cannot be explained by any nonenvironmental cause, fifteen have intermittent skin rashes, fifteen have neurological symptoms, five have nonspecific lung problems, five have digestive problems, five have cancer of various sites, and five have serious chemical sensitivity or allergic reactions. The point here is that, even when contamination is verified, most people show neither acute nor chronic toxicity. How about permanent genetic effects? Let us suppose that instead of five expected cases of a particular kind of cancer, you find ten (statistical analysis will tell you if this is "real" or not); again, almost everyone does not now have cancer. How many people currently being exposed can be expected to develop this kind of cancer in the future as a result of being exposed now? Again, very few: Perhaps twenty more instead of the ten more that would develop this kind of cancer anyway. Will these cases of cancer develop earlier than they otherwise would? Perhaps, but the multitude of factors contributing to the cancer process (chapter 3) makes this question impossible to answer with our current level of understanding. Suppose you uncover a slight excess of low birth weight and spontaneous abortion (miscarriage). The same answers can be used: Most births are not affected, many factors contribute to the final outcome, and there is a certain "natural" incidence (i.e., we cannot yet explain the mechanism). Your community group must be prepared to explain these concepts to everyone involved, so that they do not think they are cancer time bombs or that they can avoid birth defects if they move away from the area. On the other hand, if your final report concludes that there is no evidence of an environmental health problem, you may have to explain why someone develops cancer anyway. Again, the purpose of the health survey is to determine if there is a statistically "real" problem.

SUMMARY: EXCESS IN A FEW KEY CONDITIONS

The questionnaire we provide is somewhat limited in terms of assessing chronic diseases, including cancer. As we mentioned before, there are special considerations in regard to diseases that take a long time to develop. If an environmental survey eventually results in court action in an attempt to compensate the victims of chronic disease or to punish the toxic waste generator (see chapter 10), supplementary information will be necessary. For instance, a complete residential history for each victim would be taken, which would address questions of other exposures and how long a person must have lived in the community to be included as a party to the legal action (in a class action suit). On the other hand, a complete occupancy history for the community (from tax assessor rolls) and extensive tracking of people who lived in the community during times of potential exposure will also probably be necessary. All these considerations pertain to determining possible causes of the condition whose current incidence rate you have already established.

Epidemiology is largely common sense. You know your community situation better than anyone else, so rely on your own judgment in choosing which health effects to concentrate on. Remember, all you need do is accurately measure a few of the most prevalent symptoms in the community, so focus on what you have discovered from your preliminary survey. Naturally, state health officials will have to spend more effort on a cancer cluster than on skin rashes; on the other hand, they may choose to spend their limited funds on a well-documented large increase in dermatitis rather than on an unsubstantiated cluster of birth defects.

No perfect epidemiologic study has ever been conducted, and probably none will be. But if you arm yourself with an objective, rational approach and know the advantages and limitations of your study design before you begin, there is no reason your study cannot be as good as most and better than many. Remember, you owe it to yourself and to your neighbors to conduct your study as professionally as possible, whether you use the entire questionnaire or condense it to a few pages. A well-conducted study should save you considerable time, expense, and emotional stress, whether you document the existence of a problem or eliminate unfounded fears. You can do it.

SEVEN

HOW TO GET THE INFORMATION

The Questionnaire,
Question Discussion,
and Tabulation

Barbara L. Harper, Mary C. Lowery, Michael J. Scott, and Paul Mills

This chapter is divided into two main sections: the questionnaire and a discussion of each question, and instructions on coding the answers and transferring them to the tabulation forms. The questionnaire itself is presented here in its complete form. The discussion describes why each question was included, what kind of information it asks for, and how important it is. If your group does not have the resources to administer and tabulate the entire questionnaire, certain questions can be answered in advance or can be left out altogether if they clearly do not pertain to your particular situation. Coding each answer to be entered on tabulation sheets is essential for reducing to one page the amount of paperwork for each person in your sample. Each person (man, woman, or child) will use one tabulation form, so that results can be expressed individually. Thus results for a mother will include some information on her children, but the children will be tabulated by themselves so that the general health questions in section A can be tabulated for the children as well as for the parents. When you are finished, you should therefore have one tabulation form *per person*, as discussed in the next chapter. Although this chapter may look intimidating, if you proceed through each part in order, the entire procedure should become clear.

First, we need to reemphasize a few general items concerning this questionnaire. As we explained earlier, the medical terminology included in the questionnaire elicits the fact that people know they have a particular condition because a doctor has told them so. This is an indirect way of confirming diagnosis by a physician without access to physician or hospital records. Of course, responsible physicians may help families fill out the forms, but since this is often not possible, the questionnaire has been designed so as not to require a physician's assistance.

A second point to consider before beginning your survey is whether you are simply measuring adverse health effects or whether you want to examine as many variables as possible as a first step in searching for the causes of any such effects you find. Obviously, if you do not ask about occupation, you will not know if occupation contributes to adverse health effects. The questions you leave out now will have to be asked eventually, by you or by whatever agency comes to your assistance. Therefore, unless you are extremely short of volunteers, we recommend asking as many questions as you can in a single sampling. You will not have to analyze all the results right away, since your primary goal is to determine whether there is an adverse health effect, but you will have the information you need when you want to look at other variables.

Last, this questionnaire is primarily designed to ask, Who has what now? In other words, it assesses acute or permanent effects. Chronic conditions such as cancer or other progressive diseases will be detected only in those who currently have them. One question asks about household members who have died in the past five years, but other than this there is no mechanism for measuring death rates from any cause. Finding out about former household members who died more than five years ago and knowing how long they lived in the community before death is a complex procedure. Even professional epidemiologists often cannot agree on how many people lived in one particular place, worked in another, were exposed to a certain amount of some chemical, and died of a particular cause. This process entails collecting complete residential, occupational, and exposure histories as well as making a rigorous examination of death certificates, and it is generally beyond the resources of community groups. The more information you can get on annual mortality rates in past years (city, county, or state records) the better, but if you cannot obtain them on your own, these answers will have to wait until further study.

ENVIRONMENTAL HEALTH QUESTIONNAIRE

This questionnaire is designed to assess the health status of individual households. It is divided into four sections:

    A. Family description and general health, filled in for each person
    B. Occupation and life-style, all adults
    C. Reproductive history, all adult women
    D. Children's health. Sections A and D should be filled in for children.

It may be administered by an interviewer or may be self-administered. The time for completion will vary from about thirty minutes (young, single, nonparent) upward.

College students may answer appropriate sections if they are now at home, especially if they recently lived in this household full time.

Section A: The important factor in this section is whether any conditions reported have been diagnosed by a doctor.

Section B: A complete occupational history for each person is followed by more detailed questions on jobs held during the past five years. If the person has never worked, skip the occupational part and proceed to the neighborhood description.

Section C: This section and the next concern only children who currently live with you. Each adult woman (over eighteen years old) who lives in the household should answer this section. If there has never been a pregnancy, stop at question 11. If there has been a pregnancy, even if it did end in birth, answer all the questions you can in this section, since many concern early pregnancy and the time before pregnancy.

Section D: Some of these questions will not apply to infants or very young children. Answer all you can for each child up to age eighteen.

Attach a continuation page at the end of the questionnaire if more space is needed for any question, or if you have any comments on your particular situation.

Thank you for your time and patience.

For more information, call _____.

Section A. Family Description and General Health

The first part of this section inquires about some variables known to be important for epidemiologic studies. The description of the family and family medical history may be filled in once per family, but questions A11 through A19 must be answered for each person. The family medical history is concerned with blood relatives, not steprelatives. A lengthy list of symptoms and diagnosed conditions must be filled out for each person. Since these conditions may not be verified from hospital, physician, or other records, the year of diagnosis by a doctor is important. A record of major medications is also important, since drugs have many side effects and can interact with each other.

Name _____

Address _____

Telephone _____

or Identification Number

A1. Race

_____ 1. White (not Hispanic)   _____ 4. Native American
_____ 2. Black   _____ 5. Oriental
_____ 3. Hispanic   _____ 6. Other

A2. Type of neighborhood

_____ 1. Urban   _____ 4. Mixed industrial/
_____ 2. Suburban   residential
_____ 3. Town or village   _____ 5. Farm or rural

A3. Total household income

_____ 1. Below $10,000   _____ 4. $30,000–$50,000
_____ 2. $10,000–$20,000   _____ 5. Over $50,000
_____ 3. $20,000–$30,000

A4. Type of housing

_____ 1. Single-family
_____ 2. Multifamily
_____ 3. Mobile home

A5. What year did you move to your present address? _____

A6. What year did you move into this community? _____

A7. How many persons regularly live in your household? _____

A8. Has anyone (within the last five years) left this household owing to death? Who? Cause of death?

_____

_____

A9. For other reasons? Who? Reason for leaving?

_____

_____

A10. Source of water
_____ 1. City   _____ 3. Bottled
_____ 2. Well   _____ 4. Unknown

A11. Age _____

A12. Sex
_____ Male
_____ Female

A13. Height in inches _____

A14. Weight in pounds _____

A15. Last grade of school completed _____

A16. Did you serve in the armed forces?
_____ 1. Army   _____ 4. Marines
_____ 2. Navy   _____ 5. Other
_____ 3. Air Force

A17. Year entered service (do not count Reserves) _____

A18. Year left active service _____
or still in service _____

A19. Longest tour of duty
_____ 1. Europe   _____ 4. Africa
_____ 2. North America   _____ 5. Asia
_____ 3. South America   _____ 6. Other

A20. Family medical history

	Male parent or respondent	Your father	Your mother	Your brother	Your brother	Your sister	Your sister	Any first cousins	Your grandparents	Other	Female parent or respondent	Your father	Your mother	Your brother	Your brother	Your sister	Your sister	Any first cousins	Your grandparents	Other	
a																					Allergies
b																					Anemia
c																					Arthritis/gout
d																					Asthma
e																					Bleeding/bruising
f																					Cancer or tumors
g																					Convulsions/epilepsy
h																					Diabetes
i																					Drinking or drug problem
j																					Eczema
k																					Emphysema
l																					Heart trouble
m																					Hepatitis
n																					High blood pressure
o																					Frequent infections
p																					Kidney or bladder problems
q																					Mental illness
r																					Migraines
s																					Abnormal menstrual periods
t																					Psoriasis
u																					Pneumonia
v																					Polio
w																					Prostate problems
x																					Rheumatic fever
y																					Stomach or intestinal disease
z																					Stroke
aa																					Thyroid problems
bb																					Tuberculosis
cc																					Ulcers
dd																					Veneral disease
ee																					Weight problem
	1	2	3	4	5	6	7	8	9		10	11	12	13	14	15	16	17	18		

A21. Lung
Diagnosed conditions
Year of occurrence or diagnosis

_____ 1. Tuberculosis
_____ 2. Persistent bronchitis
_____ 3. Pneumoconiosis
_____ 4. Lung disease
_____ 5. Pneumonia

Symptoms
_____ 8. Persistent cough
_____ 9. Chest pains
_____ 10. Difficult or labored
       breathing
_____ 11. Wheezing or asthma

_____ 6. Emphysema
_____ 7. Other conditions

_____
_____
_____

_____ 12. Productive cough
       (phlegm, sputum)
_____ 13. Coughing up blood
_____ 14. Other symptoms

_____

A22. Cardiovascular system
Symptoms or diagnosed conditions
Year of occurrence or diagnosis

_____ 1. Heart attack
_____ 2. Heart disease
_____ 3. Rapid or irregular
       heartbeat
_____ 4. Heart murmur
_____ 5. Swollen feet or ankles
_____ 6. High blood pressure
_____ 7. Stroke

_____ 8. Low blood pressure
_____ 9. Hardening of the
       arteries
_____ 10. Vasculitis
_____ 11. Thrombophlebitis
_____ 12. Other disease of
       veins or arteries
_____ 13. Other conditions

A23. Blood
Diagnosed conditions
Year of occurrence or diagnosis

_____ 1. ITP
_____ 2. Anemia
_____ 3. Infectious
       mononucleosis
_____ 4. Malaria
_____ 5. Condition of spleen
_____ 6. Dialysis or pheresis
       (reason?)

_____

_____

_____ 7. Abnormal blood count
_____ 8. Blood transfusion
_____ 9. Coagulation or clotting
       disorder
_____ 10. Other conditions

_____

_____

A24. Digestive
Diagnosed conditions
Year of occurrence or diagnosis

_____ 1. Gallstones
_____ 2. Ulcers-any site
_____ 3. Hepatitis
_____ 4. Jaundice
_____ 5. Cirrhosis of liver
_____ 6. Other conditions of
         liver or pancreas
_____ 7. Esophageal atresia
_____ 8. Frequent nausea or
         vomiting
_____ 9. Chronic indigestion
_____ 10. Colic or abdominal
         cramps

_____ 11. Frequent diarrhea
_____ 12. Frequent constipation
_____ 13. Loss of appetite
_____ 14. Loss of weight
_____ 15. Alcohol or food
         intolerance
_____ 16. Other symptoms

_____

_____

A25. Urinary tract
Diagnosed conditions
Year of occurrence or diagnosis

_____ 1. Kidney condition

_____ 2. Bladder disease
_____ 3. Protein in urine

Symptoms

_____ 4. Frequent or painful
         urination
_____ 5. Blood in urine
_____ 6. Other symptoms

_____

A26. Endocrine/glandular system
Symptoms or diagnosed conditions
Year of occurrence or diagnosis

_____ 1. Diabetes
_____ 2. Thyroid condition
_____ 3. Any hormonal condition
_____ 4. Excessive sweating
_____ 5. Hypoglycemia

_____ 6. Other

_____

_____

A27. Skin
Diagnosed conditions
Year of occurrence or diagnosis

_____ 1. Psoriasis
_____ 2. Eczema
_____ 3. Dermatitis

Symptoms

_____ 4. Unusual rashes
_____ 5. Red, scaly, dry or itching skin
_____ 6. Unusual acne
_____ 7. Hives or boils
_____ 8. Unusual flushing
_____ 9. Patches of greater or less pigmentation
_____ 10. Easy or spontaneous bruising

_____ 11. Small, round purple or red spots
_____ 12. Other symptoms

_____

_____

_____

A28. Immune system
Symptoms or diagnosed conditions
Year of occurrence or diagnosis

_____ 1. Hay fever
_____ 2. Asthma
_____ 3. Food allergies
_____ 4. Allergic dermatitis or skin rashes

_____ 5. Frequent colds or infections
_____ 6. Chemical intolerance
_____ 7. Other

_____

A29. Head and neck
Symptoms or diagnosed conditions
Year of occurrence or diagnosis

_____ 1. Excessively oily or brittle hair
_____ 2. Unusual loss of hair
_____ 3. Nasal soreness
_____ 4. Sinus troubles or infections
_____ 5. Excessive salivation
_____ 6. Prolonged sore throat
_____ 7. Dry throat
_____ 8. Difficulty in swallowing
_____ 9. Unusual taste in mouth (e.g. metal, garlic)
_____ 10. Excessive dental cavities
_____ 11. Excessive tooth loss (other than baby teeth)
_____ 12. Swollen or sore gums
_____ 13. Eyes — red, itchy, watery, sore, dry, inflamed, other (specify)

_____ 14. Blurred vision
_____ 15. Constricted pupils
_____ 16. Corrective lens needed
_____ 17. Cataracts
_____ 18. Glaucoma
_____ 19. Ears — itching, pain, or discharge
_____ 20. Head injuries (any after effects?)

_____

_____ 21. Other

_____

_____

_____

A30. Nervous System
Symptoms or diagnosed conditions
Year of occurrence or diagnosis

_____ 1. Epilepsy or seizures	_____ 12. Anxiety
_____ 2. Frequent headaches	_____ 13. Depression
_____ 3. Frequent dizziness	_____ 14. Trouble sleeping (at
_____ 4. Weakness, fatigue	least once a week last-
_____ 5. Lethargy, drowsiness	ing six months)
_____ 6. Decreased sensory per-	_____ 15. Irritability
ception — smell, taste,	_____ 16. Hyperactivity
hearing, vision, touch	_____ 17. Restlessness or trouble
_____ 7. Color vision (What	sitting still
color is hard to see?)	_____ 18. Learning disorder
	_____ 19. Memory or personality
	changes
_____	_____ 20. Frequent nightmares
	_____ 21. Meningitis
_____ 8. Trouble discriminating	_____ 22. Peripheral neuropathy
colors in dim light	_____ 23. Other
_____ 9. Numbness, tingling,	
prickling, other sensa-	
tions on skin	_____
_____ 10. Tremors, cramps,	
spasms	
_____ 11. Problems with balance,	_____
coordination, reaction	
time, clumsiness	_____

A31. Muscles and bones
Symptoms or diagnosed conditions
Year of occurrence or diagnosis

_____ 1. Arthritis/rheumatism	_____ 9. Other muscle or bone
_____ 2. Limb pain, hand or foot	pain
_____ 3. Stiffness in joints	_____ 10. Other
_____ 4. Broken bones	
_____ 5. Numbness, weakness	
foot in arms or legs	_____
_____ 6. Leg cramps	
_____ 7. Muscular dystrophy	
_____ 8. Multiple sclerosis	_____

A32. Other
Symptoms or diagnosed conditions
Year of occurrence or diagnosis

_____ 1. Cancer
  What sites?

_____

_____ 2. Leukemia
_____ 3. Hodgkin's disease
_____ 4. Any metabolic disorder
  Specify:

_____

_____ 5. Fever
_____ 6. Chills
_____ 7. Other conditions or
  complaints

_____

_____

_____ 8. Unexplained loss or
  gain in weight
_____ 9. Twenty pounds over-
  weight or underweight
_____ 10. Frequently feel warmer
  or colder than others
_____ 11. Cysts
_____ 12. Accidents that required
  medical care (including
  athletic injuries)
_____ 13. Serious infections
  What site? _____

_____

_____ 14. Other

_____

_____

A33. Female
Diagnosed conditions
Year of occurrence of diagnosis

_____ 1. Menopause
_____ 2. Irregular periods
_____ 3. Premenstrual syndrome
_____ 4. Female hormones (estro-
  gen) prescribed
_____ 5. Disorder of cervix
_____ 6. Disorder of uterus
_____ 7. Disorders of ovaries
_____ 8. Venereal disease

_____ 9. Infertility
_____ 10. Other

_____

_____

A33. Male
Diagnosed conditions
Year of occurrence or diagnosis

_____ 1. Sterility
_____ 2. Abnormal sperm count
_____ 3. Sexual disturbances or
  problems
_____ 4. Venereal disease

_____ 5. Other

_____

_____

A34. *Major medications*
Please indicate any prescribed medication you have ever taken regularly or taken at onset of symptoms. Include pain relievers only if taken regularly for three months or more; do not include antibiotics for minor infections unless infections are recurrent and antibiotics are used at each onset. Do include antiparasitic agents. Do include medications taken for more than one month for preventive purposes (such as antimalarials or antituberculosis drugs). Indicate approximate years you took them, and especially list all those you take regularly now.

_____

_____

_____

A35. *Radiation history: approximate number and years of X rays*
1. Screening (chest, mammography, dental)

_____

_____

2. Diagnostic (what body part, how many, when)

_____

3. Therapeutic radiation (what type, what underlying condition, how many treatments, when)

_____

A36. How do you rate your general health?
_____ 1. Poor   _____ 3. Average   _____ 5. Excellent
_____ 2. Fair   _____ 4. Better than average

A37. Have there been any changes in your health in the past five years?
Examples: gradual improvement or decline in health, seasonal variations, any change (better or worse) when you leave the area for a while.

_____

_____

_____

A38. Are there any other complaints you are concerned about?

_____

_____

Section B. Occupation and Life-Style

This section includes a summary of all jobs held since age sixteen and detailed information for jobs held within the past five years (one form per job). The administrator of the survey will provide extra sheets if needed.

Summary of Occupations Since Age Sixteen

Job 1 (present job)
Place of employment _____

Department _____

What years employed? _____

Was a physical required? _____

Job 2 (previous job)
Place of employment _____

Department _____

What years employed? _____

Was a physical required? _____

Job 3
Place of employment _____

Department _____

What years employed? _____

Was a physical required? _____

Job 4
Place of employment _____

Department _____

What years employed? _____

Was a physical required? _____

Job 5
Place of employment _____

Department _____

What years employed? _____

Was a physical required? _____

Job 6
Place of employment _____

Department _____

What years employed? _____

Was a physical required? _____

Job 7
Place of employment _____

Department _____

What years employed? _____

Was a physical required? _____

Job 8
Place of employment _____

Department _____

What years employed? _____

Was a physical required? _____

Job 9
Place of employment _____

Department _____

What years employed? _____

Was a physical required? _____

Job 10
Place of employment _____

Department _____

What years employed? _____

Was a physical required? _____

Occupational Information
Please answer this question for each job held during the past five years, including self-employment, lasting six months or more.

Job_____ (from 19_____ to 19_____)

B1. Place of employment

_____

B2. Main activity of company or organization

_____

B3. Relevant activities or products

_____

B4. If industrial, production process used

_____

B5. Describe the type of place usually worked
_____ 1. Factory or plant   _____ 5. Outdoors
_____ 2. Laboratory   _____ 6. Office
_____ 3. Vehicle   _____ 7. Restaurant or hotel
_____ 4. Warehouse   _____ 8. Other

B6. Department

_____

B7. Specific tasks and materials used

_____

B8. Did you ever have to replace someone else or have to be replaced? If so, how often?

_____

B9. Describe work surroundings (number of people, noise, temperature, machines)

_____

B10. Were there dust, fumes, smoke, gases? If so, what specifically, including cigarette smoke?

_____

B11. Did you work with oils, solvents, acids, detergents? If so, what specifically?

_____

B12. Did your job involve exposure to X rays or microwaves? If so, what was their function?

_____

B13. Did you have to wear protective equipment? If so, what and why?

_____

B14. Did this job have a bad effect on your physical health? If so, how or why?

_____

B15. Was there anything you did not like to do?

_____

B16. What is the source of your drinking water at work?

_____

B17. Did any of those performing the same job have a common complaint(s) or illness?

_____

Repeat B1-B17 for each job held during the past five years.

B18. To your knowledge, are you now or have you ever been frequently exposed to any of the following chemicals at work? Give approximate inclusive dates for frequent exposures.

Job Number (see Summary of Occupations) and Inclusive Years of Exposure

1. Acrylonitrile _____

2. Arsenic _____

3. Asbestos _____

4. Benzene _____

5. Beryllium _____

6. Bis(chloromethyl)ether _____

7. Ceramic dust or talc _____

8. Coal tar pitch, volatiles _____

9. Oils, asphalt _____

10. Chemical fertilizers _____

11. Coke oven emissions _____

12. Dyes _____

13. Lacquers, varnishes _____

14. Fiberglass _____

15. Cotton, textile, wood, grain, or metal dust _____

16. Paints, glues _____

17. Organic solvents, paint thinners _____

18. Isopropyl oils _____

19. Other petroleum products _____

20. Radioisotopes or radioactive
    materials   _____

21. Insecticides, pesticides   _____

22. Herbicides, fungicides   _____

23. Chromium or chromates   _____

B19. Have you ever been told you have an occupationally related disease
or reaction? If yes, please indicate person, year recognized, and agent if
known (examples: allergic dermatitis, pneumoconiosis or lung disease,
neurological effects)

_____

_____

_____

B20. Indicate which of the following substances you have used frequently, perhaps in your hobby or around the house.

_____ 1. Plastics   _____ 17. Oil paints
_____ 2. Metals   _____ 18. Acrylic paints
_____ 3. Clay   _____ 19. Alkyd paints
_____ 4. Wood   _____ 20. Epoxy paints
_____ 5. Paper   _____ 21. Aerosol or spray paints
_____ 6. Stone   _____ 22. Lacquer, varnish
_____ 7. Glazes   _____ 23. Acid, caustics
_____ 8. Enamels   _____ 24. Solvents — turpentine,
_____ 9. Pastels   paint thinner, paint re-
_____ 10. Dyes   movers, other solvents
_____ 11. Plaster   _____ 25. Glues, adhesives, resins
_____ 12. Pigments   _____ 26. Photography chemicals
_____ 13. Feathers   _____ 27. Pesticides, insecticides,
_____ 14. Wax   fungicides, herbicides,
_____ 15. Glass   fumigants
_____ 16. Fixatives

Neighborhood Description

B21. Water

1. Does your water ever taste or smell unusual? _____

2. Is it corrosive or does it discolor cooking utensils or pipes? _____

3. Is it hard? _____

4. Does it leave a film or residue? _____

5. Do you use a water softener? _____

6. Do you use a charcoal filter or ion exchanger? _____

7. Do you add anything to soften your water? _____

B22. What is the general quality of air in your neighborhood?

_____ 1. Clear
_____ 2. Haze
_____ 3. Light smog
_____ 4. Moderate smog
_____ 5. Heavy smog
_____ 6. Occasional dust or smoke
_____ 7. Frequent dust or smoke

_____ 8. Occasional chemical smell
_____ 9. Frequent chemical smell
_____ 10. Other (description)

_____

B23. Do you know of or suspect a specific source of neighborhood pollution or contamination?

_____

_____

B24. Have you noticed any other "environmental clues" you think may be relevant (clusters of dead trees, large barren patches, oil sheen on puddles, fish kills, honeybee kills, unusual frequency of sick pets or livestock), or do you have any other pertinent information?

_____

_____

_____

B25. Indoor pollution description: Is the household regularly exposed to any of the following?

1. Tobacco smoke
_____ Never
_____ Occasionally/seasonally
_____ Frequently

2. Unvented gas space heater
_____ Never
_____ Occasionally/seasonally
_____ Frequently

3. Gas stove
_____ Never
_____ Occasionally/seasonally
_____ Frequently

4. Woodburning or coal-burning stove
_____ Never
_____ Occasionally/seasonally
_____ Frequently

5. Floor wax, furniture polish, oven cleaner
_____ Never
_____ Occasionally/seasonally
_____ Frequently

6. Roach spray, insecticides, foggers
_____ Never
_____ Occasionally/seasonally
_____ Frequently

7. Anything else? Specify

_____

_____

Lifestyle Description

B26. Is anyone in the family on a special or restricted diet? If yes, what type and why?

_____

_____

B27. Cigarettes

_____ 1. Number smoked per day
_____ 2. Year begun
_____ 3. Year quit
_____ 4. Did you inhale?

B28. Cigars

_____ 1. Number smoked per day
_____ 2. Year begun
_____ 3. Year quit
_____ 4. Did you inhale?

B29. Chewing or smokeless tobacco

_____ 1. Packs or ounces chewed per day
_____ 2. Year begun
_____ 3. Year quit
_____ 4. Did you swallow?

B30. Snuff

_____ 1. Number of dips per day
_____ 2. Year begun
_____ 3. Year quit

B31. Pipe

_____ 1. Number smoked per day   _____ 3. Year quit
_____ 2. Year begun   _____ 4. Did you inhale?

B32. Recreational drugs (number used per week)

_____ 1. Amphetamines   _____ 4. Other
         (stimulants)
_____ 2. Barbiturates   _____
_____ 3. Marijuana
                             _____

B33. Alcoholic beverages (number per week)

_____ 1. Beer
_____ 2. Wine
_____ 3. Mixed drinks

Section C. Reproductive History

All women answer this section; answer all questions that apply.

C1. Are you currently pregnant?
_____ Yes
_____ No
_____ Don't know

C2. Have you ever been pregnant?
_____ Yes
_____ No
_____ Don't know

C3. Has a doctor ever advised you not to become pregnant (again)?
_____ Yes
_____ No
_____ Don't know
If yes, what was the doctor's reason for this?

_____

C4. Have you ever been told you are sterile or have reached menopause?
_____ Sterile
_____ Menopause
_____ No
If so, year? _____

C5. Are you currently using or have you used some birth control method?

_____ 1. Pill

_____ 2. Foam, cream, jelly

_____ 3. IUD

_____ 4. Sterile—wife

_____ 5. Sterile—husband

_____ 6. Abortion

_____ 7. Other (please specify)

_____

_____ 8. Hysterectomy/vasectomy

C6. Have you ever wanted to become pregnant but been physically unable?

_____ Yes

_____ No

_____ Don't know

C7. Have you ever seen a doctor because you had trouble getting pregnant?

_____ Yes

_____ No

If yes, when? _____

What was the doctor's diagnosis?

_____ Anatomical defect

_____ Hormonal/glandular

_____ No reported abnormality

_____ Other (specify)

_____

C8. Has your husband ever seen a doctor because you had trouble getting pregnant?

_____ Yes

_____ No

_____ Don't know

If yes, when? _____

What was the doctor's diagnosis?

_____ Anatomical defect

_____ Hormonal/glandular

_____ Low sperm count

_____ Impotence

_____ No reported abnormality

_____ Other (specify)

_____

C9. How many times all together have you been pregnant? Please be sure to include all pregnancies that ended in a live birth, a miscarriage, a stillbirth, or an induced abortion.

_____

C10. How many babies have been born to you, including any who died after birth?

_____

Stop here if there have been no pregnancies. Continue if there was a pregnancy, regardless of outcome. Extra sheets provided by the survey administrator may be used for more babies.

Answer for each baby:	First	Second	Third
C11. Was your baby a boy or girl?			
C12. In what year did each pregnancy end?			
C13. Did this pregnancy result in			
1. Normal vaginal birth	____	____	____
2. Cesarean	____	____	____
3. Stillbirth	____	____	____
4. Abortion (induced)	____	____	____
5. Twins, both live	____	____	____
6. Twins, one live, one stillborn	____	____	____
7. Other multiple outcome	____	____	____
8. Tubal pregnancy	____	____	____
9. Low birth-weight baby (less than 5½ pounds or 2500 grams)	____	____	____
10. Premature birth (less than thirty-seven weeks)	____	____	____
11. Miscarriage	____	____	____
How long had you been pregnant at the time of the miscarriage?	____	____	____

C14. Did your baby/babies have any condition at birth or apparent shortly afterward that involved (please specify):

	First	Second	Third
1. Extremities (arms, legs, hands, feet)	———	———	———
2. Skin rashes or darkened skin	———	———	———
3. Moles/birthmarks	———	———	———
4. Head — molding	———	———	———
5. Eyes — abnormalities	———	———	———
6. Lips — cleft, other	———	———	———
7. Gums — cleft, born with teeth	———	———	———
8. Palate — cleft, other	———	———	———
9. Other facial features	———	———	———
10. Ears	———	———	———
11. Thorax — large, small	———	———	———
12. Lungs — not fully inflated	———	———	———
difficulty breathing	———	———	———
13. Heart — abnormal rhythm or rate	———	———	———
murmur	———	———	———
valve defect	———	———	———
other	———	———	———
14. Liver — jaundice	———	———	———
other	———	———	———
15. Spleen	———	———	———
16. Kidneys	———	———	———
17. Skeletal muscles	———	———	———
bones	———	———	———
joints	———	———	———
18. Stomach	———	———	———
19. Intestines	———	———	———
20. Throat	———	———	———
21. Genitals — male	———	———	———
female	———	———	———
22. Brain — cerebral palsy	———	———	———
other spinal	———	———	———
other nervous system condition			
mental condition	———	———	———
23. Reflexes — abnormal	———	———	———
24. Metabolic disorder	———	———	———
25. Chromosomal disorder	———	———	———

26. Any other condition apparent or occurring at birth

_____ _____ _____

C15. Did any baby require extra time in the hospital after delivery? _____ If so, why?

_____

Section D. Children's Health

Please answer each question for each child. "Children" includes persons through eighteen years of age. Answer as appropriate for the age of the child.

Household member number, to match section A _____

D1. Sex and present age of child

_____

D2. In general, would you say your child's health is excellent, good, fair, or poor?

_____

D3. Does your child seem less healthy than other children his/her age?
_____ Yes
_____ No
_____ Don't know

D4. Does your child seem to resist illness well?
_____ Yes
_____ No
_____ Intermediate

D5. Has your child ever been seriously ill? Specify:

_____

What year was this diagnosed? _____

D6. Does health limit this child in any way from doing what he/she wants to do?
_____ Yes
_____ No
_____ Don't know

Specify: _____

_____

D7. Does health limit the amount or kind of ordinary play he/she
can do?

_____

Specify: _____

_____

D8. Does health limit the kind or amount of vigorous or strenuous
activities he/she can do?

_____

Specify: _____

_____

D9. In the past year, has your child seemed to be:
_____ 1. Bothered by nervousness   _____ 5. Unable to concentrate
         or "nerves"   _____ 6. Hyperactive
_____ 2. Anxious or worried   _____ 7. Losing interest in things
_____ 3. Restless or impatient   _____ 8. Doing worse in school or
_____ 4. Depressed or moody   sports

D10. During the past year has your child gotten along well with:
_____ 1. Other children
_____ 2. The family
_____ 3. Teachers and classmates

D11. Do you feel your child has developed normally during
_____ 1. 0–4 years of age
_____ 2. 5–16 years of age

D12. Does your child have any learning or reading disorder that requires
special attention? Specify

_____

_____

D13. In the past year, has your child been doing as well academically in
school as you think he/she should or as he/she has done in the past?

D14. Does your child have any other conditions that might require special attention or adaptation? Specify

_____

_____

D15. Does your child require regular or frequent medication, injections, or supplements of any sort other than children's aspirin or vitamins? Specify reason and treatment.

_____

_____

D16. Is or was your child's diet limited by
_____ 1. Allergies   _____ 4. Other
_____ 2. Metabolic condition
_____ 3. Preference   _____

D17. Are there any other complaints or conditions that arise in your child more often than you think they should, or anything you think is not normal? Specify (refer if needed to the checklist in the first section).

_____

_____

_____

D18. Did (does) your child do well in
_____ 1. Nursery school   _____ 3. Preschool
_____ 2. Day care   _____ 4. Kindergarten

D19. Were (are) his/her height and weight normal? If not, specify how not.

_____

_____

D20. Was (is) his/her mental development normal? If not, specify.

_____

_____

D21. Have any conditions present at birth been resolved or permanently corrected? Specify (refer to reproductive history section).

_____

_____

D22. Are there any other problems or conditions that you would like to detail?

_____

_____

Questions Concerning the Administration of This Questionnaire

1. Time it took to complete _____

2. Were any questions   Question   Part   Why

Too technical?   _____ _____ _____

Confusing?   _____ _____ _____

Other?   _____ _____ _____

3. Do you think an interviewer, if present, inhibited your response to any question?
_____ Yes
_____ Somewhat
_____ No

4. Were there questions you think would be answered more honestly in general without an interviewer present?
_____ Reproductive history   _____ Other
_____ Amount smoked
_____ Amount drunk   _____
_____ Use of recreational drugs

5. Any other comments will be appreciated.

_____

_____

Attach a blank sheet if more space is required for any given answer. (Indicate section, question, and person responding.)

QUESTION DISCUSSION

Section A. Family Description and General Health

The issue of confidentiality has been discussed; your experimental design determines whether you need to know the exact location of every household. Since you are collecting individual cases within households, you will need an identification number (for tabulation purposes) for each person as well as for each household.

A1.   Some traits have definite racial or cultural associations.

A2.   The type of neighborhood will describe in part such factors as pollution, pesticide use, and water source. This is not necessary if the entire sample is the same.

A3.   Neighborhood quality can be assessed by income; income also correlates with general awareness of environmental issues, personal health care, and many other things.

A4.   A general descriptive element.

A5.   This question is necessary unless exposure is known to be less than one year.

A6.   Identifies people who have lived in more than one place within the community.

A7.   Necessary to determine sample size.

A8–9.   Necessary if you want to know whether moderate or long-term exposures might have already contributed to death rates. The second part (A9) may identify exposed persons who have been affected and moved away. The five-year limit is arbitrary; a longer time period may pick up earlier deaths.

A10.   Is everyone in the community using the same water source? If waterborne exposure is suspected, is anyone using bottled water? (Later you might ask how long they used each water source.)

A11–15.   Minimally, you will need to know the age, sex, height, weight, and educational level of each person.

A16–19.   Possibly of interest in situations of herbicide application (Agent Orange, for example). This does not include members of the Reserves.

A20.   Since many diseases run in families, this question pertains to the respondents (and spouses, if applicable) and to other family members who do not live in the household and therefore probably were not exposed. As a rule of thumb, if any condition occurs in three or more first-degree relatives of a respondent, you may decide to disregard that condition if it also appears in the respondent. In this way you will obtain a conservative estimate, since you will not be counting predisposition for a particular condition even though it may have been environmentally triggered. You will still be counting any symptom that does not appear to run in the family. However, many surveys do not assess family history at all; if you leave it out, you will than be counting environmentally triggered conditions to which a person is especially vulnerable (an equally valid measurement anyway). If you do use this question, by correlating family conditions with environmentally triggered systems, you may identify high-risk groups and thus provide an early warning system. On the whole, we recommend leaving this question in.

A21–33. For the preliminary survey you will want to assess effects on all organ systems. Even for a condensed questionnaire, health effects are the core of your entire survey, so while you initially approach your survey with the idea of measuring incidence for only a few specific conditions, remember that people can respond in different ways to the same chemical. By conducting a thorough survey from the start, you will avoid having to go back to ask about other conditions you were not aware of at first.

A34. This question asks about major medications taken regularly or continually. Many drugs have adverse side effects, and you cannot hope to pick up all such effects, but drugs taken in large amounts should be recorded here.

Section B. Occupation and Life-style

Summary of Occupations and B1–19. Complete occupational histories are required in any good epidemiologic study, owing to the large number of people with occupational exposures to toxic substances. If you have recently seen a sudden onset of acute symptoms, you will still need to ascertain current jobs to rule out an uneven employment pattern. Even if you know exactly what the chemical in question is and where it comes from, occupational exposures may contribute to the appearance and severity of symptoms. If you do not know whether there is a health problem or know there is a problem but not where it is coming from, you will need a complete job history (jobs beginning with age eighteen and lasting six months) plus the more detailed questions (B1–17) on recent jobs. If this job required a physical examination, there may be a doctor's record of it, and thus you may be able to verify past health status.

B20. Toxic exposures from arts and crafts are often underestimated.

B21. Water treatment or characteristics may vary between households.

B22. You may be able to answer this for the entire community. The answer is subjective and does not indicate frequency. Pollution may be regarded as more serious by persons who are adversely affected by it.

B23. A "discovery" question that may be more appropriate as an issue discussed at a group meeting.

B24. Same comment, but this depends more on individual observation.

B25. This is included to underline the importance of indoor pollution, and it can also indicate exposures that can be many times more toxic than outdoor pollution. Gas heaters and woodburning stoves can be particularly polluting, but their use may be consistent between your groups. Even so, we recommend leaving this question in.

Section C. Reproductive History

C1–10. The minimum core of questions that should be asked of all women of reproductive age. We know much less about the effect of chemicals on reproductive outcomes, so we probably underestimate the incidence of reproductive effects.

Section D. Children's Health

We believe this section should be used intact, since there are no reference values for general incidence of the characteristics queried. It will be of absolutely no value to assess the children of your community without assessing the children of a control community just as carefully. What if one-third of the children in your randomly selected households have allergies? The same might be true of unexposed communities. You might find discussions of the incidence of certain kinds of learning disabilities, but since we are still discovering how to measure them, the rates are not accurate. Your school board, even if willing to help, can at best give you only a vague idea of the incidence of dyslexia or the number in remedial classes or similar statistics. These rates are entirely dependent on testing for them in public schools, and their severity (or degree of correction) depends on the quality of corrective education. In a similar vein, pediatricians will not have a feeling for incidence rates of health problems, because they see only a portion of the affected children and even fewer of the unaffected. Thus you will be shortchanging your children if you have no adequate control group of unexposed children with which to compare them.

CODING THE ANSWERS FOR THE TABULATION FORMS

By coding you reduce a vast amount of information to a shorthand or code in which each possible answer to a multiple choice question is replaced by a number. Thus the answer to question A2 (type of neighborhood), which offers five choices, is coded as a number between 1 and 5. Dates will be coded as the last two digits of the year. Codes are often listed 01 to 99 merely to reserve enough spaces for each digit, not because there are 99 possible responses. The format used here describes how to code every digit; for example, for the identification numbers in section A, the first three digits represent the household number, the next two represent the person in the household, and the last digit is the code for control or exposed.

Section A. Family Description and General Health

Identification number 001–999, one number per person, or 001–999, number per household/01–99 number of each person within each household, to coordinate residence; 1 = control, 2 = exposed, or C, H, M, L for control, high, medium, low exposures. Example: 023/3/M = twenty-third household, third member, medium exposure group or stratum.

A1. Race: 1–6
A2. Neighborhood: 1–5
A3. Income: 1–5
A4. Housing: 1–3
A5. Present address: 19_____ (give last two digits of year)
A6. Year moved to community: 19_____
A7. Number of regular household members
A8. Recent death? 1 = yes, 2 = no. If yes, write in who and cause of death.
A9. Other departure? 1 = yes, 2 = no. If yes, write in who and why.
A10. Water source: 1–4
A11. Age
A12. Sex: 1 = male, 2 = female
A13. Height in inches
A14. Weight in pounds
A15. Education: 12 = high school, 16 = college, etc.
A16. Service: 1–5
A17. Year entered 19_____
A18. Year left 19_____
A19. Tour: 1–6
A20. All positive responses, such as 1p, 12d, 21ee, etc.
A21–33. In each box, write diagnosis or symptom number and year indicated (last two digits). Write in what other symptoms or conditions and cancer site. Answer A33 for male or female as appropriate. Example: for A22: 02–78; 09–76.

A34. Write in medications.
A35. Copy radiation history.
A36. General health: 1–5
A37–38. Summarize response.

Section B. Occupation and Life-style

Occupational summary: Summarize, for example as: teacher/administrator 1970–83 (arts and crafts supplies). Miscellaneous clerical jobs 1960–80 (cigarette smoke). Trucker/mechanic 1940–80, retired (degreasers, solvents). Indicate potential responses from B1–17, to be analyzed in more detail separately. Indicate major employer also: operator/Able Chemical Company 1965–82 (pesticides, respirator required). This requires a judgment on the part of the tabulator, but key exposures and major jobs noted here should be sufficient until a more thorough occupational analysis needs to be made.

B18. Job/number
B19. Occupational disease?
B20. Any positive numbers
B21. Water: 1–7 (may be more than one affirmative answer)
B22. Air: 1–10 (may be more than one affirmative answer)
B23–24. Summarize response.
B25. Indoor air: 1–7; never = 1, occasionally = 2, frequently = 3
B27–31. Smoking: number/year begun 19_____/year quit 19_____
B32. Number/how many per week
B33. Number/how many per week

Section C. Reproductive History

C1–3. 1 = yes, 2 = no, 3 = don't know
C4. 1 = sterile, 2 = menopause (year), 3 = no/year
C5. Birth control: 1-8/number for past/number for present
C6. 1 = yes, 2 = no, 3 = don't know
C7. 1 = yes, 2 = no/year/3 = anatomical, 4 = hormonal, 5 = no abnormality, 6 = other (what?)
C8. 1 = yes, 2 = no, 3 = don't know, 4 = anatomical, 5 = hormonal, 6 = sperm count, 7 = impotence, 8 = no abnormality, 9 = other (what?)
C9. Pregnancies: number
C10. Births: number
C11. Birth number/1 = boy, 2 = girl
C12. Write years of pregnancies (63, 65, 66, 68, 71, for example)
C13. Pregnancy number/1–9

C14. Baby number/defect(s) (1–26)
C15. Baby number/reason (3/jaundice, for example)

Section D. Children's Health

D1.	Age/1 = boy, 2 = girl/household member number should agree with section A
D2.	1 = excellent, 2 = good, 3 = fair, 4 = poor
D3.	1 = yes, 2 = no, 3 = don't know
D4.	1 = yes, 2 = no, 3 = intermediate
D5.	What/year
D6.	1 = yes, 2 = no, 3 = don't know
D7–8.	1 = yes, 2 = no/what
D9.	1–8 (may be more than one answer)
D10.	1–3 (indicate a negative response)
D11.	1–2 (indicate a negative response)
D12–15.	1 = yes, 2 = no
D16.	1–4 (indicate a negative response)
D17.	1 = yes, 2 = no
D18.	1–4 (indicate a negative response)
D19–20.	Summarize responses.

EIGHT

LOTS OF INFORMATION

What to Do with It,
Statistics for Nonstatisticians

Michael J. Scott and Barbara L. Harper

The next step, tabulation of data, consists of adding up the number of responses to a question or how many choices were marked. Initial totals will tell you some basic things about the groups you have surveyed, such as how many people are in each age group, how many are male and how many female, and what organ systems are most affected. Simple comparisons can be made by going back through the tabulation forms (or by drawing from your data base if you have the information on a computer) and asking questions such as how many females have a particular condition or when did the symptoms start to appear. Each question of this kind generates four groups — variable A (yes or no) cross referenced with variable B (yes or no). Thus, every time you wish to examine a different factor you must go back through the data collection forms and read the answers for the new set of factors. This is obviously a time-consuming process, but educated guesses about which factors to use to follow significant health effects should allow you to avoid many dead ends. To determine if any difference you may see between your two groups is "real" (i.e., statistically convincing to health authorities), you can apply some simple tests to see if the number of cases of something you observe is different than you would normally expect to see. The number you derive from this tells you how sure you can be that the difference you see between the exposed and unexposed groups is not due just to chance or natural variation. We have assumed that the occurrence of any event exceeding that which is expected to occur less than 10 percent of the time due to chance alone may be "significant." Comparing your results with a national or regional average requires different, but still simple, calculations. Other basic questions are also discussed: What is the normal variation in the background rate and how does it affect the ability to detect increases? If there really is a difference, how sure can I be of detecting it? Will I be able to detect a twofold increase or a fourfold increase? If I have an idea of what the normal rate for a particular condition is, how many exposed persons do I need to survey to detect a reasonable increase in that condition? How does sample size (the number of persons surveyed) affect the sensitivity of the study? What chance is there of my concluding that a difference exists between my two groups when it really does not? Though some calculations may be necessary, tables are provided to help you make some of the decisions.

This chapter will assist you in tabulating your results and organizing them so they can be easily understood. By using many examples based on the questionnaire, we will introduce the concept of comparing results between two groups and determining by simple numerical methods whether there is a real difference.

TABULATING YOUR ANSWERS
AND PRESENTING YOUR RESULTS

Using the tabulation form in the previous chapter, you will have coded all the answers from the survey and reduced the amount of paperwork to one page for each person.

The first type of question in the questionnaire is simple multiple choice. Question 1, for example, has a one-digit answer for race and will be tallied as the number of persons choosing each answer, giving you a racial profile for your communities. Comparing the exposed and unexposed communities will show you if they are similar in racial makeup, which they should be if you have selected your control group correctly. Questions A2, A3, and A4 also describe the community and should be similar for both communities; affluent suburbs are not proper control groups for poor rural areas. The total in question A7 is your sample size and should correspond to the number of completed tabulation forms you have. Questions A5 and A6 (length of residence) will be important when you need to know if conditions (cancer, for instance) occur only in persons who have lived in the area for ten years or more or occur less frequently in persons of the same age who moved there only a short time ago.

Question A11 will give you the age distribution, or how many people are in each age group. When you are finished tabulating, your results for one community may look like table 8.1. This information can also be presented as a line or bar graph (fig. 8.1). If we make a graph, it becomes apparent that in this example there are two peaks in the age distribution (called a "bimodal distribution"), which might be explained by the presence of many young families plus senior citizens' housing or a large retirement or nursing home. Since you know that the very young and the elderly are especially susceptible to environmental

Table 8.1. Example of Frequency Distribution of Persons in Various Age Groups

Age Group	Male	Female	Total
0–10	10	12	22
11–20	8	11	19
21–30	15	17	32
31–40	23	25	48
41–50	18	17	35
51–60	8	10	18
61–70	13	16	29
71–80	15	17	32
81 or more	4	6	10
Total	114	131	245

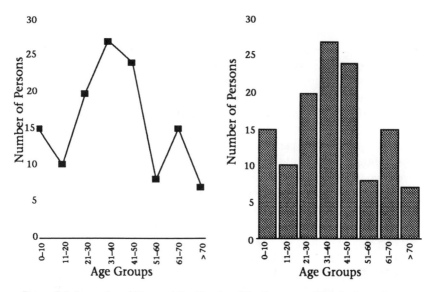

Figure 8.1 Examples of Line and Bar Graphs of the Frequency Distribution of Persons in Various Age Groups

agents, a distribution like this might suggest that you examine in more detail those up to twenty years old and the retirement-age groups. This will also be very important in comparing the age distributions between the two communities. If a community with an older average age has more symptoms than a younger community, you may not be able to compare people up through age twenty in one community with people the same age in the other. The same point pertains to examining your results by gender.

Specific health effects (A21 through A33) will initially be tallied simply as how many positive responses are recorded for each organ system. Since each person is allowed more than one symptom or condition, the total will be quite large. An initial total for each question will tell you which organ systems are most affected. At this point you can begin to do simple comparisons between number of symptoms reported and other parameters such as water source, sex, or age. You will begin to map your results on a large map or aerial photograph of your community by placing colored pins at the locations of affected persons or households. You may begin to examine specific aspects of your results such as whether males and females are affected in equal proportion, whether males are affected more severely than females, and whether older age groups are more seriously affected. You may also compare your results with year of diagnosis or first occurrence. If you noticed a picture such as that shown in figure 8.2, then you would focus on events that happened in 1980 (new factory, new pesticide, and so on). In other words, the time course of particular acute symptoms may give you valuable clues to the cause. For chronic symptoms of cancer, which have a slowly progressive course and long latency, the cause is obviously long separated from the time of diagnosis. The incidence of conditions that are aggravated little by little over the years will need to be carefully compared with that in the unexposed community. Age in particular is an important parameter, because so many conditions increase in incidence and severity with age. Thus the results from the unexposed community are extremely important in comparing health effects, most of which are expected to occur naturally to some extent and also to increase with age. An example of this might be figure 8.3.

If you did not have information from community A, often called the control group, you would not know whether the rates in community B were elevated. This is particularly important for most health-related conditions, for which there are few local, regional, state, or national data.

Several questions are "open," that is, the person writes in the answer in a free text format, listing medications, other health complaints, X rays, and so on. These are tabulated as number of positive responses, and you will need to compare symptomatic and nonsymptomatic

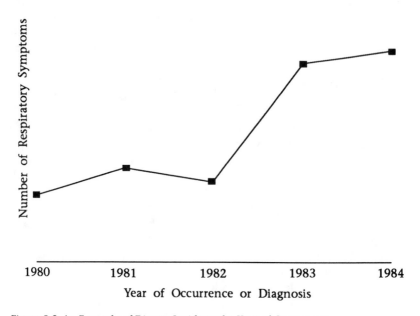

Figure 8.2 An Example of Disease Incidence by Year of Occurrence

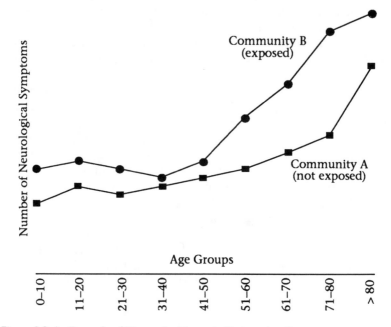

Figure 8.3 An Example of Disease Incidence in Various Age Groups

groups as well as exposed and unexposed groups. It is a circular argument whether initial medical conditions required medication that in turn aggravated other conditions, but you should know the general medication profiles of your various subsamples.

As discussed in the previous chapter, you will need to know if symptoms are related to employment, either as a direct cause or as a contributing factor. For instance, does employment in chemical factory A seem to aggravate respiratory symptoms while employment as a dry cleaner is associated with neurological complaints? This involves many painstaking comparisons and might well bring to light associations that have been overlooked. Questions B18 and B20 (occupational and nonoccupational chemical exposures) might really bring home the point that headaches and solvents go together, for example, and if your survey has no other result than improving ventilation it will have been worthwhile. Likewise, if frequent indoor pollution (B25) plus weatherproofing seems to be associated with symptoms, your survey might result in local building code changes to require certain air-exchange provisions.

Smoking, drinking, and recreational drugs are of course extremely important variables and should be handled as broad groups after tabulating specifics. For example, someone who smokes eight cigarettes a day might go in the one to ten cigarettes a day group. You are entitled to make your own classifications, but if you tabulate exact numbers, you can modify your categorical criteria without having to contact the survey respondents again. General smoking categories might be (1) heavy (over one pack a day), (2) moderate (five to twenty cigarettes a day), (3) light (fewer than five cigarettes a day), (4) quit recently (less than ten years ago), (5) quit more than ten years ago, and (6) never smoked. By looking at the raw numbers you get for cigars, pipes, snuff, and chewing tobacco, you can decide how to divide the respondents into groups (three to five groups per category). Recreational drug use is tabulated by type of drug more than by frequency (anything over once a week is positive for present purposes). Alcohol use is also divided both by type of drink and by frequency, depending on the distribution you find in your results.

When you tabulate reproductive histories and make comparisons, remember that several things other than birth defects are considered to be adverse reproductive effects. Difficulty in getting pregnant may be a sensitive indicator and has in fact been the first clue in several instances of chemical exposure. Spontaneous abortions or miscarriages are also sensitive indicators, as are prematurity and low birth weight.

A discussion of birth defects will introduce the concept of ruling out variables (factors) that do not contribute. Remember that you are not trying to assign a cause for each birth defect, but are trying instead to

Table 8.2. Sample Two-by-two Contingency Table

	Affected	
Exposed	Yes	No
Yes	Group 1	Group 2
No	Group 3	Group 4

determine if the rate of birth defects in your community as a whole is elevated with respect to your control community or to regional or national rates, and if common variables can be eliminated, thus leaving environment as a possible contributing cause. Examining one variable at a time means repeatedly dividing both your entire community and the unexposed community in many different ways. For example, you will want to examine both X-ray exposure and medication during pregnancy with respect to birth defects. For each factor you wish to examine you will divide your two communities into appropriate groups, giving you for groups each time: (1) exposed and affected, (2) exposed and not affected, (3) not exposed and affected, and (4) not exposed and not affected (table 8.2).

Additional factors such as medication may be examined separately or may be added to the first two, generating seven groups in our example (fig. 8.4). A fourth variable such as residence or occupation increases the

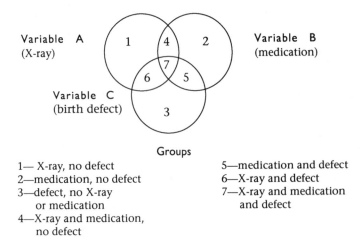

Variable A (X-ray)   Variable B (medication)   Variable C (birth defect)

Groups

1— X-ray, no defect
2—medication, no defect
3—defect, no X-ray
   or medication
4—X-ray and medication,
   no defect

5—medication and defect
6—X-ray and defect
7—X-ray and medication
   and defect

Figure 8.4 Possible Combination of Three Factors

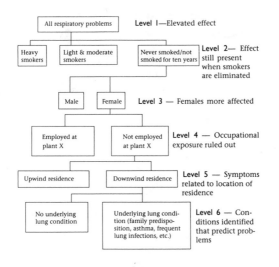

Figure 8.5 Sequential Examination of Possible Contributing Factors

number of possible combinations to fifteen, including single criteria alone, in pairs, in triplets, and all together. Comparing all these groups with one another is called multivariate analysis and will be discussed below.

An alternative to comparing each variable with every other variable at one time is a stepwise analysis that starts with the largest possible number of variables and subdivides little by little, checking for statistical significance at each step so you will know if you are on the right track. For example, in analyzing respiratory problems, divide respondents into heavy smokers, light and moderate smokers, and those who have never smoked or have not smoked for ten years or more. Repeat this process for both exposed and control groups (fig. 8.5).

You will now need to know whether there is any difference between these three groups in incidence of respiratory problems. Methods for making that decision will be discussed shortly. If there is not, lump them all back together and subdivide differently, by male and female, for example. However, if there is no difference between smokers and nonsmokers, the question still remains why nonsmokers are also affected. As you subdivide further and further, thereby defining your affected group more and more specifically, you may find that your "significant" effect disappears. In this case go back to the level of greatest significance (say females who never smoked — level 3), and compare this incidence rate with that for females who never smoked and were exposed but do not have respiratory problems, and the equivalent females from the control or unexposed population.

LOOKING FOR DIFFERENCES BETWEEN
YOUR POPULATION AND SOME STANDARD

As we pointed out previously, you cannot simply compare the incidence rate for your population with some standard and decide whether the two are different. This is because outcomes naturally vary in subpopulations. Therefore, even though the state average for a certain health problem might be ten in a thousand, your community of one thousand persons might easily have anywhere from four to sixteen cases and still be normal. A number of factors contribute to the size of the normal range, and later in this chapter we will talk about some of these factors and what should be considered in designing and analyzing your study.

Since you cannot just compare absolute numbers and rates obtained from your surveys, you will need a couple of statistical tools to help you understand both the implications and the limitations of your data. Two approaches will be presented: one is used in situations where you have data from two populations, either control and exposed or different zones in a stratified population, and the other involves comparing your data with some set of standard health statistics.

Comparing Populations: The Chi-Square Analysis

Basics   Although there are a variety of statistical procedures designed to compare one population with another, one of the most useful and easiest to perform is the chi-square analysis (pronounced ki, to rhyme with pie).

There are two basic concepts associated with chi-square. First, chi-square is structured around some concept of estimating the "expected" value for a population. If we had, for example, a population of 200 people and "knew" that half of "all people" have brown hair, we would "expect" $200 \times 0.5 = 100$ people in our population to have brown hair. Given this, the second concept is that of differences between what you actually have in your population and what you expected. This difference could be due to natural variation as mentioned earlier, or it could represent a true difference between your population and a "normal" population. For example, your population could have a unique ethnic component, such as a strong Nordic origin, that has caused it not to conform to the "normal" population standard. Chi-square uses these two factors to help you understand your population. By using chi-square you can ask whether two populations are actually the same or whether the difference observed is too big to be consistent with normal variation or chance alone.

Two-by-two Tables   The easiest way to set up a chi-square analysis is to build a simple table. We will begin with a two-by-two table based on the example given earlier (table 8.3).

Table 8.3. Sample Two-by-two Table For Chi-square Analysis

Exposure	Pulmonary Disease		
	Yes	No	Row Total
Yes	90	210	300
No	85	315	400
Column Total	175	525	700

Table 8.4. Determining Expected Frequency of Disease

Exposure	Pulmonary Disease		
	Yes	No	Row Total
Yes	90	210	300
No	85	315	400
Column Total	**175**	525	**700**
	175/700 = 0.25		

Table 8.5. Determining Expected Frequency of Disease in the Exposed Population

Exposure	Pulmonary Disease		
	Yes	No	Row Total
Yes	90	210	**300**
No	85	315	400
Column Total	175	525	700

Table 8.6. Chi-square Analysis of Data

Exposure	Pulmonary Disease		
	Yes	No	Total
Yes	90	210	300
	(75)	(225)	
No	85	315	400
	(199)	(300)	
Total	175	525	700

Note: Expected number of cases in parentheses.

A few things to note: this table looks at only two items at a time; one item is given at the top of the table and the other down the left-hand side; individual columns and rows are totaled, and these subtotals are used to reach the grand total at lower right; and the table consists of the actual number of people who meet a given requirement, not of rates, percentages, or frequencies. The location of the two criteria (exposure and pulmonary disease) is not mandatory (exposure could have been on top), but we suggest that for standardization you keep the health outcome at the top and the exposure criteria on the left side.

This table represents what was actually observed. The next step is to determine what was to be expected had both the exposed and the unexposed populations behaved in the same way with respect to pulmonary disease. To do this we take the total number of pulmonary disease cases and divide that by the grand total (table 8.4).

This gives us a frequency for the occurrence of pulmonary disease. If exposure has nothing to do with pulmonary disease, then 0.25, or one-fourth, of the exposed population should have a health problem, and three-fourths should not. Since there are a total of 300 people in the exposed population (table 8.5), we would expect $300 \times 0.25 = 75$ of them to have the pulmonary disease and $300 - 75 = 225$ not to have the disease. The same approach is used for the unexposed population with $400 \times 0.25 = 100$ expected to have the disease and $400 - 100 = 300$ expected not to have the disease.

If you now go back to the original two-by-two table and put the expected numbers in parentheses in each appropriate box, you will be ready to begin the analysis of your data (table 8.6).

Mathematical Tables The chi-square process evaluates the difference between the observed and expected values in each cell, performing a mathematical function on that difference, and adding up the results cell by cell to reach a total called a chi-square statistic. The theory of the chi-square is beyond the scope of this book; you can refer to the statistics section of a library to learn more about the procedure. The basic thrust of the test is to determine the difference between the observed number of people in a given cell (O) and the expected number of people for that cell (E): you then multiply that difference times itself, $(O-E) \times (O-E)$ or $(O-E)^2$, and divide that result by the value expected for that cell, $(O-E)^2/E$.

This is carried out for each cell, then these numbers are added together. A quick computation table keeps the math organized and allows you to progress at a pace that can be handled by any simple calculator (table 8.7).

Using the Chi-square Statistic The value of the chi-square statistic in this example is 7.00. The problem is that this number in itself means

Table 8.7. Computation Table For Calculating Chi-square

Exposure	Pulmonary Disease	E	O	O $-$ E	$(O-E)^2$	$(O-E)^2/E$
Yes	Yes	90	75	15	225	3.00
Yes	No	210	225	15	225	1.00
No	Yes	85	100	15	225	2.25
No	No	315	300	15	225	0.75
Total						7.00

Note: O = observed; E = expected

very little. To make some sense out of this, you must go to the chi-square distribution table (table 8.8).

Before using the chi-square distribution table, there are a few things you need to know. The table is constructed around two items of information, the chi-square statistic, which you already have and know how to obtain, and a number called the degrees of freedom (df), which we will expand upon shortly; for now, this example has one degree of freedom.

The chi-square distribution table is entered along the row corresponding to the degrees of freedom your test has. Once you have the correct row, you read along that row looking for a number close to your chi-square statistic. For our example, the number for degrees of freedom (df) is one, so you use the first row in the body of the table and read along until you find a number close to 7.00, your chi-square statistic. From the table, 7.00 falls between 6.64 and 10.83. From here you read straight up to the column headings; 6.64 reads up to .01, and 10.83 yields the number .001. These two numbers are called p-values, and they are the standard to use in trying to determine if two groups are different.

P-Values P-values are a statement about probability — specifically, the probability that the difference you observe is due solely to chance or natural variation and that your two groups are actually the same. Remember that probability ranges from zero to one, a probability of zero (.00) implying that something will never happen and a probability of one (1.00) implying that it will always happen. Another way to view p-values is to say they represent a measure of your belief that the two groups under study are actually the same. For the example, the p-value is somewhere between .01 and .001, or very close to .00. Therefore it is very unlikely that the two groups, exposed and unexposed, are the same with respect to the outcome of pulmonary disease.

Table 8.8. Chi-square Distribution Table

df	.99	.98	.95	.90	.80	.70	.50	.30	.20	.10	.05	.02	.01	.001
1	0.00016	0.00063	0.0039	0.016	0.064	0.15	0.46	1.07	1.64	2.71	3.84	5.41	6.64	10.83
2	0.02	0.04	0.10	0.21	0.45	0.71	1.39	2.41	3.22	4.60	5.99	7.82	9.21	13.82
3	0.12	0.18	0.35	0.58	1.00	1.42	2.37	3.66	4.64	6.25	7.82	9.84	11.34	16.27
4	0.30	0.43	0.71	1.06	1.65	2.20	3.36	4.88	5.99	7.78	9.49	11.67	13.28	18.46
5	0.55	0.75	1.14	1.61	2.34	3.00	4.35	6.06	7.29	9.24	11.07	13.39	15.09	20.52
6	0.87	1.13	1.64	2.20	3.07	3.83	5.35	7.23	8.56	10.64	12.59	15.03	16.81	22.46
7	1.24	1.56	2.17	2.83	3.82	4.67	6.35	8.38	9.80	12.02	14.07	16.62	18.48	24.32
8	1.65	2.03	2.73	3.49	4.59	5.53	7.34	9.52	11.03	13.36	15.51	18.17	20.09	26.12
9	2.09	2.53	3.32	4.17	5.38	6.39	8.34	10.66	12.24	14.68	16.92	19.68	21.67	27.88
10	2.56	3.06	3.94	4.86	6.18	7.27	9.34	11.78	13.44	15.99	18.31	21.16	23.21	39.59
11	3.05	3.61	4.58	5.58	6.99	8.15	10.34	12.90	14.63	17.28	19.68	22.62	24.72	31.26
12	3.57	4.18	5.23	6.30	7.81	9.03	11.34	14.01	15.81	18.55	21.03	24.05	26.22	32.91
13	4.11	4.76	5.89	7.04	8.63	9.93	12.34	15.12	16.98	19.81	22.36	25.47	27.69	34.53
14	4.66	5.37	6.57	7.79	9.47	10.82	13.34	16.22	18.15	21.06	23.68	26.87	29.14	36.12
15	5.23	5.98	7.26	8.55	10.31	11.72	14.34	17.32	19.31	22.31	15.00	28.26	30.58	37.70

Note: df = degrees of freedom.

The question arises of how small the p-value needs to be before you conclude that your two groups are different. A matter of debate in the scientific and statistical communities, the standard response is that the p-value should be equal to or less than .05. This is equivalent to accepting a one in twenty risk of being wrong in claiming a difference when in fact a difference does not exist. This reflects the conservative tendency of scientific professionals not to state that a difference exists unless there is a significant amount of evidence to support such a conclusion. However, since you are not out to establish indisputable evidence, but rather want to raise warning flags concerning potential health problems, if you get a p-value of less than .10 you should make note of that, and if the p-value is less than .02 you should seriously suspect that a difference (which implies a problem) exists between the two groups being studied.

Variations on the Two-by-two Format The example previously given is a good sample of the use of the chi-square analysis. However, in some situations you may have measured an outcome on a scale that is not simply an either/or combination (yes/no responses), but rather a range of responses, such as pulmonary problems requiring hospitalization, pulmonary problems requiring only prescription medication, and no evidence of pulmonary problems. The contributing factor being tested may also involve more than two alternatives, as when a stratified population has three or more "zones" (strata). The chi-square analysis can still be carried out on this type of material, in the same manner as before (table 8.9).

The computation table (table 8.10) is constructed as before, with the $(O-E)^2/E$ number generated for each cell and the result for each cell added to get the chi-square statistic. The only difference comes in using the chi-square distribution table — specifically, the degrees of freedom. Degrees of freedom is a mathematical or physical concept that for our purposes is related to the number of subjects or categories under study. As the dimensions of the original data table change, so do the degrees of freedom. The new degrees of freedom can be obtained by adding up the number of rows (R) and columns (C), subtracting one from each, $(R-1)$ and $(C-1)$, then multiplying these two numbers $(R-1) \times (C-1)$. Therefore this example, which uses a three-by-three table, has $(3-1) \times (3-1) = 4$ degrees of freedom. When you look along the row for four degrees of freedom to find a value near your chi-square statistic of 21.21, you run off the table. There is no number that large in the row for four degrees of freedom. You can conclude from this that the probability that the three zones have the pulmonary pattern they do simply by chance is less than .001 (the smallest p-value in the column heading on the far right). You must then strongly suspect

Table 8.9. Chi-square Example with an Exposure Gradient Divided into Three Zones and Two Levels of Symptoms

| Zone | Pulmonary Problem | | | Total |
	Hospitalization Needed	Medication Needed	None	
1	30	70	100	200
	(24.3)	(51.4)	(124.3)	
2	30	60	160	250
	(30.4)	(64.3)	(155.4)	
3	25	50	175	250
	(30.4)	(64.3)	(155.4)	
Totals	85	180	435	700

Note: Overall proportions for each of the health outcomes are:
Pulmonary disease requiring hospitalization   85/700 = 0.12
Pulmonary disease requiring prescription medication   180/700 = 0.26
No evidence of pulmonary disease   435/700 = 0.62

Table 8.10. Overall Proportions for Each of the Health Outcomes in Table 8.9

Pulmonary Problem	O	E	O − E	(O − E)²	(O − E)²/E
Zone 1					
Hospitalization	30	24.3	5.3	28.1	1.16
Medication	70	51.4	20.6	424.4	8.26
None	100	124.3	24.3	590.5	4.75
Zone 2					
Hospitalization	30	30.4	0.4	0.2	0.00
Medication	60	64.3	4.3	18.5	0.29
None	160	155.4	4.6	21.2	0.14
Zone 3					
Hospitalization	25	30.4	5.4	29.2	0.96
Medication	50	64.3	14.3	204.5	3.18
None	175	155.4	19.6	384.2	2.47
Total					21.21

Note: O = observed; E = expected.

that, whatever the difference is between the three zones, it is significantly affecting the development of pulmonary problems within each zone.

Comparing Your Population with Established Health Statistics

Occasionally, obtaining a comparison population is difficult, or suitable local health statistics exist that make a comparison population unnecessary. In these cases you will compare the results from your study with reported standards for the health outcomes you are interested in. Since these health statistics are presented as rates of various sorts, one of the easiest ways to deal with your data is to generate a "reasonable bound" on the health statistic rate for a given health problem. The limits for this "reasonable bound" are determined by the frequency distribution of the group under study. Back to an example mentioned earlier: If the health statistics for a given disease showed a rate of ten per thousand, then in any population of one thousand people it would not be unexpected to see from four to sixteen cases of that disease, owing to normal variation within populations. Conversely, if you find sixteen cases of this disease in a population of one thousand people, even though your rate is sixteen per thousand you cannot say with reasonable certainty that your population is any different from a "normal population" that has a rate of ten per thousand. If this is confusing, a short test period of flipping a coin in series of ten tries, as described in chapter 5, should point out that, though the average number of heads you get when flipping the coin ten times is five, you actually see anywhere from two to eight heads in any given set of ten flips. In fact, in only about one-fourth of the sets of ten will you actually get five heads. The survey you have done is like a single series of ten flips. You may end up with exactly the published rate for some disease (just like getting five heads), you may get a number slightly different from the published rate (like seeing three or seven heads), or you may get a number that seems significantly different from the published rate (like getting all heads). Setting a "reasonable bound" on the estimate of the rate for a health outcome lets you put a range around the published statistic so you can see if the observed rate for your population is within this bound. If your observed rate falls outside this range, then you must suspect that your population is different from the population used to generate the published health statistics. The possible advantages and pitfalls of using published health statistics have been discussed in previous chapters, and you should refresh your understanding of these if necessary. Unlike the chi-square analysis on two different populations, this technique, though it points out a potential problem, is weaker in its ability to suggest a possible cause.

The mathematical process for generating this "reasonable bound" is based on two factors: the "normal" rate for the health problem and the number of people in your population who could potentially develop that problem. The normal rate (P), in decimal notation, is multiplied by one minus that rate $(1-P)$ and divided by the number of susceptible people in your population (N), then the square root of this number is taken:

$$\sqrt{\frac{(P)\ (1-P)}{N}}.$$

This is considered the standard error of your estimate of a proportion (the rate of the disease). Most of the time (more than 90 percent) the estimate of the disease rate you get should fall within 1.65 times this standard error from the published rate:

$$1.65 \times \sqrt{\frac{(P)\ (1-P)}{N}}.$$

For example, with a published rate of 0.06 (six per hundred) and a population size of 1,000:

$$1.65 \times \sqrt{\frac{(P)\ (1-P)}{N}} = .0124.$$

Therefore, if the rate you observe is between 0.0476 and 0.0724, or 48 and 72 per thousand, then you cannot say that your population is different from the "normal" population used to generate the health statistics. If your observed rate falls outside this reasonable bound, then you must take note of the situation, and if it falls well outside this range you should be concerned. In this case our range was 60 ± (plus or minus) 12 cases per thousand. If your observed rate is outside this range by more than half again the bound (12), that is, 0.5 × 12 = 6, this is a very important observation that suggests your population is significantly different from the normal population.

Since the calculations involved can be tedious and certain standard situations can be anticipated, table 8.11 has been generated to help you quickly estimate a reasonable bound for a few standard population sizes and rates. Remember that the population sizes down the left side represent the number of people you surveyed who could potentially develop a particular health problem, and the proportions across the top are the decimal representation of the normal rate as reported in published health statistics. The bounds used in this table are the same as those presented in the mathematical computation. Since you are generally interested in determining a directional difference, such as an increase in pulmonary disease or a decrease in number of births, the table gives a directional bound. Instead of using 1.65 times the standard error of the estimate (SEE), which gives a bidirectional measure and encompasses about 90 percent of the expected outcomes. If your actual population size or proportion for the health outcome does not appear in the table, you may do some sort of simple extrapolation by comparing your numbers with those that most closely bracket your data. Once again, these are ranges about a set proportion, and you still must solve the equation (background proportion + bound) or (background proportion − bound), where bound is equivalent to

$$1.28 \times \sqrt{\frac{(P)\,(1-P)}{N}},$$

which has been solved for you in this table. If your proportion (rate) falls near the edge of the reasonable bound, this constitutes a warning that the situation needs to be investigated further. If your proportion (rate) falls outside the bound by more than half again the size of the bound − that is, outside (background proportion ± 1.5 × bound) − then significant evidence exists to warrant special attention as to why your population is so different from the "normal" population. But keep in mind at all times the limitations of using published health statistics and realize that this evidence alone is not sufficient to attribute blame concerning the cause of the health problem; rather, it simply shows that the health problem is "real."

OTHER STATISTICAL CONSIDERATIONS

Although the mathematical portions of statistics are fairly straightforward, a few aspects pertaining to experimental design and data interpretation need to be discussed. One factor, alluded to in the chapter on experimental design (chapter 5), is the concept of "power." The other factor is the role of "false positive" results in the analysis of data. We will briefly explain these concepts here so that you can appreciate the limits they can put on your study.

Power

With regard to a study and analysis, "power" means the ability to detect a difference between two populations given that the difference does ex-

Table 8.11. Natural Variation around Published Proportions with a Variety of Population Sizes

	Expected Proportions From Published Health Statistics							
Population Size	.00001	.00002	.00004	.00008	.00016	.00032	.00064	.0013
50	.00057	.00081	.00114	.00162	.00229	.00324	.00548	.0065
100	.00040	.00057	.00081	.00114	.00162	.00229	.00324	.0046
150	.00030	.00047	.00066	.00093	.00132	.00187	.00264	.0037
200	.00029	.00040	.00057	.00081	.00114	.00162	.00229	.0032
250	.00026	.00036	.00051	.00072	.00102	.00145	.00205	.0029
300	.00023	.00033	.00047	.00066	.00093	.00132	.00187	.0026
350	.00022	.00031	.00043	.00061	.00087	.00122	.00173	.0024
400	.00020	.00029	.00040	.00057	.00081	.00114	.00162	.0023
450	.00019	.00027	.00038	.00054	.00076	.00108	.00153	.0022
500	.00018	.00026	.00036	.00051	.00072	.00102	.00145	.0020
600	.00017	.00023	.00033	.00047	.00066	.00093	.00132	.0019
700	.00015	.00022	.00031	.00043	.00061	.00087	.00122	.0017
800	.00014	.00020	.00029	.00040	.00057	.00081	.00114	.0016
900	.00013	.00019	.00027	.00038	.00054	.00076	.00108	.0015
1,000	.00013	.00018	.00026	.00036	.00051	.00072	.00102	.0014
1,200	.00012	.00017	.00023	.00033	.00047	.00066	.00093	.0013
1,400	.00011	.00015	.00022	.00031	.00043	.00061	.00087	.0012
1,600	.00010	.00014	.00020	.00029	.00040	.00057	.00081	.0011
1,800	.00010	.00013	.00019	.00027	.00038	.00054	.00076	.0011
2,000	.00009	.00013	.00018	.00026	.00036	.00051	.00072	.0010
2,500	.00008	.00011	.00016	.00023	.00032	.00046	.00065	.00091
3,000	.00007	.00010	.00015	.00021	.00030	.00042	.00059	.00094
3,500	.00007	.00010	.00014	.00019	.00027	.00039	.00055	.00077
4,000	.00006	.00009	.00013	.00018	.00026	.00036	.00051	.00072
4,500	.00006	.00009	.00012	.00017	.00024	.00034	.00048	.00068

ist. Although a number of things can contribute to a study's sensitivity (power), here we will deal only with three statistical factors: population, or more specifically sample size, natural variation, and the magnitude of the difference one is trying to detect. Since the equations needed to derive a measure of power are complicated, we will not get involved with them. Instead, table 8.12 presents a collection of possible study situations. With some orientation you should be able to use the table to help you design your study or to put your results in proper context.

The table is structured around two numbers: the background rate (proportion) for a given health effect is listed down the left side, and the relative increase over the background rate is across the top. The fig-

Table 8.11.
(*continued*)

				Expected Proportions From Published Health Statistics				
Population Size	.0026	.0051	.0102	.0205	.0410	.0819	.1638	.3277	.6554
50	.0091	.0129	.0182	.0256	.0359	.0496	.0670	.0850	.0860
100	.0065	.0091	.0129	.0181	.0254	.0351	.0474	.0601	.0608
150	.0053	.0075	.0105	.0148	.0207	.0287	.0387	.0491	.0497
200	.0046	.0065	.0091	.0128	.0179	.0248	.0335	.0425	.0430
250	.0041	.0058	.0081	.0115	.0160	.0222	.0300	.0380	.0385
300	.0037	.0053	.0074	.0105	.0146	.0203	.0274	.0347	.0351
350	.0035	.0049	.0069	.0097	.0136	.0188	.0253	.0321	.0325
400	.0032	.0046	.0064	.0091	.0127	.0176	.0237	.0300	.0304
450	.0030	.0043	.0061	.0085	.0120	.0165	.0223	.0283	.0287
500	.0029	.0041	.0058	.0081	.0113	.0157	.0212	.0269	.0272
600	.0026	.0037	.0053	.0074	.0104	.0143	.0193	.0245	.0248
700	.0024	.0035	.0049	.0069	.0096	.0133	.0179	.0227	.0230
800	.0023	.0032	.0046	.0064	.0090	.0124	.0168	.0212	.0215
900	.0022	.0030	.0043	.0060	.0085	.0117	.0158	.0200	.0203
1,000	.0020	.0029	.0041	.0057	.0080	.0111	.0150	.0190	.0192
1,200	.0019	.0026	.0037	.0052	.0073	.0101	.0137	.0173	.0176
1,400	.0017	.0024	.0034	.0048	.0068	.0094	.0127	.0161	.0163
1,600	.0016	.0023	.0032	.0045	.0063	.0088	.0118	.0150	.0152
1,800	.0015	.0022	.0030	.0043	.0060	.0083	.0112	.0142	.0143
2,000	.0014	.0020	.0029	.0041	.0057	.0078	.0106	.0134	.0136
2,500	.0013	.0018	.0026	.0036	.0051	.0070	.0095	.0120	.0122
3,000	.0012	.0017	.0024	.0033	.0046	.0064	.0086	.0110	.0111
3,500	.0011	.0015	.0022	.0031	.0043	.0059	.0080	.0102	.0103
4,000	.0010	.0014	.0020	.0029	.0040	.0056	.0075	.0095	.0096
4,500	.00096	.0014	.0019	.0027	.0038	.0052	.0071	.0090	.0091

ures that constitute the body of the table are the number of people you would need to look at in both the exposed and the control populations in order to have an 80 percent chance of demonstrating that a difference does exist. For example, for a health problem with a background rate of 0.02 (twenty per thousand), if you wanted to be able to detect a twofold increase (doubling) in your population, you would have to look at 874 people in your population and 874 people from a control population.

When we examine the table, two points become apparent. First, the larger the background rate for a given health problem, the smaller the study size needed to demonstrate a relative change in incidence. This

Table 8.12. Population Sizes for Exposed and Control Groups Needed to Have an 80 Percent Chance of Demonstrating a Significant Difference Between Two Populations

Background Rate	Relative Increase Over Background Rate							
	2	4	6	8	10	12	14	16
.00001	1,900,000	345,000	170,000	110,000	83,853	66,338	54,802	46,650
.00002	930,000	170,000	86,444	56,703	41,923	33,165	27,398	23,322
.00004	460,000	85,755	43,217	28,347	20,958	16,579	13,695	11,657
.00008	230,000	42,872	21,604	14,170	10,475	8,286	6,844	5,825
.00016	120,000	21,430	10,798	7,081	5,234	4,139	3,418	2,909
.00032	57,862	10,709	5,394	3,536	2,613	2,066	1,706	1,451
.00064	28,915	5,349	2,693	1,764	1,303	1,029	850	722
.00128	14,442	2,669	1,342	878	648	511	421	358
.00256	7,206	1,328	667	435	320	252	207	176
.005	3,587	659	329	214	157	123	100	85
.01	1,778	324	160	103	75	58	47	39
.02	874	156	76	48	34	25	20	16
.04	422	73	34	20	13	9	7	5
.05	340	57	26	15	10	6	4	3
.10	155	23	9	4	1			
.15	93	12	3					
.20	62	6						
.25	44	3						
.30	31							
.35	23							
.40	16							
.45	11							
.50	7							

results from the magnitude of the difference that accompanies "relative change." Second, as the severity of the difference changes (i.e., a twofold versus a fourfold increase), so does the number of people needed to demonstrate an effect. Table 8.13 represents the study size that will give you a 50 percent chance of demonstrating that something is going on.

These tables are important from both a pre- and a poststudy perspective. For prestudy purposes, if you know the background rate for the particular health problem that interests you and have in mind the type of increase you would like to be able to detect in your population (say a twofold increase, or doubling over normal), then tables 8.12 and 8.13 will tell you the size of the study necessary to have an 80 percent or a 50 percent chance of demonstrating such an effect. Therefore you can plan the size of your study to give yourself the degree of power you want. Increasing the number of people in your study will always increase your power. These tables can also help you realize the limitations of your study. For studies involving rare health conditions you must study a large number of people to have even a small chance of seeing sizable increases over background rates. In this situation you must either accept this potential problem and continue with the study, remembering that you don't actually know how great the effect is in your community, or eliminate this section of your study, which unfortunately doesn't help anyone. You may easily find yourself working on something with little hope of success. Seriously evaluate the process beforehand so as to appreciate the work that lies ahead. If, after the fact, you are unable to demonstrate a health problem in your community, remind yourself of the power of your study. Also remember that it is not uncommon for studies with very little power to be conducted and that just because you could not demonstrate a difference between your population and some "normal" population does not necessarily mean no problem exists.

Last, if you partition your population into subpopulations based on contributing factors such as smoking history, age, or sex, some of the sensitivity gained from focusing on more susceptible subgroups may in part be offset by a drop in power. Don't go too far in delineating highly specific subgroups of your population.

False Positives

A "false positive" occurs when a difference appears to exist between two populations, or between the study population and some standard proportion, when in fact there is no real difference at all. This goes back to the role of natural variation and the fact that we must use some standard for decision making. As discussed earlier, scientists use a p-value of

Table 8.13. Population Sizes for Exposed and Control Groups Needed to Have a 50 Percent Chance of Demonstrating a Significant Difference Between Two Populations

Background Rate	Relative Increase Over Background Rate							
	2	4	6	8	10	12	14	16
.00001	810,000	150,000	75,765	49,699	36,745	29,070	24,015	20,442
.00002	410,000	75,162	37,880	28,848	18,371	14,533	12,006	10,220
.00004	200,000	37,579	18,938	12,422	9,184	7,265	6,001	5,108
.00008	100,000	18,787	9,467	6,209	4,590	3,631	2,999	2,553
.00016	50,724	9,391	4,732	3,103	2,293	1,814	1,498	1,275
.00032	25,355	4,693	2,364	1,550	1,145	906	748	636
.00064	12,671	2,344	1,180	773	571	451	373	317
.00128	6,329	1,169	588	385	284	224	185	157
.00256	3,158	583	292	191	141	111	91	77
.005	1,572	289	144	94	69	54	44	37
.01	780	142	70	45	33	26	21	17
.02	383	69	33	21	15	11	9	7
.04	185	32	15	9	6	4	3	2
.05	149	25	12	7	4	3	2	1
.10	68	10	4	2	1			
.15	41	5	2					
.20	28	3						
.25	19	1						
.30	14							
.35	10							
.40	7							
.45	5							
.50	3							

.05 to determine whether their results are significant. This means that about five percent of the time it is expected that the results could have occurred by chance alone. The investigators should understand that some fraction of the time their claim that an adverse health effect was "caused" by an agent may not be correct. This is because it is so difficult to prove certain types of material; sometimes you can do no more than collect a significant amount of evidence. The scientific community has come to accept this false-positive rate as an appropriate trade-off between making an incorrect decision (false positive) when no difference exists and doing so when in fact a difference does exist (false negative).

With the statistical methods given in this chapter, a false positive rate of one in ten (10 percent) has been accepted. This means that about 10 percent of your comparisons will come out as possibly significant. Therefore, that one or two indicators of health show increased levels compared with some "normal" group does not necessarily mean that a real difference, or problem, exists. Once again this is a trade-off. Ideally you want no false positives, yet you need some standard so you can at least begin to identify possible health problems. As we mentioned in discussing chi-square and reasonable bounds, a p-value of about .10 constitutes a warning that you should look further. With a p-value of less than .02, or if the "reasonable bound" is more than one and one-half times the bound width away from the normal rate, then a significant amount of evidence exists that a problem (the observed difference in health status between two populations) is real. You need temperance and understanding when analyzing your data. Any comparison that shows a warning flag (p-value of .10 or less) should be looked at further to determine if specific subpopulations exist that are experiencing the bulk of the increase in adverse health conditions.

FURTHER STUDY

The next chapter discusses several possible next steps, including pursuing further study by governmental or academic investigators. Yet another alternative is for you to use more rigorous and powerful statistical tools. A paper introducing and explaining such tools, designed for use by laypersons and accompanied by simple computer programs, is available at the following address:

Dr. J. I. Rosenblatt
Director, Office of Biomathematics
619 Shriners Burns Institute
University of Texas Medical Branch
Galveston, TX 77555-1220

There will be a small charge to cover shipping and handling costs.

WHERE DO YOU GO FROM HERE?

Exploring Options for Further Study and Further Action

Ellen K. Silbergeld

Community health studies are primarily organizing and consciousness-raising tools that are effective as part of an overall community based strategy for change. Their use in this context is discussed elsewhere in this book; this chapter will provide some suggestions for using these studies to find out more or different information on associations between exposures to hazardous waste releases and the health of your community. It is unfortunately the case that most health professionals and public health or environmental officials look upon community health studies with suspicion and disdain; health studies are considered complex undertakings and the professionals tend to doubt that non-professionals could actually uncover any valid or useful information. However, some health professionals and government officials who have come to recognize that the "local knowledge" of community residents provide invaluable information frequently unknown to outside investigators. Ideally, at some point, we will be able to forge effective working relationships between alert community health detectives and sympathetic officials. At present, this kind of relationship has been difficult, if not impossible to establish.

Now that it is clear where the health survey fits into the overall process, you can move from the thinking phase to the doing phase.

After you complete an investigation of health effects in your community, you will be faced with choices for action. Here we assume that you decide something more must be done. This may include obtaining further information on health, getting the source of toxic chemicals cleaned up, or obtaining compensation for damage to property or health. First, and most important, remember your commitments to your friends and neighbors and arrange for a full presentation of study results to all who are potentially affected. Remember to deal sensitively and discreetly with everyone involved.

Your choices are obviously influenced by the outcome of the study. In all cases, successful mobilization of resources to attain your goals ultimately depends upon the effectiveness of your organization and your persistence in political action.

OBTAINING FURTHER INFORMATION

After completing your health survey, you may want to enlist the assistance of organizations or people with greater resources, more access to medical information, and medical or clinical skills and facilities. Citizens in Alabama and in Michigan involved the Centers of Disease Control in extensive and long-term health studies of DDT and PCBs. In other cases, universities have been sources of experts to assist in analyzing community health studies and in designing further investigations.

It is important to realize that as soon as others are involved in further health studies in your community, control and direction pass out of your hands. Their goals and objectives may not be the same as yours, since in many cases they need to satisfy the more exacting criteria of scientific research, and they may be affected by economic and political pressures. It usually takes such organizations a relatively long time to get their further studies under way, in part because they must submit any projects to clinical research committees or other forms of review, and in part because they have to coordinate people or departments within their institutions.

Your relations with such outside investigators will be most successful if you keep in mind that both sides have gains and losses in working together. You retain the ultimate power of not agreeing to participate — a powerful weapon in negotiating an acceptable and comprehensive study, because the research can be irreparably damaged if large numbers of people decline to take part. On their side, they have the power to determine the scope of the study, the types of questions to be answered, and the methods of data analysis. You can and should demand to take as active a role as possible in the analysis of the study, but you should respect their need to conduct it independently. The value of their work will largely depend upon others' perception of its objectivity and independence. Before you agree to participate, make sure the goals of the study are acceptable to you and you are satisfied with schedules, procedures, access to information, and the like.

Further studies may be necessary to resolve important issues of concern to your community or to provide various types of information on health effects, such as biopsies to determine individual exposure more precisely. Three types of resources are available for assistance in conducting further research: private medical services (including hospitals, health maintenance organizations, and private physicians); universities, schools of public health, and medical schools; and public health departments in the local, county, state, and federal levels.

Private medical services can get interested in conducting community health studies, particularly if they are involved in preventive health care and, most importantly, if they are responsible for the medical expenses of many people in the community. For example, the Kaiser Permanente health care organization in Santa Clara County, California has taken part in studying whether there has been an increase in birth defects associated with exposure to 1,1,1-trichloroethane in drinking water.

Universities, schools of public health, and medical schools, particularly those with departments of community medicine or epidemiology, may be interested in conducting intensive studies of community health. Among the schools of public health and medical schools that have already been involved in such studies are those of the State University of New York at Binghamton, Johns Hopkins University, Harvard, Boston University, the University of Massachusetts, the University of California at Los Angeles, and the University of Texas.

Public health agencies include local public health offices, county and state agencies, and federal Public Health Service (Centers for Disease Control [CDC]). These organizations are set up by law and funded by taxes specifically to protect public health and investigate potential causes of community illness. Often they can bring to their work extensive resources, personnel, and experience.

The Agency for Toxic Substances and Disease Registry (ATSDR), a new agency within the Public Health Service, was established by Congress in the Superfund law to provide information, conduct health investigations, maintain registries, and conduct research on the health effects of toxic substances and hazardous wastes in the environment. After a slow beginning, hindered by interference from the White House and EPA, ATSDR is beginning to respond to citizen petitions and other requests for information and health assessments in communities near hazardous waste sites. The agency is required by Congress to study all communities at all National Priority List (NPL) sites, and to respond to petitions from communities for assessments and investigations. In 1989 and 1990, ATSDR conducted over 280 health assessments at 246 NPL sites. In addition, ATSDR is required to establish registries to follow the longterm consequences of exposure to specific chemicals. ATSDR has to date established four registries of persons living in the Missouri dioxin-contaminated communities (including Times Beach) and 13 registries of persons living in communities where drinking water was contaminated with trichloroethylene. Other registries on lead and other solvents are being set up. ATSDR also publishes profiles on chemicals frequently found at hazardous waste sites. These toxicological profiles are fairly good summaries of information on health risks and exposures, but tend to be rather conservative.

Communities have had varied experiences with ATSDR and its studies. One problem is that ATSDR rarely conducts any new sampling or analysis at sites, but uses data from state sources, EPA, and responsible parties. This information may not be complete or in an appropriate form for using in an epidemiological study. Also, in many communities, people are understandably wary of working with federal officials on health studies at the same time as they are trying to get action from the federal government towards effective cleanup. While health effects are not a necessary finding in order for cleanup to occur, many communities have experienced situations where the alleged lack of health effects has been cited as a reason to delay or dilute cleanup efforts.

It is difficult to recommend a particular source for obtaining assistance with further health studies. Unfortunately, all organizations can be hampered by political and other pressures, and every organization is constrained by the funds available. You need to investigate work the group has done on similar topics, which you do get by requesting copies of publications describing their research. Keep in mind that every study of your community in a sense reduces the probability of further studies, so that as far as possible you need to ensure that the best possible study is done on this second round.

It is always useful to notify the federal Public Health Service of your study, because they maintain data banks on health and potential dangers to health. Even if you get no initial action from this source, your request may be acted on later (for example, if other similar results are observed or there is a chemical fire at a dump site). Moreover, your letter serves as official notification of your study and your concerns, which may be useful in the future.

GETTING A CLEANUP

One of the main reasons for communities to undertake health studies is the existence of an obvious source of chemical exposure, such as a hazardous waste dump. Even if your health study does not conclusively show adverse health effects in your community, you may still be concerned about getting the dump site cleaned up. To accomplish this you have several resources. The principal one is a federal law, the Comprehensive Rehabilitation and Environmental Compensation and Liability Act of 1980 (CERCLA), better known as Superfund.

Your state may have, and certainly should have, its own "Superfund" law to finance the state's share of the federal program and to provide for dump sites not covered by the federal cleanup (such as sites with lower priority in the national ranking system).

Superfund provides the EPA with the authority and the funding to identify such dump sites, develop action plans, and clean up the waste. Unfortunately, as with anything else, it takes persistence and political organization to get Superfund to work in your community. See chapter 11 for books, hotlines, and organizations concerning Superfund.

As a federal program, Superfund can be difficult to activate. Many states now also have their own Superfund programs, designed to provide for dump site cleanups. You need to consult your state department of environmental protection or natural resources to find out the details of such programs and how to activate them. If your state government offices are not helpful, an inquiry through a state representative may be more effective.

The Public Health Service has new resources provided through Superfund specifically to conduct health studies and to set up long-term health registries of people likely to have been exposed to toxic chemicals from hazardous waste dump sites. It took a lawsuit by the Environmental Defense Fund to accomplish this, but EPA will soon be forced to release millions of dollars for these purposes. The regional offices of EPA are listed in chapter 11.

COMPENSATION

If in the course of your study you establish that you or others may have suffered specific health damage or that your property has depreciated as a result of exposure to toxic substances, you have the right to seek compensation.

From a scientific medical point of view, we should make the following points. Legal suits are strongest under these three conditions:

• Fairly serious health effects have occurred (children born with birth defects, persons developing liver disease, for example).
• Chemical exposure has been directly measured in people or in their food or drinking water.
• The chemicals detected are already well defined and, ideally, already regulated or banned as toxic.

In situations where potential health effects — such as increased risk of cancer — are alleged, or where toxic substances have not yet been measured directly in people or are a complex mixture not yet fully investigated, it will be more difficult to build a case, but this has successfully been done in at least one instance.

At present the federal Superfund law does not provide for this type of compensation (known as victim compensation), though it does contain provisions covering damage to natural resources and the environment.

There is considerable interest in Congress in expanding Superfund or creating a new law to address the issue of compensation for damage to health by dump site exposure.

What communities have sought compensation for chemical exposure? In Kellogg, Idaho, parents sued a smelter company (Gulf and Western) for dumping so much lead in their community that their children were severely poisoned. Several of these cases have been settled out of court. Citizens in Triana, Alabama, have won cases against Olin for dumping DDT in their community and contaminating their food supply. In San Jose, California, families have sued Fairchild Industries for contaminating their drinking water with trichloroethane, holding that several of their children's birth defects were associated with this exposure. There are many citizens' suits against Hooker Chemical Company in Hyde Park and Niagara Falls, New York.

To determine the advisability of bringing a legal suit for compensation and to judge the strength of your case, you need legal counsel. In addition, there is at least one organization of lawyers who have specialized in this area of law and can be consulted by citizens: Trial Lawyers for Public Justice in Washington, D.C.

NEXT

There is more to do. Chemical contamination of the environment has only recently been recognized as one of the most important concerns of our modern life, in large part as a result of citizens' urgent concern about their communities and their health. Action continues to depend upon the focused political expression of that concern.

Action is needed in two directions. First, we must work more quickly and comprehensively to correct the problems caused by past mismanagement. At Price's landfill in New Jersey, trichlorethylene, lead, benzene, and other toxic chemicals have been moving through the ground toward the drinking water supply of Atlantic City. EPA has stockpiled activated carbon to place in municipal water systems in an attempt to remove these chemicals once they reach the aquifer. In Dade County, Florida, chemicals escaping from the 58th Street landfill have already contaminated several well fields that provide drinking water for Hialeah Gardens and the suburbs of Miami. Although those wells have been shut down, the chemicals are continuing to migrate, posing a threat to other water supplies.

By not eliminating the source of the contamination, these are policies of retreat. Relying on these policies, we shall surrender more and more of our country and its resources to an irreversible state of chemically induced degradation and loss. It is essential that we move toward policies of toxic-use reduction and source control so that risks are not transferred from production sites to waste disposal and ultimately to our air, water, and food. Communities must bring pressure to bear upon polluters to change manufacturing processes upstream before hazardous wastes are generated. Some states now have toxic use reduction policies in law. In addition, industries are now required to disclose how much and what chemicals they are releasing into air, water, and landfills. This information, the *Toxics Release Inventory* (TRI), must be provided annually by manufacturers to EPA and state agencies. In turn, the inventory is available as an on-line database at the National Library of Medicine, on tapes, and diskettes, and as a printed report. Call the EPA Right-to-Know Hotline (800-535-0202) for more information.

The TRI provides very valuable data on toxics releases, which can be important for your health studies as well as for campaigns to reduce toxics in your community. By getting this information in computer format, you can run your own analysis as has been done by the National Wildlife Federation and by students at the University of Maryland, among others. Some community environmental organizations have used this information to publicize particularly large polluters; the light of publicity has already influenced such big chemical companies as DuPont and Monsanto to commit to major reductions in toxics releases.

Your community knows firsthand it may not possible to move away soon enough, to close down wells fast enough. What can you do to counter these policies of retreat?

• If your state has no Superfund law, work to get one written, proposed, and passed by your state legislature.
• If you have identified a source of chemical contamination, work to get it corrected—through federal and state Superfund programs, or through state and federal laws on pollution control if it is an active source.

The other important direction for your efforts is preventative and toward the future. We must prevent the conditions that permit chemical contamination to occur. This means more than keeping industries or disposal facilities out of your community because of their potential to pollute the environment. There are laws and regulations that can effectively prevent dangerous or incompetent operation of such sources. You can

• Attend local and state National Pollution Discharge System (NPDES) discharge permit hearings and be actively informed about the conditions under which industries operate in your community. Citizens in

Michigan have been very effective at overseeing the way Dow Chemical Company will be permitted to discharge its wastes.

• Demand public hearings for any new hazardous waste dump, at which the industry or waste disposal company must present details on its operations that might affect your community. Citizens in Calcasieu, Louisiana, and in South Baltimore, Maryland, have used this process to get a great deal of information on the intentions of waste disposal managers in their communities.

• Join local and national networks to effectively inform Congress of your support for strong laws to regulate environmental protection and handling—the Clean Air Act, Clean Water Act, Resource Conservation and Recycling Act, and Toxic Substances Control Act all require periodic reauthorization. Widespread citizen pressure will save these laws from being weakened or restricted.

WHAT KIND OF EVIDENCE DO YOU NEED?

Legal Implications of Acute and Chronic Effects

William E. Townsley

Anyone reading this handbook has probably asked:

• Why are my neighbors and I being forced to defend ourselves against a toxic assault taking place in our own homes, schools, churches, parks, and public streets?
• Why haven't public health authorities been given the responsibility and the resources to protect us?
• Why has the public given the toxic waste generator a major role in ascertaining the harm from its toxic waste? Isn't it rather foolish to assign this responsibility to a party with such an obvious conflict of interest?
• Do victims of toxic harm have any legal rights?
• What can we, the public, do to better protect ourselves?

As we discuss issues raised by these questions, you will better understand why effective protection depends upon adequate identification of toxic harm, its victims, and its causes.

As more and more information accumulates on the role a toxic agent plays in causing harm, such a causal role may progress from mere speculation to distinct possibility, onward to probability, and at times even to virtual certainty. The facts necessary to build a reliable bridge between speculation and certainty are often available only to the toxic waste generator (TWG). Therefore, the TWG can prevent, stall, or weaken this evidentiary bridge by neglecting to compile necessary data such as exposure information, and by withholding information needed for epidemiologic studies.[1]

---

[1] Throughout this chapter I will express a number of views and conclusions based on my personal involvement in chronic disease litigation in which many of the nation's leading petrochemical companies gave testimony and other evi-

The TWG, in its adversary relationship with the public, has often promoted ignorance and uncertainty as to the identity of toxic harm, its victims, and its causes. The resulting ignorance and uncertainty have been effectively used to thwart public regulation of the TWG and enable it to evade its responsibility to toxic-harm victims.

In this chapter we will discuss a hypothetical toxic-harm claim so as to illustrate some of the complex legal and factual considerations involved. Our hypothetical claim will involve a victim, exposed both inside and outside the work place, who has chronic disease (cancer) allegedly caused by contamination of the ambient air by neighborhood industries over a long period of time.

We should keep in mind that toxic-harm victims, both inside and outside the work place, have fared poorly in obtaining legal relief. Occupational disease kills over 100,000 workers every year and three or four times that many are disabled. Yet only five percent of occupational disease victims are compensated and for that percent the compensation is little and late.

While cancer is the toxic harm in our hypothetical claim, we should recognize that cancer may not prove to be the most serious type of damage. We know that there is also reproductive, developmental, and neurological harm, but we have no idea of the magnitude and, unfortunately, too little is being done to understand the nature and proportion of such harm.

Not to be dismissed are the controversial acute health effects, as well as enhanced risk of chronic disease, being alleged with greater frequency, particularly by residents near toxic waste sites. It's no surprise that among this large population at risk many people experience debilitating anxiety. While this chapter does not focus on this area of concern, the reader should be aware that recent and current litigation is addressing some of the complex legal issues involved.[2]

After presenting and reviewing the hypothetical claim, I will further

---

dence of their activities in ascertaining the cancer dangers arising out of their operations. The industry evidence included toxicity and epidemiological studies, and a paucity of exposure data.

[2] *Sterling v. Velsicol Chemical Corporation*, 855 F2d 1188 (6 Cir. 1988), involving contamination of drinking water from chemical waste site and allowing recovery for fear caused by increased risk of toxic harm, but denying recovery for an enhanced risk of harm where no admissible expert testimony that such harm was probable; *Ayers v. Jackson Township*, 515 A.2d 287 (N.J. 1987), where water supply contaminated by township landfill, with recovery allowed for cost of medical surveillance and nuisance damages, but denied for anxiety and enhanced risk.

analyze how and why the public has found itself underprotected in dealing with toxic harm. Then I will offer a relatively simple plan as a partial solution.

In this chapter I have given few references, since the material is not written for the legal community and scientific material has been adequately discussed and referenced in other chapters. Moreover, my own views and conclusions have been strongly influenced by knowledge and experience gained from personal involvement in cancer litigation.

DUTY OF THE TOXIC WASTE GENERATOR
TO ASCERTAIN DANGERS

A toxic waste generator (TWG) has a legal duty to ascertain the dangers arising out of its operations, including the disposal of its toxic waste into the atmosphere, into the waterways, and on and into the earth.[3] The TWG can perform this legal duty (1) by identifying, measuring, and recording the exposure creating possible risks; (2) by conducting appropriate toxicity studies; (3) by conducting well-designed epidemiologic studies of populations at risk; (4) by developing and using effective methods of biological monitoring; and (5) by keeping abreast of pertinent medical and scientific literature and new developments.

Unfortunately the TWGs, for the most part, have ignored their legal duty to discover the dangers created by their toxic waste. For example, the great majority of commercial chemicals have never been tested for risk of causing chronic disease or for causing reproductive, developmental, and neurological harm. The TWGs have failed to conduct adequate epidemiologic studies of their employees, even in respect to workplace exposure to confirmed animal carcinogens. This breach of duty has prevented an adequate identification of toxic harm, its victims, and its causes. Instead of being punished for their duty breach, the TWGs have been rewarded in at least two respects: in avoiding the expense of performing their duty, and in escaping virtually all responsibility to their toxic-harm victims.

STATEMENT OF A HYPOTHETICAL CLAIM

Jim Brewster, age thirty-two, has recently been told by his physician that he has brain cancer, a type identified as glioblastoma multiforme. The prognosis is poor.

---

[3] See *Borel v. Fibreboard Paper Products Corp.*, 403 F2d 1076 (5th Cir. 1976), upholding a duty of a manufacturer to test for dangers and to keep abreast of medical and scientific literature.

At age five, Jim moved to Jackson, Texas, and his father went to work for Able Chemical Company's large petrochemical complex there. After Jim graduated from Jackson High School, he too went to work for Able Chemical and is now assistant operator of a unit that makes ethyl benzene. Other units at Able make benzene, styrene, vinyl chloride, and polyvinyl chloride.

From age five until he was about fourteen, Jim lived about one mile northwest of Able Chemical. His other two residences have been two and three miles from Able. Adjoining Able is Baker Chemical Company, the other substantial petrochemical complex in Jackson that also produces the products named above. Jim's residences have been approximately the same distance from Baker as from Able.

Jim is aware that a recent epidemiologic study of Able workers by a government agency revealed an incidence of brain cancer significantly above that in the general population. Also, another epidemiologic study of a similar but distant petrochemical plant showed a significant excess of brain cancer. Both Able Chemical and the distant company did their own epidemiologic studies and reached a contrary conclusion, finding that no such excess existed.

Jim talked to a lawyer who had recently won a workers' compensation case for the widow of an Able Chemical worker who died from brain cancer. After the lawyer reviewed the pertinent data and records, he told Jim that he had a good chance of winning a workers' compensation claim and perhaps even a fair chance on a traditional suit against Able and Baker jointly.

Jim's lawyer saw a chance to prove that a contributing cause to Jim's brain cancer was his exposure, both inside and outside the work place, to the carcinogenic waste of Able and Baker, which contaminated the ambient air.

With this simplified version of the facts, let's examine some of the evidence problems and some pertinent principles to be applied to the facts.

RECONSTRUCTING PAST TOXIC EXPOSURE

Jim's lawyer will consult with various scientists (such as industrial hygienists, toxicologists, industrial chemists, meteorologists) to assist him in the difficult and expensive task of reconstructing, as available evidence permits, the toxic exposure from both Able Chemical and Baker Chemical to which Jim was subjected from 1955 (when he moved to Jackson) until his brain cancer was diagnosed in 1982.

Based on experience, Jim's lawyer is not surprised to learn that very little air sampling and analysis for specific compounds has ever been performed in Jackson, and that the few exposure data available are virtually useless. Likewise, the air monitoring data within the Able and Baker facilities have been found grossly inadequate.

If the emissions data were reasonably accurate during the disease latency and exposure period (twenty-seven years), and if necessary meteorological data were available, Jim's primary exposure expert might undertake atmospheric modeling in an effort to scientifically quantify past exposures. While such modeling may be too difficult and expensive in most cases, expert evidence on the atmospheric transport of industrial pollutants will help explain the disease risk to populations outside the work place.

The attorney, through court procedures, will obtain from Able Chemical (and also Baker Chemical) a plot plan of the Jackson plant(s) showing various process units, storage facilities, shipping locations, and all emission points; a pertinent history on each process unit since 1955; pertinent material balances; emissions inventories filed with the Texas Air Control Board; air emissions data furnished to federal agencies; and all air monitoring records on select compounds.

The exposure expert will review any government studies (by EPA, OSHA, NIOSH, or state and local regulatory agencies) of emissions from the plants of Able and Baker and from other plants with similar process units.

Some toxic substances have known odor thresholds and have such distinct odors that many workers can recognize their presence. These workers may testify about the existence and frequency of such detectable odors in the areas where Jim lived and moved about.

Jim's attorney will be able to secure a broad estimate of the carcinogenic waste of Able and Baker that contaminated the ambient air where Jim lived and worked. Such an estimate may include total hydrocarbons as well as select compounds that are known or likely carcinogens. The exposure data, once compiled, must be reviewed by Jim's cancer causation expert, who will determine whether they are adequate, when considered together with epidemiologic, toxicologic, and other data, to prove (more likely than not) that such exposure was a contributing, legal cause of Jim's brain tumor.

Able and Baker may complain about the imprecision of the reconstructed exposure data, but such complaints should fall on deaf ears. After all, they had a duty to ascertain the dangers arising out of their operations, and had they performed such duty they necessarily would have compiled the exposure data, which would then have been available (by subpoena) to the toxic-harm victims. In other words, after breaching its duty to compile such exposure data, a TWG should not be heard to complain about the quality of the reconstructed data. In the interest of justice, the court should appoint a master to reconstruct the exposure data at the expense of the derelict TWG. The master (master in chancery) is a judicial officer appointed by courts of equity to assist the court, including hearing testimony and making reports which, when approved by the presiding judge, become the decision of the court.

We will assume that the exposure data have been reconstructed, that the court has found the methods satisfactory, and that the data have been admitted into evidence.

PROVING LEGAL CAUSATION

Jim will be required to prove that his exposure to the toxic waste of Baker Chemical (while outside the work place) and Able Chemical (both inside Able and outside) was a legal cause of his brain tumor. Other facts must also be established, but proving legal causation is a major hurdle for the toxic-harm victim. Under some legal theories (e.g., strict liability) the claimant must prove only that the exposure in question was a "producing cause," while under other legal theories (e.g., negligence) proving "proximate cause" will be required.

There may be several legal causes of an event or condition (such as toxic harm). To prove "producing cause" some jurisdictions require only proof of "cause-in-fact," which means the harm would not have occurred at the time it did but for the exposure in question; other jurisdictions require proof that the cause was a "substantial factor" in bringing about such harm; and still others require both cause-in-fact and substantial factor evidence.

To prove "proximate cause," the claimant, in addition to proving producing cause, must also show that the TWG should have foreseen that the same or similar harm might reasonably have occurred because of such exposure. Some jurisdictions will permit the claimant to lump the combined effect of the toxic exposures of the various TWG defendants and then prove (more likely than not) that such combined effect was a legal cause of the harm, leaving it to each defendant to separate, if it can, its contribution, if any, to the total toxic harm. However, other jurisdictions will still require the claimant to prove the contribution of each TWG defendant to the total harm.

Jim must present expert opinion evidence that his toxic exposure from Able and Baker caused his brain tumor. The expert[4] may acknowl-

---

[4]There is a disagreement among the various jurisdictions as to whether a Ph.D. expert will be allowed to give an opinion on individual causation even though his qualifications may be vastly superior to those of a treating physician on the issue of causation.

edge that several factors probably contributed to Jim's cancer and may be of the opinion that one of those factors was Jim's exposure to the toxic waste of Able and Baker that contaminated the ambient air. Of course no one can say with absolute certainty what caused Jim's brain tumor, and the law does not require such certainty. Jim must only prove (through his expert) that the toxic exposure was more likely than not a contributing, legal cause.

Epidemiologic Studies

While not always the best, epidemiologic studies are the most acceptable evidence of cancer causation by toxic exposures. These studies have been described in earlier chapters. Epidemiologic studies may link a certain type of cancer with a certain compound (e.g., leukemia with benzene), or with a certain industry (e.g., brain cancer with the petrochemical industry), or with a certain occupation (e.g., respiratory cancer with pipefitting).

The design of an epidemiologic study is critical and vitally affects validity. For any epidemiologic study to merit serious consideration in a legal setting, it should be made available for peer review; that is, be subject to critical review by other epidemiologists.

The strength of a positive epidemiologic study is expressed in statistical terms. Scientific significance (high degree of certainty) and legal significance (more likely than not) are not the same thing.[5] A nonpositive epidemiologic study should not be regarded as evidence that no risk exists, but rather should be considered as failing to establish a risk. The courts are now accepting (as they should) positive epidemiologic studies as supporting an inference of a causal connection between exposure and toxic harm.[6] The TWG can be expected to oppose such use of statistical evidence when unfavorable, since it may make the TWG responsible to its toxic-harm victims. The TWG, of course, wants to avoid this responsibility and can successfully do so as long as the victims are denied sufficient causation evidence.

Jim's causation expert, as a basis for his professional opinion, may rely upon several types of evidence, one being government epidemiologic studies showing a significant excess of brain cancer among petro-

[5] Some courts have attempted to define the degree of probability of the causal association in an epidemiological study before such study can be utilized to support a finding of causation. See the ill-considered opinion of *Brock v. Merrell Dow Pharmaceuticals Inc.*, 874 F.2d 307 (5 Cir. 1989).

[6] Some courts now hold that causation must be supported by some epidemiological data.

chemical workers. The expert for Able and Baker will be critical of the government studies and will seek to use the industry-sponsored epidemiologic studies to rebut causation. The industry-sponsored studies will lack credibility if their design is poor or if their data have not been made available for peer review. Jim's expert may strengthen his opinion with epidemiologic studies not involving the petrochemical industry or the implicated compounds. An example would be studies showing that neighborhood populations are subjected to the same risks (though to a lesser degree as distance increases) as the workers within a given plant.

The court (judge) will determine whether the causation expert can give an opinion, and if so, whether the judge can use such epidemiologic studies in arriving at an opinion. The jury, by contrast, will determine the weight to be given any such study. The jury can accept a study's findings as factual, reject the study in toto, or accept some parts and reject others. Such evaluation will be reflected in the weight the jury gives to the opinion of the causation expert.

Toxicity Studies

Toxicity studies may be relevant in proving that the carcinogenic waste of Able and Baker was a legal cause of Jim's brain cancer. Significantly, our nation makes major public health decisions based on the results of animal studies. This shows our high degree of confidence in the validity of extrapolation from animals to man. In our hypothetical case, Jim's causation expert may use toxicity studies, along with other evidence, to strengthen his opinion on the causal link between Jim's brain tumor and his toxic exposure to the chemical waste of Able and Baker. In some instances a causation expert would seem justified in relying upon toxicity studies alone to support an opinion of legal causation.[7] An example would be where an animal carcinogen is very potent, the cancer victim has a history of substantial exposure to that particular carcinogen, the victim's cancer is similar (organ and type) to that induced by the carcinogen in animal species, and the type of cancer is not common.

Epidemiologic studies remain the evidence of choice even though they, unfortunately, require a victim body count. Yet, well-designed two-year animal studies may have greater overall validity than many epidemiologic studies, particularly those epidemiologic studies with inadequate exposure data and insufficient power. The uncertainty in extrapolation is arguably smaller than the uncertainty from confounding factors, uncontrolled conditions, inadequate exposure data, and in-

---

[7] However, a growing number of cases have flatly stated that animal studies alone are not sufficient to support an opinion of causation.

sufficient power that beset many epidemiologic studies. Where animal studies of a chemical prove to be nonpositive, the TWG may argue that such studies are valid evidence of the safety of the substance. However, when such studies prove positive, the TWG will be critical of extrapolation, both as to species, and as to dosage. Again we see the TWG, in an adversary relationship with the public, seeking to place the burden of uncertainty on its potential victims.

While toxicity studies, standing alone, may not support an opinion of legal causation in Jim's case, such studies will give added strength to an opinion on causation. Toxicity data will show that certain compounds in the toxic waste of Able and Baker have an affinity for the brain. Moreover, one of the compounds (vinyl chloride monomer) is a potent animal (and human) carcinogen, with the brain as one of the target organs. Also, styrene would be suspected of making a contribution because of its similarity to vinyl chloride in chemical structure and because styrene (or its metabolites) is a likely carcinogen and/or promotor.

Jim's causation expert may not wish to isolate vinyl chloride as a legal cause but may prefer to implicate the total chemical emissions, which contain not only known and suspected carcinogens, but also a number of untested (or inadequately tested) compounds. The expert can correctly point out that, while vinyl chloride monomer is very likely a causal factor, there are still other carcinogens and promoters in such toxic waste that will likewise make their contribution to Jim's brain tumor.

Structure-Activity Data

The causation expert, having a background in toxicology, knows that the great majority of chemical compounds found in the environment have never been tested for carcinogenicity. This failure to test has created a need to predict, as scientifically as possible, the toxic effects of untested chemicals. This need has been partially met by studying the reactivity of untested compounds with DNA and by classifying the various chemicals according to their molecular structure. These predictive tools cannot support a conclusion that a given chemical is or is not a carcinogen, but such characteristics can be considered when evaluating toxicity and epidemiologic studies.

The Role of Principles of Carcinogenesis in Legal Causation

All doses of carcinogens, no matter how small, likely contribute to the total carcinogenic effect. Jim's expert may point out that the effect of multiple carcinogens is usually at least additive, and in some instances is synergistic. This means that Jim's exposure to vinyl chloride, benzene, and other carcinogens in the toxic waste of Able and Baker likely had a causal role in his brain tumor. Moreover, there may have been noncarcinogenic substances present that played a causal role as cancer promoters. Keep in mind that most, if not all, carcinogens are also cancer promoters. However, not all promoters are carcinogens.

The intensity and duration of the dosage of carcinogens affect the latency period of cancer — the time between initial exposure and tumor formation. The greater the cumulative dosage of carcinogens, the shorter the latency period; and of course, a reduced dosage will extend the latency period. Proving legal causation is made easier by the well-accepted principle of carcinogenesis that dosage directly affects the cancer latency period. By this principle, Jim's expert can state with confidence that Jim's brain tumor would not have appeared when it did except for his toxic exposure. In other words, without the exposure from Able and Baker, Jim's tumor would have appeared either at a later date or not at all. Cause-in-fact is thereby established.

THEORIES OF LIABILITY OF TOXIC WASTE GENERATORS WHO CONTAMINATE THE AMBIENT AIR

Society has an ongoing role of declaring and balancing interrelated rights and duties among parties. The "rights" protect one's person and property and confer certain privileges. The "duties" delineate one's responsibility when one's acts and omissions affect the rights of others.

Jim would claim a right, at least in his own home, to breathe air not contaminated with the carcinogenic waste of Able Chemical and Baker Chemical. Jim's remedy for an infringement of that right might be of an equitable nature, of a legal nature, or both. An injunction to prevent such contamination of the ambient air with known carcinogens would be characterized as an equitable remedy. Monetary damages for any proven harm from such contamination would be called a legal remedy. While society permits the toxic waste generator to discharge, at least to some extent, its carcinogenic waste into the environment, such a license does not insulate the TWG against liability for monetary damages to its toxic-harm victims but merely protects it against certain equitable remedies such as injunctions. In resolving disputes involving harm from the interaction between "rights and duties," society can be said to play a role in the allocation of risks. In allocating risks, "strict liability" is applied in some situations. Thus the risk is placed on the party who causes the harm. The victim will still be required to prove certain facts, including legal causation, and the party causing the harm still has available certain defenses. Strict liability may be applicable to toxic harm caused by a TWG in some circumstances and not in others. The rules in identical situations often differ among the various states. This means that Jim may have an effective legal remedy in Texas but not in Louisiana. Differently stated, Able and Baker may be strictly liable to its toxic-harm victims in one state but not in another. Of course, the balance of political power among the parties may affect the allocation of risks.

Several legal theories employ the strict liability concept. In our example involving contamination of Jackson's ambient air with carcinogens, strict liability theories would include trespass (an intentional invasion by a physical agent), some forms of nuisance, ultrahazardous activities, and what may be simply called a pollution tort for intentional invasions. In our example the word "intentional" would simply mean an awareness by Able and Baker that their activities necessarily involved the discharge of chemical waste into the ambient air. The trespass theory is an attractively simple remedy for contamination of the ambient air. In different states trespass has been both applied and rejected.[8] A principal inadequacy of "ultrahazardous activity" as a basis for strict liability lies in the uncertainty whether a given activity is to be deemed ultrahazardous. Such uncertainty could be reduced with a definition including all activities creating a foreseeable risk of toxic harm.

Where toxic harm is caused by the migration of a TWG's toxic waste through air or water, the law of nuisance is used most frequently to determine its responsibility, if any. Nuisance law is ordinarily invoked where one party uses his property (e.g., for the operation of a chemical plant) in a manner that disturbs another party in the use and enjoyment of his property. Some types of interference constitute a private nuisance as a matter of law (e.g., an interference prohibited by statute). Other types of interference may constitute a private nuisance only when deemed unreasonable (e.g., odors). Where reasonable people may differ on whether a given interference is unreasonable, the dispute will be resolved by the fact finder (e.g., jury). The consensus on reasonableness may differ in different areas.

If a TWG, in disposing of its toxic waste, interferes with the enjoyment and use of public property, a public nuisance may be found to exist. An individual can recover on the basis of a public nuisance only when the harm is different from that experienced by the general public. Liability based on nuisance may be affected by whether a release of toxic waste is intentional (e.g., for normal process, fugitive and storage

---

[8] *Martin v. Reynolds Metals Co.*, 221 Ore. 86, P 2d 790, 974 (1959), applying trespass; *Arvidson v. Reynolds Metal Co.*, 125 F. Suppl. 481 (S.D. Wash. 1954), rejecting trespass theory.

emissions from a chemical plant) or unintentional (e.g., from an explosion). Court decisions are often inconsistent in describing the nature and scope of nuisance law and its application to given facts.

Referring again to our hypothetical case, we will assume that Jim's brain tumor was caused by Able and Baker's contaminating the ambient air with low-level doses of carcinogenic substances. Jim will claim that the invasion of his home with carcinogens unleashed by Able and Baker constituted an absolute nuisance with strict liability on their part for his resulting brain tumor. Moreover, Jim will claim that such carcinogenic contamination of Jackson's ambient air created a public nuisance resulting in special harm to him.

On the other hand, Able and Baker will point out that their operations have economic benefits for the city of Jackson and its residents; that their operations are in all respects lawful; that the public regulates, by issuing permits, the disposal of their toxic waste and that they have at all relevant times been in compliance with their permits; and that therefore they have acted as reasonable and prudent chemical companies in their release of carcinogenic substances into the ambient air of Jackson.

Negligence law is commonly used in balancing conflicting rights (or allocating risks) where one party, in the use of his property, causes harm to another. "Reasonableness" is the key concept in resolving such conflicts. Negligence is defined as the failure to exercise ordinary care — the care a prudent party would ordinarily exercise under the same or similar circumstances.

"Reasonable" persons may differ among themselves on whether certain conduct by a party is reasonable or unreasonable. Under negligence law a party is responsible only for the unforeseeable consequences of his conduct. No liability attaches for consequences that are remote or inconceivable.

New technology and its effect often challenge the capacity of existing legal theories to resolve newly created conflicts. Usually a traditional theory is sufficiently adaptable, but sometimes a new theory will offer greater clarity and less confusion by directly addressing the conflict. An outstanding opinion in a Texas case formulated an express legal theory on harm from intentional air and water pollution.[9]

In factual disputes, the controlling facts must be determined by the judge or jury. A single set of facts may give rise to more than one legal basis of liability. Ordinarily a claimant can allege alternative facts and as many causes of action (legal theories providing remedies) as the alleged facts may confer.

[9] *Atlas Chemical Industry, Inc. v. Anderson*, 514 S.W.2d 309 (Tex. Civ. App. 1974) affirmed 524 S.W.2d 681 (Tex. 1975).

What legal theories will Jim use against Able and Baker? Jim's first choice may be to ask that strict liability be applied for a pollution tort arising from harm caused by the intentional discharge of carcinogens into the ambient air. A second choice would be to contend that the disposal of carcinogenic waste is an ultrahazardous activity and that therefore strict liability attaches. A third choice would be for Jim to contend that Able and Baker committed a trespass by setting in motion carcinogenic waste, knowing that it would invade nearby homes, churches, schools, and other places where people had a right to be.[10] A fourth choice would be to argue that such contamination of the ambient air with carcinogenic substances created both a public and a private nuisance. A fifth basis of recovery against Able and Baker would be to claim that Jim's harm was caused by negligence on their part, particularly as to the nature and quantity of the carcinogenic waste showered on the town of Jackson.

Regardless of the legal theories used, Jim (through his attorney and experts) should identify and roughly quantify the carcinogenic waste of Able and Baker to which he was exposed and then prove (more likely than not) that such exposure was a legal cause of his brain tumor.

FINDING A LAWYER FOR THE TOXIC HARM VICTIM

In most areas where toxic harm occurs, there will probably be one or more lawyers who will have the experience, resources, and motivation to handle any indicated litigation. Usually such a lawyer will be available for a conference without cost or obligation to the victim. If the damages are significant and there is a fair chance of recovery, the lawyer will ordinarily be willing to take the case with his fee being an agreed percentage of any recovery; if there is no recovery, then no fee is paid.

The lawyer chosen should have the experience and resources to adequately handle personal injury and disease litigation and preferably should have experience in preparing and presenting evidence establishing past toxic exposure and evidence supporting a causal link between that exposure and the plaintiff's harm. A lawyer with the desired qualifications may be identified through publicity, or by making inquiries of experienced scientific experts, of representatives of environmental organizations, personal attorneys, and knowledgeable courthouse workers.

Some lawyers accept toxic-harm claims and then refer the cases to other lawyers who perform the work under an agreement whereby the fee is split. Since toxic claims are relatively new, complex, and expen-

---

[10] *Atlas Chemical Industry, Inc. v. Anderson*, supra.

sive, a lawyer will sometimes accept a case directly that he would turn down as a referral. Therefore the victim may be better served by contracting only with the lawyer who will perform all or a significant portion of the legal services.

HOW DID THINGS GET THIS WAY?

The discussion of our hypothetical case illustrates the complexity of litigating a toxic-harm claim. Such complexity, together with the enormous expense, explains why so few claims have been made. The exception has been in the case of asbestos related disease.

We have allowed toxic waste generators (TWGs) to inflict, with virtual impunity, toxic harm on millions of people as well as to do inestimable environmental harm. Kept powerless by political inaction, we, for many years, permitted our ambient air, surface water, groundwater, and the good earth to be freely appropriated as random dump sites for toxic waste. When enough influential citizens sensed the ongoing harm and got a glimpse of the specter of a toxic avalanche with the potential for doing us all in, the public gained sufficient political strength for regulatory legislation. This legislation, as expected, was opposed by the TWGs, who apparently had come to view themselves as entitled to unleash their toxic waste into the environment without restraint.

As the evidence of toxic harm mounted and the potential consequences of the toxic avalanche became better perceived, more regulatory legislation was enacted to protect public health and the environment. While the public has greatly benefitted from the major environmental laws, the TWGs have significantly reduced the laws' effectiveness with their vast legal and political resources. The TWGs, of course, do not want toxic harm to occur, but their concern for such harm remains subservient to their desire to generate and dispose of toxic waste with as little restraint and responsibility as possible.

WE EXPECT TOO MUCH OF THE TOXIC WASTE GENERATOR

The toxic waste generator feels threatened by the discovery that its operations may contribute to disease. When vinyl chloride monomer became recognized as a carcinogen, the affected TWGs assumed a defensive adversary posture, minimizing the risk and opposing regulatory efforts by the federal government. The TWGs have done little to discover cancer morbidity or suggested reproductive harm among populations exposed to vinyl chloride monomer. Brain cancer has been suggested as a risk among petrochemical workers producing vinyl chloride, but this suggestion instantly prompted an adversary reaction by the affected TWGs, followed by their preparing rebuttal evidence from "proprietary" data.

The TWGs again and again have effectively resisted public regulations aimed at preventing toxic harm. They spent millions of dollars to fight reduced benzene exposure and in recent years have spent millions to weaken environmental regulations such as the Clean Air Act. Some TWGs have openly obstructed public investigations of cancer dangers to their own workers. In fact, the TWGs have even opposed efforts by their own workers to investigate disease dangers in the work place. We, the public, have expected too much of the toxic waste generators.

It is naive to expect a serious effort by the TWGs to use part of their profits to discover disease dangers that would invite regulatory action and liability to their toxic-harm victims. Through purposeful neglect, the TWG can promote ignorance and uncertainty about toxic harm. Such neglect, though not benign, is something the corporate entity can live with. The TWG is a private corporate entity. Its mission is profit, and it resists detracting factors. The public should realistically accept the TWG for what it is. Consistent with its corporate nature and mission, the TWG has made it abundantly clear that it wants an arrangement with society whereby the TWG has these rights: to engage in industrial activities creating risks of toxic harm; to unilaterally determine the acceptable levels of exposure to its toxic waste, thereby avoiding public regulation and interference; to avoid any penalty for breaching its common-law duty to discover disease dangers from its operations; to place the burden of toxic harm on the victims and the public; and to prevent others from discovering toxic harm by withholding information needed to compile exposure data, identify victims, and establish causal relations.

Once the public accepts the corporate nature of the TWG, we can proceed to fashion a plan offering some measure of protection against toxic harm and then, with much greater frequency, make the TWG responsible to its toxic-harm victims.

A PROPOSAL TO BETTER PROTECT THE PUBLIC

To better identify toxic harm and to allocate its cost, a special tax should be levied against the toxic waste generator to finance the public performance of its common-law duty. After all, creating risks of widespread toxic harm is not an absolute right, but rather a privilege that society can withhold or confer with reasonable conditions. One such condition should be compelling the TWG to disclose all information helpful in compiling exposure data on populations at risk and identifying toxic-harm victims. Public health investigators should compile such exposure data and should conduct appropriate studies to ascertain any causal relation between such exposure and harm. If the public took over the TWG's common-law duty, data worthy of confidence would be created, and the TWG would be freed of a troublesome conflict of interest.

For the time being the TWG should be penalized, but fairly so, for having legally wronged its victims. One act of legal restitution would be for the courts to appoint masters, at the TWG's expense, to compile exposure data where there is reasonable basis for believing a plaintiff victim has sustained harm that may have been caused by toxic exposure created by the defendant TWG. Such exposure data, with appropriate modifications, could thereafter be utilized by other plaintiffs.

Because of its breach of duty, the TWG should be denied (in legal jargon, estopped) use of the statute of limitations to defeat the legal rights of a victim or his beneficiaries. The breach of duty by the TWG has left plaintiffs with evidence problems in proving legal causation. Fairness would be served by applying judicial innovations as well as traditional legal tools such as presumptions to such evidence problems.

CONCLUSION

The burden of toxic harm will continue to increase for these reasons:

• The continuing generation of enormous quantities of toxic waste.
• The vast quantities of toxic waste currently in the environment, including innumerable dump sites where such waste is either doing its damage or is on standby, threatening harm.
• The many ultimate victims from past exposure where incipient, time-dependent disease is still evolving toward morbidity.
• The legacy of accumulating inheritable mutations.

We are in dire need of a public strategy to reduce the burden of toxic harm and to do justice to the individual victims. Our society prides itself on concern for the individual, including the protection of life, the integrity of mind and body, and the defense of property. This societal protection has been grossly inadequate to cope with the mounting toxic onslaught of the past thirty-five years.

We have failed to adequately identify the various forms of toxic harm, and we remain ignorant of its magnitude. We are not likely to secure better protection until we arm ourselves with the data necessary to reveal the nature and extent of this toxic harm. Of elementary importance (and the most neglected) is the necessary exposure data. Such data are needed to better identify the population at risk, to improve the design of toxicity studies, and to enhance the design and evaluation of epidemiologic studies.

We, the public, have utterly failed our toxic-harm victims. We have naively entrusted the TWGs to create and record vital exposure data and to properly study their employee populations at risk. Predictably, the TWGs have avoided programs to ascertain disease dangers. Identifying toxic dangers would only invite regulation and liability. Instead the TWG, for its own economic protection, has used its resources to exonerate its accused chemicals.

I propose a new policy whereby dependable data would be created to effectively identify and prevent toxic harm. Such data would be created by public health personnel at TWG expense. The newly created data, together with a just, innovative judiciary would offer toxic-harm victims legal relief with much greater frequency. The cost of toxic harm to the extent of such relief, plus the cost of creating the necessary data, would finally be properly allocated. Once the cost is fixed, the TWG, consistent with its purpose of profit, will more seriously undertake prevention measures to reduce its own financial burden.

ELEVEN

RESOURCE GUIDE

Sabrina F. Strawn

If you are just now wanting to learn more about hazardous substances—
what they are and who else is concerned about them—this guide will
help direct you to all sorts of information sources. If you are already
involved, you will appreciate these words to the novice: No one can
possible know all about toxic substances. The subject area is enormous
and information gaps still exist. This is intended only as a guide, not a
mandatory reading list. Moreover, the most useful resources often are
personal contacts.

PUBLICATIONS
  AIR
  EMERGENCY PLANNING AND COMMUNITY
  RIGHT-TO-KNOW
  EPIDEMIOLOGY
  HAZARDOUS WASTE—EFFECTS
  HAZARDOUS WASTE—MANAGEMENT
  INCINERATION
  INFORMATION SOURCES
  ORGANIZING
  PESTICIDES
  RISK ASSESSMENT
  STATUTES, REGULATIONS AND LEGAL ISSUES
  TOXIC CHEMICALS (see HAZARDOUS WASTE)
  WATER
  WORKPLACE ISSUES
PUBLISHERS' ADDRESSES
PERIODICALS
OTHER RESOURCES
HOTLINES

COMPUTER-RELATED SERVICES
ORGANIZATIONS
U.S. GOVERNMENT OFFICES

PUBLICATIONS

Air

Michael H. Brown, *Toxic Cloud: The Poisoning of America's Air*, New York: Harper & Row, 1987. ($9.95)

Emergency Planning and Community-Right-to-Know

See also STATUTES.

Chemical Manufacturers Association, several publications and videos. Call or write for titles and costs.

Citizens Fund, *Poisons in Our Neighborhoods: Toxic Pollution in the United States*, Washington, D.C.: Citizens Fund, 1990. ($25.00)

Susan G. Hadden, *A Citizen's Right to Know: Risk Communications and Public Policy*, Boulder, Colorado: Westview Press, 1989. ($28.50)

Stephen Lester, et al., *Using your Right to Know*, Arlington, Virginia: Citizens Clearinghouse for Hazardous Wastes, 1989. ($9.95)

Carol Steinsapir and others, *Hazardous Neighbors?* New York, NY: Community Environmental Health Center, Hunter College School of Health Sciences, 1989. (5.00)

U.S. Department of Transportation, *Emergency Response Guidebook.* n.p., n.d. (free)

U.S. Environmental Protection Agency, Office of Pesticides and Toxic Substances, several publications including annual reports on the toxics release inventory. Call the SARA Hotline for information.

Working Group on Community Right To Know, newsletter and several packets. Call or write for titles and costs.

Epidemiology

Phil Brown, "Popular Epidemiology: Community Response to Toxic-Waste Induced Disease" *Science, Technology and Human Values*, vol. 12, (Summer/Fall 1987) pp. 78–85 . Reprinted in *Environmental Health Monthly*, vol. 2 (February 1990). Obtain from the Citizens Clearinghouse for Hazardous Waste.

Gary D. Friedman, *Primer of Epidemiology*, 3rd edition, New York: McGraw-Hill, 1987. ($19.95)

John R. Goldsmith, *Environmental Epidemiology: Epidemiological Investi-*

gation of Community Health Problems, Boca Raton, Florida: CRC Press, 1986. ($110)

Philip Hauser, *Social Statistics in Use*, New York: Russell Sage Foundation, 1975. ($37.50)

Abraham M. Lilienfeld and David E. Lilienfeld, *Foundations of Epidemiology*, 2nd edition, New York: Oxford University Press, 1980. ($22.95 paper)

Judith S. Mausner and Anita K. Bahn, *Epidemiology: An Introductory Text*, 2nd edition, Philadelphia: W.B. Saunders, 1985. ($29.95)

Brian MacMahon and Thomas F. Pugh, *Epidemiology: Principles and Methods*, Boston: Little, Brown, 1970. ($29.50)

Proceedings of the National Conference on Clustering of Health Events, Atlanta, Georgia, February 1989, *American Journal of Epidemiology*, vol. 132, supplement no. 1, 1990.

Lynn A. Gloecker Ries, et al., *Cancer Statistics Review*, 1973–1987, Bethesda, Maryland: National Cancer Institute, 1990, Pub. No. 90–2789. (free)

Dona Schneider, *Completeness and Accuracy of Cancer Mortality and Incidence Data*, Monticello, Illinois: Vance Bibliographies, 1989. ($6.25)

Janet Tanur, et al., *Statistics: A Guide to the Unknown*, 3rd edition, n.p.: Brooks-Cole, 1989. ($16.95)

Hazardous Waste—Effects

Julian B. Andelman and Dwight W. Underhill, *Health Effects from Hazardous Waste Sites*, Chelsea, Michigan: Lewis Publishers, 1987. ($49.95)

Nicholas A. Ashford and Claudia S. Miller, *Chemical Sensitivity: A Report to the New Jersey Department of Health*, 1989. (available from National Center for Environmental Health Strategies, $15.00 non-members)

Alvin C. Bronstein and Phillip L. Currance, *Emergency Care for Hazardous Materials Exposure*, St. Louis: C.V. Mosby Company, 1988. ($22.95)

Earon S. Davis, ed., *Ecological Illness Law Report*, vols. 1–5, 1983–1988. Write for prices. Other publications also available.

Michael Edelstein, *Contaminated Communities: The Social and Psychological Impacts of Residential Toxic Exposure*, Boulder, Colorado: Westview Press, 1988. ($33.00)

Samuel S. Epstein, Carl Pope, and Lester O. Brown, *Hazardous Waste in America*, San Francisco: Sierra Club, n.d. . ($12.95 non-members)

Ernest Hodgson, et al., eds., *Dictionary of Toxicology*, New York: Van Nostrand Reinhold, 1988. ($73.95)

Peter Montague, *Hazardous Waste News*, Princeton, N.J.: Environmental Research Foundation, weekly newsletter. ($18/year)

National Research Council, Committee on Environmental Epidemiology, *Environmental Epidemiology, Volume 1: Public Health and Haz-*

ardous Wastes, Washington, D.C.: National Academy Press, 1991. ($29.95)

National Institute for Occupational Safety and Health (NIOSH) *Pocket Guide to Chemical Hazards*, 1990, (DHHS (NIOSH) Publication No. 90–117). (free)

Janette Sherman, *Chemical Exposure and Disease: Diagnostic and Investigative Techniques*, New York: Van Nostrand Reinhold, 1988. ($52.95)

U.S. Environmental Protection Agency, *Toxicology Handbook*, Rockville, Maryland: Government Institutes, Inc. n.d. ($49.00)

Arthur C. Upton, Theodore Kneip, and Paolo Toniolo, "Public Health Aspects of Toxic Chemical Disposal Sites," *Annual Review of Public Health* 10:1–25, 1989.

Henry M. Vyner, *Invisible Trauma: The Psychosocial Effects of the Invisible Environmental Contaminants*, Lexington, Massachusetts: Lexington Books, 1988. ($29.00)

Hazardous Waste—Management

Ronny J. Coleman and Kara Hewson Williams, *Hazardous Material Dictionary*, Lancaster, PA: Technomic Publishing Co., Inc., 1988. ($39.00)

Paul and Ellen Connett, *Waste Not*, Canton, New Jersey: Work on Waste, weekly newsletter. ($25/year)

L. Epstein, *Leaking Underground Storage Tanks — Secondary Containment*, Washington, D.C.: Environmental Defense Fund, 1988. ($2.50)

Harry M. Freeman, *Standard Handbook of Hazardous Waste Treatment and Disposal*, New York: McGraw-Hill, 1988. ($95.00)

Benjamin A. Goldman et al., *Hazardous Waste Management: Reducing the Risk*, Washington, D.C.: Island Press, 1985. ($64.95 cloth, $34.95 paper)

Ben Gordon and Peter Montague, *A Citizen's Toxic Waste Audit Manual*, Chicago, Illinois: Greenpeace, 1989. ($5.00 donation)

W. Gordon and J. Bloom, *Deeper Problems: Limits to Underground Injection as a Hazardous Waste Disposal Method*, New York: Natural Resources Defense Council, 1985. ($7.50)

Roger D. Griffin, *Principles of Hazardous Materials Management*, Chelsea, Michigan: Lewis Publishers, Inc., 1989. ($45.00)

S. Guyer and D. Roe, *Approaches to Source Reduction of Hazardous Waste: Practical Guidance from Existing Policies and Programs*, Washington, D.C.: Environmental Defense Fund, 1988. ($30 non-members)

Hazardous Waste Handbook Series, five volumes, New York: Executive Enterprises Publications Co., Inc. 1989. ($175)
Volume I Hazardous Waste Generator Obligations Under RCRA
Volume II PCB Management Under TSCA
Volume III Health Risk Assessment at Superfund Sites

Volume IV Managing Underground Storage Tanks
Volume V Hazardous Waste Regulations: Enforcement and Liability
Thomas E. Higgins, Hazardous Waste Minimization Handbook, Chelsea, Michigan: Lewis Publishers, 1989. ($49.95)
Household Wastes: Issues and Opportunities, Concern, Inc., n.d. ($5.50)
Gary F. Lindgren, Managing Industrial Hazardous Waste, Chelsea, Michigan: Lewis Publishers, 1989. ($59.95)
Peter Montague, What Chemicals Each Industry Uses, Princeton, New Jersey: Environmental Research Foundation, 1989. ($25.00)
Natural Resources Defense Council, et al., Hazardous Waste Surface Impoundments: The Nation's Most Serious and Neglected Threat to Groundwater, New York: Natural Resources Defense Council, 1983. ($5.00)
Office of Technology Assessment, Assessing Contractor Use in Superfund — Background Report, Washington, D.C.: Government Printing Office, 1989, #052-003-01147-6. ($2.50)
——, Are We Cleaning Up? Ten Superfund Case Studies — Special Report, Washington, D.C.: Government Printing Office, 1988, #052-003-01122-1. ($3.75)
——, Coming Clean: Superfund Problems Can Be Solved, Washington, D.C.: Government Printing Office, 1989, #052-003-01166-2. ($10.00)
——, From Pollution to Prevention: A Progress Report on Waste Reduction — Special Report, Washington, D.C.: Government Printing Office, 1987, #052-003-01071-2. ($2.75)
——, Serious Reduction of Hazardous Waste, National Technical Information Service, 1986, #PB 87–139 622/AS. ($38.00, summary available free from Office of Technology Assessment.)
Russell W. Phifer and William R. McTigue, Jr., Handbook of Hazardous Waste Management for Small Quantity Generators, Chelsea, Michigan: Lewis Publishers, 1988. ($44.95)
Aileen Schumacher, A Guide to Hazardous Materials Management: Physical Characteristics, Federal Regulations, and Response Alternatives, Westport, Connecticut: Greenwood Press, 1988. ($49.95)
Todd G. Schwendeman and H. Kendall Wilcox, Underground Storage Systems: Leak Detection and Monitoring, Chelsea, Michigan: Lewis Publishers, Inc., 1988. ($44.95)
Waste: Choices for Communities, Concern, Inc. n.d. ($5.50)
Roy F. Weston and University of Massachusetts Environmental Science Program, Remedial Technologies for Leaking Underground Storage Tanks, Chelsea, Michigan: Lewis Publishers, 1988. ($49.95)

Incineration

Calvin R. Brunner, P.E., Handbook of Hazardous Waste Incineration, n.p.: Tab Professional and Reference Books, 1989. ($45.00)

Harry M. Freeman, ed., *Incinerating Hazardous Wastes*, Lancaster, Pennsylvania: Technomic Publishing Company, 1988. ($49.00)

Information Sources

The Directory of National Environmental Organizations, St. Paul, Minnesota: U.S. Environmental Directories, 1988. ($35.00)
Environmental Health and Toxicology: A Bibliography of Printed Reference Sources, Center for Environmental Health and Injury Control, July 1989. (free)
League of Women Voters, *Hazardous Waste Goes to the Movies* (*catalog of audiovisual materials*), 1986, #414. ($.35 non-members)
Sierra Club, *Federal Government Offices*. ($.50 non-members)
U.S. Environmental Protection Agency, Office of Information Resources Management, *Information Resources Directory*, Fall 1989. (free)

Organizing

Douglas Amy, *The Politics of Environmental Mediation*, New York: Columbia University Press, 1987. ($30.00)
Ruth Caplan and the staff of Environmental Action, *Our Earth, Ourselves: The Action Oriented Guide to Help You Protect and Preserve Our Environment*, New York: Bantam Books, 1990. ($10.95)
Caron Chess, *Winning the Right to Know: A Handbook for Toxics Activists*, Washington, D.C.: National Center for Policy Alternatives, 1983. ($9.95)
Citizens Clearinghouse for Hazardous Wastes, numerous publications. Call or write for titles and costs.
Clean Water Fund of North Carolina, *Environment for Cooperation: Building Community/Worker Coalitions*, Asheville, North Caroline: Clean Water Fund of North Carolina, 1990. ($3.00)
Gary Cohen and John O'Connor, eds., *Fighting Toxics: A Manual for Protecting Your Family, Community, and Workplace*, Washington, D.C.: Island Press, 1990. ($31.95 cloth, $19.95 paper)
Environmental Research Foundation, numerous publications. Write or call for list.
Brad Erickson, ed., *Call to Action: Handbook for Ecology, Peace and Justice*, San Francisco: Sierra Club, 1990. ($12.95 non-members)
Adeline Gordon Levine, *Love Canal: Science, Politics and People*, Lexington, Massachusetts: Lexington Books, 1982. ($14.00)
National Toxics Campaign, numerous publications. Write or call for list.
John O'Conner, et al., *The Citizens Toxic Protection Manual*, Boston, Massachusetts: National Campaign Against Toxic Hazards, 1987. ($30.00)

Jeremy Rifkin, ed. *The Green Lifestyle Handbook: 1001 Ways You Can Heal the Earth*, New York: Henry Holt and Company, Inc., 1990. ($10.95)

Susan Sherry, *High Tech and Toxics: A Guide for Local Communities*, Washington, D.C.: National Center for Policy Alternatives, 1985. ($25.95)

Sierra Club, *Toxics Campaign Brief.* ($1.00 non-members)

Pesticides

See also STATUTES.

R. Grover, ed., *Environmental Chemistry of Herbicides*, vol. I, Boca Raton, Florida: CRC Press, 1988. ($135.00)

League of Women Voters, *America's Growing Delimma: Pesticides in Food and Water*, 1989, pub #887. ($4.95 non-members)

National Research Council, *Alternative Agriculture*, Washington, D.C.: National Academy Press, 1989. ($24.95)

Northwest Coalition for Alternatives to Pesticides, several publications including periodicals. Call or write for titles and costs.

Natural Resources Defense Council, several publications. Call or write for titles and costs.

Risk Assessment

C. Richard Cothern, Myron A. Mehlman, and William L. Marcus, eds., *Risk Assessment and Risk Management of Industrial and Environmental Chemicals*, Princeton, New Jersey: Princeton Scientific Publishing Co., 1988. ($65.00)

Suresh H. Moolgavkar, *Scientific Issues in Quantitative Cancer Risk Assessment*, Boston: Birkhauser, 1990. ($42.50)

Dennis J. Paustenbach, *The Risk Assessment of Environmental and Human Health Hazards: A Textbook of Case Studies*, New York: Wiley, 1989. ($130.00)

Curtis C. Travis, ed., *Carcinogen Risk Assessment*, New York: Plenum Press, 1988. ($59.00)

United States Congress, Office of Technology Assessment, *Identifying and Regulating Carcinogens*, Chelsea, Michigan: Lewis Publishers, 1988. ($55.00)

Statutes, Regulations and Legal Issues

General

Frank B. Cross, *Environmentally Induced Cancer and the Law: Risks, Regulation, and Victim Compensation*, New York: Quorum Books, 1989. ($45.00)

Earon S. Davis and Valerie A. Wilk, *Toxic Chemicals: The Interface Between Law and Science*, 1982. (available from Ecological Illness Law Report, $9.50)

Directory of State Environmental Agencies, Washington, D.C.: Environmental Law Institute, 1985. ($22.50)

Environmental Law Handbook, Rockville, Maryland: Government Institutes, 1989. ($59.95)

Environmental Statutes, Rockville, Maryland: Government Institutes, 1989. ($49.50 cloth, $36.50 paper)

Going to Court in the Public Interest: A Guide for Community Groups, Washington, D.C.: League of Women Voters, 1983, #244. ($.85 nonmembers)

Deborah Hitchcock Jessup, *Guide to State Environmental Programs*, Washington, D.C.: Bureau of National Affairs, 1990. ($48.00)

David R. Jones and Jeffrey Tryens, *Legislative Sourcebook on Toxics*, Washington, D.C.: National Center for Policy Alternatives, 1986. ($14.95)

Wallace E. McClain, Jr., ed., *U.S. Environmental Laws*, 1990 edition, Washington, D.C.: Bureau of National Affairs, 1990. ($58.00)

David W. Schnare and Martin T. Katzman, eds. *Chemical Contamination and Its Victims: Medical Remedies, Legal Redress, and Public Policy*, New York: Quorum Books, 1989. ($45.00)

Transportation of Hazardous Materials: A Management Guide for Generators and Manufacturers, Rockville, Maryland: Government Institutes, 1989. ($69.00)

Jeffrey Tryens, ed., *The Toxics Crisis: What the States Should Do*, Washington, D.C.: National Center for Policy Alternatives, 1983. ($9.95)

Sidney M. Wolf, *Pollution Law Handbook*, Westport, Connecticut: Greenwood Press, 1988. ($55.00)

Emergency Planning and Community Right-to-Know

Community Right-to-Know Deskbook, Washington, D.C.: Environmental Law Institute, 1988. ($75.00)

George G. Lowry and Robert C. Lowry, *Lowry's Handbook of Right-to-Know and Emergency Planning*, Chelsea, Michigan: Lewis Publishers, 1988. ($74.95)

Hazardous Waste/Toxic Substances

Sue M. Briggum, et al., *Hazardous Waste Regulation Handbook*, New York: Executive Enterprises Publications Co., Inc. 1986. ($90.00)

Mary Devine Worobec and Girard Ordway, *Toxic Substances Control Guide: Federal Regulation of Chemicals in the Environment*, Washington, D.C.: Bureau of National Affairs, 1989. ($37.50)

Superfund Desk Book, Washington, D.C.: Environmental Law Institute, 1986. ($80.00)

Pesticides

John D. O'Conner, Jr., et al., eds., *Pesticide Regulation Handbook*, New York, NY: Executive Enterprises Publications Co., Inc., 1987. ($75.00)

Water

Edward J. Calabrese and Charles E. Gilbert, eds., *Safe Drinking Water Act: Amendments, Regulations, and Standards*, Chelsea, Michigan: Lewis Publishers, 1989. ($49.95)

Environmental Law Institute, *Clean Water Deskbook*, Washington, D.C.: Environmental Law Institute, 1988. ($80.00)

Russell S. Frye, et al. *Clean Water Act Update*, New York: Executive Enterprises Publications Co., Inc., 1987. ($59.95)

Jessica Landman, *Citizen's Handbook on Water Quality Standards*, New York, NY: Natural Resources Defense Council, May 1987. ($4.00)

Smith and Schnacke, L.P.A. and Beveridge & Diamond, P.C., *Clean Water Act Permit Guidance Manual*, New York: Executive Enterprises Publications, Co., Inc. 1984. ($75.00)

Water

See also STATUTES.

Drinking Water: A Community Action Guide, Washington, D.C.: Concern, Inc., n.d. ($5.50)

W. Wesley Eckenfelder, Jr., *Industrial Water Pollution Control*, 2nd edition, Hightstown, New Jersey: McGraw-Hill, 1989. ($47.00)

Groundwater: A Community Action Guide, Washington, D.C.: Concern, Inc., n.d. ($5.50)

Groundwater: A Citizen's Guide, Washington, D.C. League of Women Voters, 1986, #803. ($1.75 non-members)

G. William Page, *Planning for Groundwater Protection*, Troy, Missouri: Academic Press, Inc., 1987. ($49.95)

Chester D. Rail, *Groundwater Contamination: Sources, Control, and Preventative Measures*, Lancaster, Pennsylvania: Technomic Publishing Co., Inc., 1989. ($39.00)

Safety on Tap: A Citizen's Drinking Water Guide, Washington, D.C. League of Women Voters, 1987, #840. (7.95 non-members)

Sierra Club Legal Defense Fund, *The Poisoned Well: New Strategies for Groundwater Protection*, Washington, D.C.: Island Press, 1989. ($31.95 cloth, $19.95 paper)

Workplace Issues

Division of Consumer Health Education, Department of Environmental and Community Medicine, Robert Wood Johnson Medical School,

Health and Safety in Small Industry, Chelsea, Michigan: Lewis Publishers, 1989. ($39.95)

Dow Chemical Company, *Industrial Hygiene: The Science and Art of Protecting Worker Health*, Midland, Michigan: Dow Chemical Company, n.d. (free)

Richard Kazis and Richard L. Grossman, *Fear at Work: Job Black-mail, Labor and the Environment*, New York: Pilgrim Press, 1982. ($10.95)

The Labor Institute, *OCAW-Labor Institute Hazardous Waste Workbook*, New York, NY: Apex Press, 1990. ($25.50)

William F. Martin, et al., *Hazardous Waste Handbook for Health and Safety*, Stoneham, Massachusetts: Butterworth, 1987. ($32.50)

National Institute for Occupational Safety and Health, quarterly announcements of publications. (free)

Occupational Safety and Health Administration, *A Guide to Worker Education Materials in Occupational Safety and Health volumes I & II*. (free)

Ronald M. Scott, *Chemical Hazards in the Workplace*, Chelsea, Michigan: Lewis Publishers, 1989. ($39.95)

PUBLISHERS' ADDRESSES *(FOR ORDERS)*

Academic Press
465 South Lincoln Dr.
Troy, MO 63379
800-321-5068

Apex Press
P.O. Box 337
Croton, NY 10520
212-953-6920

Bantam Books
414 E. Golf Road
Des Plaines, IL 60016
800-223-6834

Birkhauser
P.O. Box 2485
Secaucus, NJ 07094
201-348-4033

Brooks-Cole
Wadsworth Customer Service Center
7625 Empire Drive
Florence, KY 41042
800-354-9706

Bureau of National Affairs
Distribution Center
300 Raritan Center Parkway
P.O. Box 7816
Edison, NJ 08818-7816
201-225-1900
201-417-0482 (fax)

Butterworth Publishers
80 Montvale Avenue
Stoneham, MA 02180
800-366-2665

Center for Environmental Health and
    Injury Control
U.S. Department of Health and
    Human Services
Public Health Service
Centers for Disease Control
Information Resources Management
    Atlanta, GA 30333

Chemical Manufacturers Association
Publications Fulfillment
2501 M Street NW
Washington, D.C. 20037
202-887-1100

Citizens Fund
1300 Connecticut Avenue, NW
Washington, D.C. 20036
202-857-5168

Clean Water Fund of North Carolina
138 E. Chestnut Street
Asheville, NC 28801
704-251-0518

Citizens Clearinghouse for Hazardous
  Wastes
P.O. Box 6806
Falls Church, VA 22040
703-237-2249

Columbia University Press
136 South Broadway
Irvington-on-Hudson, NY 10533
914-591-9111

Concern
1794 Columbia Road NW
Washington, D.C. 20009
202-328-8160

CRC Press
2000 Corporate Blvd NW
Boca Raton, FL 33431
800-272-7737

Dow Chemical USA
Literature Services
2400 James Savage Road
Midland, MI 48640

Ecological Illness Law Report
P.O. Box 6099
Wilmette, IL 60091-6099

Environmental Defense Fund
1616 P Street NW, Suite 150
Washington, D.C. 20036
202-387-3500

Environmental Law Institute
1616 P Street NW, Suite 200
Washington, D.C. 20036
202-328-5150
202-328-5002 (fax)

Environmental Research Foundation
P.O. Box 73700
Washington, D.C. 20056-3700
202-328-1119

Executive Enterprises
Publications Co., Inc.
22 W. 21st Street
New York, NY 10010-6904
212-645-7880

Government Institutes
966 Hungerford Drive #24
Rockville, MD 20850
301-251-9250

Government Printing Office
Superintendent of Documents
Department 36-BM
Washington, D.C. 20402-9325
202-783-3238
202-275-0019 (fax)

Greenpeace
1017 W. Jackson Boulevard
Chicago, IL 60607
312-666-3305

Greenwood Press
88 Post Road W., Box 5007
Westport, CT 06881
203-226-3571

Harper & Row
10 East 53rd Street
New York, NY 10022
800-242-7737
800-982-4377 (Pennsylvania)

Henry Holt and Company, Inc.
115 West 18th Street
New York, NY 10011
800-247-3912

Hunter College
School of Health Sciences
425 East 25th, Box 596
New York, NY
212-481-4355

Island Press
Box 7
Covelo, CA 95428
800-828-1302
707-983-6414 (fax)

League of Women Voters
1730 M Street NW
Washington, D.C. 20036
202-429-1965

Lewis Publishers, Inc.
121 South Main Street
P.O. Drawer 519
Chelsea, MI 48118
1-800-525-7894

Lexington Books
D.C. Heath and Company
125 Spring Street
Lexington, MA 02173

Little, Brown
200 West Street
Waltham, MA 02154
800-343-9204

McGraw-Hill
Princeton Road
Hightstown, NJ 08520
800-722-4726

C.V. Mosby Company
11830 Westline Industrial Drive
St. Louis, MO 63146

National Academy Press
2101 Constitution Avenue NW
Washington, D.C. 20418
800-624-6242

National Campaign Against Toxic
   Hazards
20 East Street, Suite 601
Boston, MA 02111
617-482-1477

National Cancer Institute
Office of Cancer Communications
Building 31, Room 10A24
Bethesda, MD 20892

National Center for Environmental
   Health Strategies
1100 Rural Avenue
Voorhees, NJ 08043
609-429-5358

National Center for Policy
   Alternatives
2000 Florida Avenue, NW
Washington, D.C. 20009
202-387-6030
202-387-8529 (fax)

National Institute for Occupational
   Safety and Health
Publications Dissemination
4676 Columbia Parkway
Cincinnati, OH 45226-1998
513-533-8287

National Technical Information
   Services
5285 Port Royal Road
Springfield, VA 22161-0001
703-487-4650

National Toxics Campaign
20 East Street, Suite 601
Boston, MA 02111
617-482-1477

National Wildlife Federation
1400 16th Street, NW
Washington, D.C. 20036
800-432-6564

Natural Resources Defense Council
49 West 20th Street
New York, NY 10011
212-727-2700

Northwest Coalition for Alternatives
   to Pesticides
P.O. Box 1393
Eugene, OR 97440
503-344-5044

Occupational Safety and Health
   Administration
Office of Publication Distribution
Room S-1212 Third and
   Constitution Avenue NW
Washington, D.C. 20210

OMB Watch
2001 O Street, NW
Washington, D.C. 20036
202-659-1711

Office of Technology Assessment
   Publications
U.S. Congress
Washington, D.C. 20510-8025
202-224-8996

Office of Toxic Substances
TSCA Assistance Office (TS-799)
U.S. Environmental Protection
   Agency
401 M Street SW
Washington, D.C. 20460
202-554-1406

Oxford University Press
Distribution Center
2001 Evans Road
Cary, NC 27513
800-451-7556

Pilgrim
36–01 43rd Avenue
Long Island City, NY 11101

Plenum Press
233 Spring Street
New York, NY 10013-1578
800-221-9369

Quorum Books
88 Post Road West
Box 5007
Westport, CT 06881
203-226-3571

Russell Sage Foundation
Cornell University Press
P.O. Box 6525
Ithaca, NY 14851
800-666-2211

Sierra Club
Department SA
P.O. Box 7959
San Francisco, CA 94120
415-291-1600

W.B. Saunders
6277 Sea Harbor Drive
Orlando, FL 32821
800-5445-2522

Technomic Publishing Co., Inc
851 New Holland Avenue
Box 3535
Lancaster, PA 17604
800-233-9936

U.S. Department of Transportation,
Research and Special Programs
DHM-S1
400 Seventh Street SW
Washington, D.C. 20590
202-420-2301

U.S. Environmental Directories
P.O. Box 65156
St. Paul, MN 55165

U.S. Environmental Protection
Agency
Office of Information
Resources Management
401 M Street SW, PM-218B
Washington, D.C. 20460
202-382-5224

U.S. Public Interest Group
215 Pennsylvania Avenue, SE
Washington, D.C. 20003

Van Nostrand Reinhold
7625 Empire Drive
Florence, KY 41022
606-525-6600

Vance Bibliographies
P.O. Box 2158
Mansfield, OH 44905
217-762-3831

Westview Press
5500 Central Avenue
Boulder, CO 80301
303-444-3541

Wiley
1 Wiley Drive
Somerset, NJ 08873
201-469-4400

Work on Waste, USA
82 Judson Street
Canton, NJ 13617
315-379-9200

Working Group on Community Right
To Know
c/o U.S. Public Interest Research
Group
215 Pennsylvania Avenue
Washington, D.C. 20003
202-546-9709

PERIODICALS

Buzzworm: The Environmental Journal
P.O. Box 6853
Syracuse, NY 13217-7930
$18.00/year, bimonthly
E The Environmental Magazine
Subscription Department
P.O. Box 6667
Syracuse, NY 13217-7934
800-825-0061
$20.00/year, bimonthly
Environmental Action
1525 New Hampshire Avenue, NW
Washington, D.C. 20036
202-745-4871
$20.00/year, bimonthly

Environmental Health Monthly
Citizens Clearinghouse for Hazardous Wastes, Inc.
See organizations list below for address.
$35 health professionals, $15 grassroots groups
EPA Journal
Editor, A-107 to subscribe:
401 M Street SW Superintendent of Documents
Washington, D.C. 20460 Government Printing Office
$20.00/year, bimonthly Washington, D.C., 20402
National Air Toxics Information Clearinghouse
National Air Toxics Information Clearinghouse
Pollutant Assessment Branch
Office of Air Quality Planning and Standards
U.S. Environmental Protection Agency
Research Triangle Park, N.C. 27711
919-541-5519
free, bimonthly
Nutrition Action Healthletter
Center for Science in the Public Interest
See organizations list below for address.
$19.95/year (frequent articles on pesticides and additives)

Many groups such as Sierra Club, Natural Resources Defense Council, and Citizens Clearinghouse for Hazardous Wastes, to name a few, circulate a magazine or newsletter to their members.

OTHER RESOURCES

Many of the books and periodicals noted above may be available at nearby libraries or through inter-library loan. The local public library, college and university libraries, and medical school libraries can be invaluable resources. Many other institutions also have libraries: Regulatory agencies such as the Environmental Protection Agency (national and regional offices), hospitals, and even local law offices have collections that may be opened to you upon your request. Libraries not only have books on the shelves but also information specialists trained in research techniques. Ask for help. You will be better able to use the library's resources and so save yourself time and frustration.

Regulatory agencies, schools, and other groupings of professionals such as hospitals and law offices have another resource that may be at your disposal — experts. Many activist groups can provide you with referrals to helpful experts and advice in ways to interact with professionals.

HOTLINES

Acute Hazards/CEPP Hotline (EPA)	800-535-0202
Cancer Information Services	800-422-6237
(National Cancer Institute)	
Chemical Referral Center	800-262-8200
(Chemical Manufacturers Association)	
Consumer Product Safety Commission	800-638-2772
Drinking Water Hotline (EPA)	800-426-4791
Department of Transportation Hotline	202-366-4488
EPA Public Information Center	202-475-7751
Laidlaw Environmental Services	800-845-1019
(information on waste disposal)	
League of Conservation Voters Toxics	800-922-5672
Hotline	
National Animal Poison Control	217-333-3611
Center	
National Poison Control Center Hotline	202-625-3333
(see your phone book for your	
regional center)	
National Response Center	800-424-8802
(to report chemical spills)	
National Institute of Occupational Safety	800-356-4674
and Health General Information	
Natural Resources Defense Council	800-648-6732
Toxic Substances Information Line	(New York) 212-687-6862
Occupational Safety and Health	202-523-8148
Administration Public Inquiry	
Pesticide Hotline (EPA funded)	800-858-7378
Superfund Hotline (EPA)	800-424-9346
SARA Hotline	800-535-0202
(for information on emergency	
planning and community right-to-	
know, EPA)	
Toxic Substances Control Act	202-382-7835
Tips and Complaints (EPA)	
Toxic Substances Control Act Hotline	202-554-1404
(EPA)	
Health Hotline list available from	800-638-8480
MEDLARS Management System	(Maryland) 301-496-6293
National Library of Medicine	
8600 Rockville Pike	
Bethesda, MD 20894	

COMPUTER-RELATED SERVICES

Econet
International
e-mail and bulletin board
1200, 2400 baud (7 data bits, 1 stop bit, odd parity)
No telephone charges (access through Telenet),
$15 sign-up fee, $10/month for one hour of off-peak time
Write for information and user id.
  Institute for Global Communications
  3228 Sacramento Street
  San Francisco, CA 94115
  415-923-0900

Environet
Large number of users
e-mail and bulletin board
300, 1200, 2400 baud (8 data bits, no parity)
415-861-6503 (bulletin board line)
Toll-free number available for grass root groups
For others, long distance phone charges only user cost
  Sign up using bulletin board.
  Operated by Greenpeace Action

HMIX (Hazardous Materials Information Exchange)
Bulletin board
300, 1200, 2400 (8 data bits, 1 stop bit, no parity)
708-972-3275 (bulletin board line)
Long distance phone charges only user cost
  Call 800-752-6367 (800-367-9592 in Illinois) for information.
  Sponsored by the Federal Emergency Management Agency and
  the U.S. Department of Transportation

NTIS Catalog of Data Files on Environmental Health
  National Technical Information Services
  5285 Port Royal Road
  Springfield, VA 22161-0001
  703-487-4650

RACHEL (Remote Access Chemical Hazards Electronic Library)
1. Abstracts from newspapers, primarily New York Times
2. New Jersey Department of Health chemical fact sheets
3. U.S. Coast Guard's Chemical Hazard Response Information Center
Manual covering about 1055 chemicals
4. Information on landfills

5. Information on incinerators
6. New technologies, recycling, pollution prevention
7. Information on particular waste-handling companies
8. Public policies, and
9. General reference information about toxics.
300, 1200, 2400, 9600 baud (7 data bits, even parity)
202-328-1065 RACHEL line
Long distance phone charges only user cost
Write for user id.
  Environmental Research Foundation
  P.O. Box 73700
  Washington, D.C. 20056-3700
  202-328-1119

TOXNET
National Library of Medicine databases
Of particular interest are the Hazardous Substances Databank, which
has peer-reviewed health and safety information on more than 4,200
chemicals, and the Toxic Release Inventory. This database contains all
the SARA Title III Community Right-to-Know reports. For the first time
information on toxic releases is available: by company, by
geographical area, by chemical, etc.
300, 1200, 2400 baud (even parity, 7 data bits, 1 stop bit, full duplex)
no telephone charges, free user id, only costs are search fees
Call or write for user id and training materials.
  MEDLARS Management Section
  National Library of Medicine
  8600 Rockville Pike
  Bethesda, MD 20894
  800-638-8480

*Some Publicly Available Sources of Computerized Information on
Environmental Health and Toxicology*, Center for Environmental Health
and Injury Control, June 1989. (free)

ORGANIZATIONS

Air and Waste Management
  Association
P.O. Box 2861
Pittsburgh, PA 15230
412-232-3444

Alaska Center for the
  Environment
700 H Street, Suite 4
Anchorage, Alaska 99501
907-274-3621, 907-274-4145 (fax)
serves Alaska

California Institute for Rural Studies
4570 California Avenue, #120
Bakersfield, CA 93308
805-395-1409

Center for Health Services
Station 17, Vanderbilt University
Nashville, TN 37332
615-322-4188
serves TN, KY, VA, WV, NC, LA, AR

Center for Science in the
Public Interest
1501 16th Street NW
Washington, DC 20036-1499
202-332-9110
202-265-4954 (fax)

Central States Education
Center
809 Fifth
Champaign, IL 61820
217-344-2371
serves primarily Illinois and Indiana

Citizens Clearinghouse for
Hazardous Wastes
P.O. Box 6806
Falls Church, VA 22040
703-237-2249

Clean Water Action
317 Pennsylvania Ave, SE
Washington, D.C. 20003
202-547-1196

Community Assistance Program in
Environmental Toxicology
Department of Resource
Development
Michigan State University
East Lansing, MI 48824
517-355-3414, 517-353-8994 (fax)

Community Environmental
Health Center
Hunter College
425 E. 25th Street, Box 596
New York, NY 10010
212-481-4355, 212-481-8795 (fax)
serves New York City

Connecticut Fund for the
Environment
152 Temple Street
New Haven, CT 06510
203-865-2677
serves Connecticut

Environmental Action
1525 New Hampshire Avenue NW
Washington, D.C. 20036

Environmental Defense Fund
257 Park Avenue S.
New York, NY 10010
212-505-2100

Environmental Health Network
P.O. Box 1628
Harvey, LA 70058
504-362-6574

Environmental Law Institute
1616 P Street, Suite 200
Washington, D.C. 20036
202-328-5150

Environmental Resource
Project
University of North Carolina at
Chapel Hill
Chapel Hill, NC 27599-7410
919-966-3335, 919-966-7141 (fax)
serves North Carolina

Friends of the Earth
218 D Street SE
Washington, D.C. 20003
202-544-2600

Greenpeace, U.S.A.
1436 U Street NW
Washington, D.C.
202-465-1177

Inform
381 Park Avenue S
New York, NY 10016
212-689-4040

Louisiana Environmental Action
Network
P.O. Box 66323
Baton Rouge, LA
70896-6323
504-928-1315

National Center for Policy
Alternatives
2000 Florida Avenue, NW
Washington, D.C. 20009
202-387-6030
202-387-8529 (fax)

National Audubon Society
950 Third Avenue
New York, NY 10022
212-832-3200

National Coalition for Alternatives to
Pesticides
P.O. Box 1393
Eugene, OR 97440
503-344-5044

National Coalition Against the Misuse
of Pesticides
530 Seventh Street SE
Washington, D.C. 20003
202-543-5450

National Environmental Health
Association
720 S. Colorado Blvd.,
Suite 970
Denver, CO 80222
303-756-9090

National Toxics Campaign
20 East Street, Suite 601
Boston, MA 02111
617-482-1477

National Wildlife Federation
1400 16th Street NW
Washington, D.C. 20036-2266
202-797-6800

Natural Resources Defense Council
40 West 20th Street
New York, NY 10011
212-727-2700

Rocky Mountain Student
Environmental Health Project
Colorado State University
Department of Environmental Health
Fort Collins, CO 80523
303-491-7038, 303-491-1815 (fax)
serves Rocky Mountain region

Sierra Club
730 Polk Street
San Francisco, CA 94109
415-776-2211

Southwest Research and Information
Center
P.O. Box 4524
Albuquerque, NM 87106
505-262-1862
serves southwestern U.S.

Texans United
3400 Montrose, Suite 225
Houston, TX 77006
713-529-8038

Texans United
11520 North Central
Expressway, Suite 133
Dallas, TX 75243
214-343-6090

Texas Center for Policy Studies
P.O. Box 2618
Austin, TX 78768
512-474-0811

Toxics Assistance Program
University of Texas Medical Branch
2.104 Ewing Hall, J-10
Galveston, TX 77550
409-772-9110
serves Texas and Louisiana

Toxic Communications and
    Assistance Project
Department of Natural Sciences
Albany State College
Albany, Georgia 31705
912-430-4811
serves Georgia, Alabama and Florida

U.S. Public Interest Group
215 Pennsylvania Avenue, SE
Washington, D.C. 20003
202-546-9707

Water Pollution Control Federation
601 Wythe Street
Alexandria, VA 22314-1994
703-684-2400

Working Group on Community Right
    to Know
c/o U.S. PIRG
215 Pennsylvania Avenue, SE
Washington, D.C. 20003
202-546-9707

U.S. GOVERNMENT OFFICES

Agency for Toxic Substances and Disease Registry
Public Health Service
U.S. Department of Health and Human Services
Atlanta, GA 30333
404-639-0615

U.S. Environmental Protection Agency (USEPA)
401 M Street, S.W.
Washington, D.C. 20460
202-260-2090

U.S. Environmental Protection Agency Regions

Region 1
Connecticut, Maine, Massachu-
setts, New Hampshire, Rhode
Island, and Vermont
John F. Kennedy
Federal Building, Room 2203
Boston, MA 02203
617-565-3715

Region 2
New Jersey, New York, Puerto
Rico, and Virgin Islands
Jacob K. Javitz Federal Building
26 Federal Plaza
New York, NY 10278
212-264-2657

Region 3
Delaware, District of Columbia,
Maryland, Pennsylvania, Virginia,
and West Virginia
841 Chestnut Building
Philadelphia, PA 19107
215-597-9800
800-438-2474

Region 4
Alabama, Florida, Georgia, Ken-
tucky, Mississippi, North Carolina, South Carolina,
Tennessee
345 Courtland Street, NE
Atlanta, GA 30365
404-347-4727
800-241-1754

Region 5
Illinois, Indiana, Michigan, Minnesota, Ohio, Wisconsin
230 South Dearborn Street
Chicago, Il 90904
312-353-2000
800-621-8431
800-572-2525 (IL)

Region 6
Arkansas, Louisiana, New Mexico,
Oklahoma, Texas
First Interstate Bank Tower at
Fountain Place
1445 Ross Avenue, Suite 1200
Dallas, TX 75202
214-655-6444

Region 7
Iowa, Kansas, Missouri,
Nebraska
726 Minnesota Avenue
Kansas City, KS
913-236-2800
800-223-0425
800-221-7749 (KS)

Region 8
Colorado, Montana, North
Dakota, South Dakota, Utah,
Wyoming
999 18th Street, Suite 500
Denver, CO 80202-2405
303-293-1603
800-525-3022

Region 9
Arizona, California, Hawaii,
Nevada, American Somoa, Guam
215 Fremont Street,
San Francisco, CA 94105
415-744-8071

Region 10
Alaska, Idaho, Oregon,
Washington
1200 Sixth Avenue
Seattle, WA 98101
206-442-1200

APPENDIX

Rates of Cancer and Birth Defects

Barbara L. Harper

We have stressed throughout this manual that it is imperative to survey an unexposed or control population in exactly the same manner and with the same care as you survey your own community. As a poor second choice, we are providing some national rates or sources of such information, with all the drawbacks inherent in such figures.

Most of the symptoms or conditions uncovered by a community health survey will be acute, temporary, or subclinical, meaning undetectible by standard medical tests. Generally speaking, there is almost no information on these kinds of conditions other than rough guesses published by national associations (professional or lay) for particular diseases, or by insurance companies who have to pay for much of the associated medical care, or as results of large health surveys (such as HANES — a survey of adults conducted by the Public Health Service, the Framingham heart study, and others) to which professionals or officials should have access. A few serious diseases must be reported to the Centers for Disease Control. These "notifiable" diseases include aseptic meningitis, encephalitis (primary and postinfectious), gonorrhea, hepatitis, Legionellosis, leprosy, malaria, measles, meningococcic infections, mumps, pertussis, rubella (German measles), syphillis, toxic shock syndrome, tuberculosis, tularemia, typhoid fever, typhus, rabies, and some low-frequency illnesses (plague, polio, anthrax, tetanus, etc.).

Some information is available from the Public Health Service concerning health care use (how many times people see a doctor, how long they are hospitalized, what operations they have, and so on). Most of the rates calculated from these studies concern the major fatal diseases. Inquiries can be addressed to U.S. Department of Health and Human Services, Public Health Service, Office of Health Research, Statistics, and Technology, or Office of Disease Prevention and Health Promotion, National Center for Health Statistics, 3700 East West Highway, Hyattsville, Maryland 20782, tel. (301) 436-6247. Tables A.1, A.2, and A.3 are excerpted from a Public Health Service publication, *Vital and Health Statistics*, a serial available from libraries at many medical schools or schools of public health.

National averages of leading causes of death give some information on major health conditions, and presumably each patient has had a disease for a while before dying from it (table A.1). However, these and the following rates (tables A.2-A.6) include only patients who die, whereas community health surveys are concerned almost entirely with health before death. Note that the same source, National Center for Health Statistics (NCHS), lists the total death rate for 1978 both as 883 per 100,000 (table A.4) and as 606 per 100,000 (table A.5).

These same rates from NCHS (*Vital and Health Statistics,* 1978) are cited by other sources (American Cancer Society, for example), as different yet (table A.6).

This should give you an idea of the accuracy of such rates. On the whole, published cancer rates average from 17 to 23 percent of all causes of death. Another problem in comparing death rates is that, for instance for cardiovascular diseases, it is not clear whether ischemic heart disease includes atherosclerosis and angina as well as heart attacks, whether cerebrovascular disease includes both cerebral hemorrhage and cerebral thrombosis, whether arteriosclerosis and hypertension are included under the umbrella of major cardiovascular disease, and so on.

Cancer statistics have also been widely published. Probably the most accurate rates were determined by the National Cancer Institute as part of the SEER (Surveillance and Epidemiology End Results) reports. The most recent SEER statistics are reported in Lynn A. Gloeckler Ries, et al., eds., *Cancer Statistics Review, 1973–1987,* Bethesda, MD: NCI, 1990. The rates are determined using cancer registries from geographical areas covering nearly ten percent of the U.S. population. These areas were selected for their population-based cancer reporting systems and for demographic characteristics.

The American Cancer Society also publishes annual cancer statistics, and these figures vary greatly from the National Cancer Institute for particular sites. One can see how the controversy arises concerning whether cancer rates are increasing or decreasing. Is two-year or five-year survival a "cure?" Are these rates calculated from "new cases" or from "deaths?" Does postponing death by effective treatment mean that future rates will rise? Have all cancer cases been reported and all cancer deaths accurately recorded?

It should be apparent that a single national average for a particular condition or cancer site will not be very useful for purposes of a community health survey. The first point to remember is that cancer rates in general increase with age (table A.9). The second point is that some cancers incidence rates peak at different ages (leukemia peaks in childhood, then again in old age). Therefore rates for each group are needed for comparisons.

Another factor that must be taken into account is the geographic distributions both of some malignant and of some non-malignant conditions. The most striking example of this is ischemic heart disease (disease due to obstruction or constriction of coronary arteries), with rates taken from Mason, et al. (1975a; cited by W. Villanueva in *Discover* magazine, September 1982, p. 82). The east/west variation makes it clear that a national incidence rate might not be at all comparable to the rate in your community. The best example of a population-based tumor registry is the Connecticut Tumor Registry, Connecticut State Department of Health, Hartford, Connecticut.

There are many other examples of geographic differences: intestinal infectious disease is more common in the Southwest; tuberculosis is more common in Appalachia and southern Texas and among American Indians; multiple sclerosis shows a north/south gradient. These statistics, while they can be used for illustration, lack some precision because the information comes from death certificates from 1965–71, based on a 1960 census population and extrapolated to later years, and some information comes from death certificates in rural areas where there might have been no medically trained coroner or medical examiner.

The third type of national rates you might need are for birth defects or congenital malformations. In general these rates are more accurate because each case must be reported when recognized, and most conditions are fairly easy for a trained pediatrician to recognize. Again, there are some geographic gradients, especially for spina bifida and hip dislocation, as reported by the Centers for Disease Control (1980) in congenital malformations surveillance reports. For comparison, rates from Bloom (1981) are given for congenital anomalies seen in over 30,000 births at the Boston Hospital for Women. Some rates show more than a two-fold difference from the Centers for Disease Control figures, for which we currently have no explanation. In addition, minor anomalies may escape notice during the first year and thus be underreported (table A.10).

In conclusion, discrepancies in incidence and mortality rates collected by various groups and widely quoted or misquoted demonstrate the difficulty of accurately measuring background rates of major diseases or conditions. However, for rare conditions they may be the only information available, in which case we must choose what appears to be the most accurate data set to use in calculating how many cases would be expected in a smaller population. For acute or less serious conditions, there is very little reliable (quantitative) information upon which either you or state health officials can base calculations, so there is no alternative to collecting it yourself.

Table A.1. Death Rates from Specified Causes, by Race and Sex: United States, 1987 (per 100,000)

Cause of Death	Total Both Sexes	Total Male	Total Female	White Both Sexes	White Male	White Female	All Other Races Both Sexes	All Other Races Male	All Other Races Female
All causes	872.4	934.7	813.1	895.5	947.8	845.5	745.8	861.5	640.0
Major cardiovascular diseases	395.9	396.6	395.2	414.7	413.0	416.3	293.1	304.7	282.4
Hypertension	3.3	3.0	3.7	3.0	2.7	3.4	5.0	4.7	5.4
Cerebrovascular diseases	61.6	49.8	72.7	63.2	49.9	75.8	52.7	49.2	55.8
Arteriosclerosis	9.2	7.1	11.2	10.1	7.6	12.4	4.7	4.1	5.1
Cancer	195.9	214.8	178.0	203.3	220.5	186.9	155.5	183.3	130.1
Accidents	39.0	54.7	24.2	38.8	53.6	24.6	40.5	60.6	22.0
Motor vehicle accidents	19.8	28.6	11.5	20.2	28.8	11.9	17.9	27.7	9.3
All other accidents	19.2	26.1	12.7	18.6	24.8	12.6	22.6	33.4	12.8
Influenza and pneumonia	28.2	28.1	28.3	29.7	28.9	30.6	19.6	23.8	15.9
Cirrhosis of the liver	10.8	14.4	7.3	10.6	14.1	7.2	11.8	16.0	7.9
Diabetes mellitus	15.8	13.7	17.9	15.3	13.5	17.0	19.0	15.0	22.7
Suicide	12.7	20.5	5.2	13.7	22.1	5.7	6.9	11.6	2.5
Homicide	8.7	13.4	4.2	5.4	7.9	3.0	26.5	43.9	10.7
Chronic obstructive pulmonary diseases	32.2	39.7	25.1	35.3	43.0	27.9	15.2	20.9	10.0

Source: Adapted from National Center for Health Statistics, *Vital Statistics of the United States 1987, Vol. II Mortality Part A*, Washington, DC: Public Health Service, 1990.

Table A.2. Death Rates for Various Age Groups, by Race and Sex: United States, 1987 (per 100,000)

Age Group	Total			White			All Other Races		
	Both Sexes	Male	Female	Both Sexes	Male	Female	Both Sexes	Male	Female
All ages[a]	872.4	934.7	813.1	895.5	947.8	845.5	745.8	861.5	640.0
Under 1 year	1018.5	1128.8	902.2	845.1	942.1	742.9	1757.0	1938.0	1571.5
1–4	51.6	57.5	45.4	46.4	52.0	40.5	73.6	81.1	65.8
5–14	25.6	31.9	19.0	24.1	30.0	17.9	31.8	39.9	23.5
15–24	99.4	146.1	51.7	93.8	137.3	49.1	124.9	186.6	63.5
25–34	133.2	192.6	73.8	115.7	167.8	62.6	225.7	331.6	129.5
35–44	214.1	291.8	138.6	184.2	249.6	119.3	396.7	570.9	248.4
45–55	498.0	644.2	359.8	451.9	582.8	325.7	786.7	1057.9	559.4
55–64	1241.3	1624.6	900.3	1182.1	1552.8	848.5	1677.2	2181.8	1265.1
65–74	2751.3	3617.8	2062.6	2688.9	3548.4	2001.8	3286.6	4230.8	2571.2
75–84	6282.5	8224.4	5117.6	6247.8	8212.2	5075.2	6629.7	8340.0	5542.5
85 and older	15320.8	18031.1	14260.9	15580.5	18434.9	14486.9	12683.3	14514.5	11809.8

[a]Figures for age not stated are included in "all ages" but not distributed among age groups.
Source: Adapted from National Center for Health Statistics (1990).

Table A.3. Leading Causes of Death in the United States, 1987
(Rates per 100,000 population)

		Rate	Percent of total deaths
	All causes	872.4	100.0
1	Diseases of heart	312.4	35.8
2	Malignant neoplasms	195.9	22.5
3	Cerebrovascular diseases	61.6	7.1
4	Accidents and adverse effects	39.0	4.5
	Motor vehicle accidents	19.8	2.3
	All other	19.2	2.2
5	Chronic obstructive pulmonary conditions	32.2	3.7
6	Pneumonia and influenza	28.4	3.3
7	Diabetes mellitus	15.8	1.8
8	Suicide	12.7	1.5
9	Chronic liver disease and cirrhosis	10.8	1.2
10	Atherosclerosis	9.2	1.1
11	Nephritis, nephrotic syndrome, and nephrosis	9.1	1.0
12	Homicide and legal intervention	8.7	1.0
13	Septicemia	8.2	.9
14	Certain conditions originating in perinatal period	7.5	.9
15	Human immunodeficiency virus infection	5.5	.6
	All other causes	115.4	13.2

Source: National Center for Health Statistics (1990).

Table A.4. Leading Causes of Death in the United States, 1978

		Number of Deaths	Death Rate per 100,000
	All causes	1,927,788	883.4
1	Heart diseases	729,510	334.3
2	Cancer	396,992	181.9
3	Cerebrovascular diseases	175,629	80.5
4	Accidents	105,561	48.4
	Motor vehicle accidents	52,411	24.0
	All other	53,150	24.4
5	Influenza and pneumonia	58,319	26.7
6	Diabetes mellitus	33,841	15.5
7	Cirrhosis of the liver	30,066	13.8
8	Arteriosclerosis	28,940	13.3
9	Suicide	27,294	12.5
10	Diseases of early infancy	22,033	10.1
	All other causes	319,603	146.5

Source: National Center for Health Statistics. Cited in *Hammond Almanac* (1983).

Table A.5. **Leading Causes of Death in the United States, 1978**

	Cause of Death	Percentage of Total Deaths	Death Rate per 100,000
	All causes	100.0	606
1	Heart disease	34.3	208
2	Cancer	22.1	134
3	Stroke	7.5	45
4	Accidents	7.3	44
5	Influenza and penumonia	2.5	15
6	Suicide	2.0	12
7	Diabetes mellitus	1.7	10

Source: National Center for Health Statistics, "Final Mortality Statistics, 1978," *Monthly Vital Statistics Report,* vol. 29, no. 6, suppl. 2, 17 September 1980.

Table A.6. **Leading Causes of Death in the United States, 1978**

	Cause of Death	Percentage of Total Deaths	Death Rate per 100,000
	All causes	100.0	810.0
1	Heart disease	37.8	300.4
2	Cancer	20.6	169.9
3	Cerebrovascular diseases	9.1	70.8
4	Accidents	5.5	45.8
5	Pneumonia and influenza	3.0	23.6
6	Chronic obstructive lung diseases	2.6	21.2
7	Diabetes mellitus	1.8	14.2
8	Cirrhosis of the liver	1.6	13.4
9	Arteriosclerosis	1.5	11.1
10	Suicide	1.4	11.6
11	Diseases of infancy	1.1	12.1
12	Homicide	1.1	8.7
13	Aortic aneurysm	0.8	5.8
14	Congenital anomalies	0.7	6.8
15	Pulmonary Infarction	0.6	4.6

Source: National Center for Health Statistics, Vital Statistics of the United States, 1978, as cited by the American Cancer Society, *Cancer Statistics,* vol. 33, no. 1, 1983.

Table A.7. Cancer Incidence as Percent of Total, 1983–1987, by Site, Sex, and Race—SEER Program

Site	All Races Both Sexes	All Races Males	All Races Females	Whites Both Sexes	Whites Males	Whites Females	Blacks Both Sexes	Blacks Males	Blacks Females
All Sites	436,520 100.0%	219,469 100.0%	217,051 100.0%	377,271 100.0%	188,022 100.0%	189,249 100.0%	35,978 100.0%	19,491 100.0%	16,487 100.0%
Oral & Pharynx	3.0	4.1	1.9	2.9	3.9	1.9	3.7	5.0	2.0
Esophagus	1.0	1.4	.6	.9	1.2	.5	2.7	3.8	1.5
Stomach	2.3	2.8	1.8	2.0	2.5	1.6	3.1	3.5	2.7
Colon/Rectum	14.1	14.0	14.0	14.3	14.3	14.3	12.4	10.8	14.4
Liver & Intrahep	.7	1.0	.5	.6	.7	.4	.9	1.2	.6
Pancreas	2.6	2.6	2.7	2.6	2.5	2.6	3.5	3.1	3.9
Larynx	1.2	1.9	.4	1.2	2.0	.4	1.7	2.5	.8
Lung & Bronchus	15.0	19.5	10.4	14.9	19.1	10.5	18.9	25.0	11.7
Melanoma of Skin	2.8	2.9	2.6	2.9	3.0	2.7	.2	.1	.3
Breast	15.0	.2	29.6	15.2	.2	30.2	13.0	.2	28.2
Cervix Uteri	1.3	–	2.6	1.1	–	2.3	2.4	–	5.2
Corp & Uter, NOS	3.2	–	6.4	3.3	–	6.7	2.0	–	4.4
Ovary	2.0	–	3.9	2.1	–	4.1	1.4	–	3.1
Prostate Gland	10.2	20.4	–	10.1	20.3	–	12.8	23.5	–
Testis	.6	1.3	–	.7	1.4	–	.1	.3	–
Urinary Bladder	4.6	6.8	2.4	4.9	7.3	2.5	2.4	3.0	1.7
Kidney & Ren Pelv	2.1	2.6	1.6	2.1	2.7	1.6	2.0	2.3	1.7
Brain & Nerv Sys	1.6	1.7	1.4	1.6	1.8	1.5	1.0	1.2	1.0
Thyroid Gland	1.2	.6	1.8	1.2	.6	1.7	.7	.3	1.2
Hodgkin's Disease	.8	.9	.7	.8	.9	.7	.6	.7	.5
Non-Hodgkin's Lym	3.4	3.6	3.2	3.5	3.8	3.3	2.2	2.2	2.2
Multiple Myeloma	1.1	1.2	1.0	1.1	1.1	1	2.1	2.0	2.2
Leukemia	2.7	3.0	2.4	2.7	3.1	2.4	2.3	2.3	2.3

Source: Adapted from Lynn A. Gloeckler Ries, et al., eds. *Cancer Statistics Review, 1973–1987,* Bethesda, MD: NCI, 1990.

Table A.8. Cancer Mortality as Percent of Total, 1983–1987, by Site, Sex, and Race—SEER Program

Site	All Races			Whites			Blacks		
	Both Sexes	Males	Females	Both Sexes	Males	Females	Both Sexes	Males	Females
All Sites	2,118,533	1,145,954	972,579	1,970,686	1,003,460	867,226	229,835	132,286	97,549
	100.0%	100.0%	100.0%	100.0%	100.0%	100.0%	100.0%	100.0%	100.0%
Oral & Pharynx	2.0	2.6	1.4	1.9	2.5	1.4	2.7	3.6	1.5
Esophagus	1.9	2.6	1.1	1.6	2.2	1.0	4.3	5.6	2.5
Stomach	3.4	3.7	3.0	3.2	3.5	2.8	4.6	5.0	4.1
Colon/Rectum	12.9	11.7	14.5	13.3	12.1	14.6	10.6	8.6	13.3
Liver & Intrahep	1.4	1.5	1.2	1.3	1.4	1.2	1.8	2.0	1.5
Pancreas	5.1	4.9	5.5	5.1	4.9	5.4	5.3	4.7	6.1
Larynx	.8	1.3	.3	.8	1.2	.3	1.2	1.6	.5
Lung & Bronchus	25.2	33.5	15.5	25.3	33.7	15.7	24.6	32.6	13.8
Melanoma of Skin	1.2	1.3	1.1	1.3	1.4	1.2	.2	.2	.3
Breast	8.6	.1	18.7	8.8	.1	18.9	7.4	.1	17.2
Cervix Uteri	1.1	–	2.5	1.0	–	2.1	2.3	–	5.4
Corp & Uter, NOS	1.4	–	3	1.4	–	2.9	1.7	–	4.1
Ovary	2.6	–	5.6	2.8	–	5.8	1.7	–	4.1
Prostate Gland	5.5	10.3	–	5.2	9.8	–	8.1	14.2	–
Testis	.1	.2	–	.1	.2	–	.1	.1	–
Urinary Bladder	2.3	2.9	1.6	2.4	3.1	1.6	1.7	1.7	1.7
Kidney & Ren Pelv	1.8	2.1	1.5	1.9	2.2	1.6	1.3	1.4	1.2
Brain & Nerv Sys	2.2	2.3	2.2	2.3	2.4	2.3	1.2	1.1	1.3
Thyroid Gland	.2	.2	.3	.2	.2	.3	.2	.1	.3
Hodgkin's Disease	.5	.5	.4	.3	.5	.5	.3	.3	.3
Non-Hodgkin's Lym	3.0	2.9	3.2	3.2	3.1	3.4	1.6	1.6	1.7
Multiple Myeloma	1.6	1.5	1.7	1.5	1.4	1.6	2.4	2.2	2.8
Leukemia	3.9	4.0	3.8	4.0	4.2	3.9	2.9	2.7	3.2

Source: Adapted from Gloeckler Reis, et al. (1990).

Table A.9. Age-specific Rates of Cancer, 1987

Age Group	Rates per 100,000
All Ages	171.5
0–4	3.5
5–14	3.4
15–24	5.0
25–34	12.0
35–44	46.1
45–54	170.7
55–64	427.0
65–74	860.1
75–84	1316.4
85+	1627.2

Source: Adapted from Gloeckler Reis, et al. (1990).

Table A.10. Incidence of Selected Congential Malformations per 10,000 Births

Malformation	North-east	North Central	South	West	Total U.S.
Central nervous system					
Anencephaly					
1970–73	5.1	4.9	5.8	5.1	5.2
1979	3.3	3.9	3.5	3.3	3.6
1980	3.7	3.1	3.8	2.5	3.3
Spina bifida without anencephaly					
1970–73	6.9	7.1	8.7	5.6	7.2
1979	5.1	5.1	5.1	4.4	5.0
1980	3.8	5.1	6.9	4.0	5.2
Hydrocephalus without spina bifida					
1970–73	4.7	4.8	5.0	4.2	4.7
1979	4.8	4.6	4.7	4.0	4.6
1980	3.9	3.9	4.6	3.4	4.0
Cardiovascular					
Transportation of great vessels					
1970–73	0.9	0.8	0.7	0.9	0.8
1979	1.1	1.1	0.8	1.2	1.0
1980	0.9	0.7	0.8	0.5	0.7

Malformation	North-east	North Central	South	West	Total U.S.
Ventricular septal defect					
1970–73	5.8	4.6	4.5	7.1	5.2
1979	12.2	10.7	8.6	12.5	10.7
1980	14.5	11.3	10.3	12.4	11.7
Patent ductus arteriosus					
1970–73	4.6	4.6	4.3	8.5	5.1
1979	16.8	17.9	13.7	19.7	16.8
1980	17.1	15.8	16.1	19.2	16.7
Craniofacial					
Cleft palate without cleft lip					
1970–83	5.7	5.4	4.7	5.6	5.3
1979	4.3	5.7	5.2	4.9	5.2
1980	3.9	5.2	4.6	5.4	4.9
Cleft lip with or without cleft palate					
1970–73	9.2	10.6	9.2	11.2	10.0
1979	5.7	8.6	7.7	7.8	7.7
1980	6.6	8.4	7.7	8.9	8.0
Musculoskeletal					
Clubfoot without CNS anomalies					
1970–73	33.6	33.5	21.5	23.1	29.4
1979	30.8	28.7	20.1	20.9	25.3
1980	30.2	29.8	21.5	18.7	25.7
Reduction deformity					
1970–73	2.9	3.0	3.1	4.0	3.1
1979	3.6	3.7	3.1	4.0	3.6
1980	4.4	3.9	3.4	3.8	3.8
Hip dislocation without CNS anomalies					
1970–73	12.2	8.4	6.5	13.9	9.6
1979	27.4	21.2	18.7	32.6	23.6
1980	30.7	20.7	18.5	29.1	23.1
Gastrointestinal					
Tracheoesophageal fistula					
1970–73	1.7	1.4	1.8	1.7	1.6
1979	1.8	1.8	1.5	2.1	1.7
1980	1.9	2.2	1.7	1.9	2.0
Rectal atresia stenosis					
1970–73	4.2	3.5	3.1	3.6	3.6
1979	3.8	2.9	2.9	2.9	3.1
1980	4.1	3.6	3.2	2.6	3.4
Genitourinary					
Renal agenesis					
1970–73	0.9	0.8	0.8	0.8	0.8
1979	1.0	1.3	1.0	1.5	1.2
1980	0.9	1.5	1.2	1.0	1.2

Table A.10. (*continued*)

Malformation	North-east	North Central	South	West	Total U.S.
Hypospadias (per 10,000 male births)					
1970–73	45.5	42.7	38.4	41.3	42.2
1979	53.0	48.9	45.8	48.8	48.7
1980	58.7	53.8	45.8	44.8	50.8
Chromosomal					
Down's syndrome					
1970–73	9.7	8.3	6.6	8.9	8.3
1979	8.0	7.9	7.2	6.9	7.6
1980	8.7	7.4	5.7	8.6	7.3

Source: Centers for Disease Control, *Congenital Malformations Surveillance,* January–December 1979, issued December 1980; January–December 1980, issued February 1982.

Table A.11. Frequency of Selected Reproductive Outcomes

Outcome	Frequency per 100	Unit
Azoospermia	1	Men
Birth weight <2,500 g	7	Livebirths
Failure to conceive after one year of unprotected intercourse	10–15	Couples
Spontaneous abortion, 8–28 weeks of gestation	10–20	Pregnancies or women
Chromosomal anomaly among spontaneously aborted conceptions 8–28 weeks	30–40	Spontaneous abortions
Chromosomal anomalies among amniocentesis specimens to unselected women over 35 years	2	Amniocentesis specimens
Stillbirth	2–4	Stillbirths & livebirths
Birth defects	2–3	Livebirths
Chromosomal anomalies in livebirths	0.2	Livebirths
Neural tube defects	0.01–1	Livebirths & stillbirths
Severe mental retardation	0.4	Children to age 15 years

Source: Adapted from A. D. Bloom, ed., *Guidelines for Studies of Human Populations Exposed to Mutagenic and Reproductive Hazards* (White Plains, N.Y.: March of Dimes Birth Defects Foundation, 1981).

Table A.12. Major Malformations Common among Newborn Infants

Malformation	Rate per 1,000
Anencephaly	1.04
Myelomeningocele	0.33
Congenital hydrocephalus	0.36
Transposition of the great arteries	0.26
Ventricular septal defect	1.17
Hypoplastic left heart	0.23
Patent ductus arteriosus	0.72
Cleft palate	0.33
Cleft lip and cleft lip with cleft palate	0.78
Undescended testes	1.21
Hypospadias — first degree	2.12
Hypospadias — second or third degree	0.52
Clubfoot — all types	2.05
Talipes equivovarus	1.01
Metatarus adductus	0.49
Calcaneovalgus	0.55
Congenital dislocation of the hip	0.78
Polydactyly — type B	2.15
Down's syndrome	1.53

Note: Prevalence of all major malformations is 26/1,000. These data are derived from surveillance of 30,681 infants of at least twenty weeks gestational age born at Boston Hospital for Women.

Source: Adapted from A. D. Bloom, ed. (1981).

Table A.13. Sample Size of Comparison Groups Needed to Detect a Certain-fold Increase with 95% Certainty over a Background Frequency of 3, 7, or 15 Cases per 100 Events (Such as Births)

Frequency	Sample Size of Comparison Groups	Increase in Frequency Detectable with 95% Power
3	50	7.7-fold
	100	5.3-fold
	250	3.3-fold
	300	3.2-fold
7	50	4.6-fold
	100	3.4-fold
	250	2.3-fold
	300	2.3-fold
15	50	3.0-fold
	100	2.4-fold
	250	1.8-fold
	300	1.7-fold

Source: Adapted from A. D. Bloom, ed. (1981).

REFERENCES CITED IN THE TEXT AND ADDITIONAL SUGGESTED READING

American Cancer Society. 1990. Cancer statistics, 1990. *Ca — A Cancer Journal for Clinicians* 40:9–26.

Andelman, J.B. and D.W. Underhill. 1987. *Health Effects From Hazardous Waste Sites*. Chelsea, Michigan: Lewis Publishers.

Bahn, Anita K. 1972. *Basic Medical Statistics*. New York: Grune and Stratton.

Barton, J., et al. 1981. Characteristics of respondents and non-respondents to a mailed questionnaire. *American Journal of Public Health* 70:308–11.

Bennett, A.E. and K. Ritchie. 1975. *Questionnaires in Medicine: A Guide to their Design and Use*. London: Oxford University Press.

Berdie, D.R. and J.F. Anderson. 1974. *Questionnaire: Design and Use*. Metuchen, N.J.: Scarecrow Press.

Blomquist, H.K., K.H. Gustavson, and G. Holmgren. 1981. Mild mental retardation in children in a northern Swedish county. *Journal of Mental Deficiency Research* 25:169–86.

Bloom, A.D., ed. 1981. *Guidelines for Studies of Human Population Exposed to Mutagenic and Reproductive Hazards*. New York: March of Dimes Birth Defects Foundation, Medical Education Division.

Bloom, A.D, L. Spatz, and N.W. Paul. 1989. *Genetic Susceptibility to Environmental Mutagens and Carcinogens*. Monograph No. 2; Environmental Health Institute. White Plains, New York: March of Dimes Birth Defects Foundation.

Calabrese, E.J. 1978. *Pollutants and High Risk Groups*. New York: John Wiley.

Caldwell, Glyn G. 1990. Twenty-two years of cancer cluster investigations at the Centers for Disease Control. *American Journal of Epidemiology* 132:S43-S47.

Centers for Disease Control. 1980. *Congenital Malformations Survey, January-December 1979*. Washington, D.C.: U.S. Department of Health, Education, and Welfare.

Connors, D. 1960. *Community development: A guide to action*. Oakville, Ont.: Development Press.

Cook, J. and R. Wigley. 1975. *Community health: Concepts and issues*. New York: Van Nostrand.

Cowan, W.M. 1979. The development of the brain. *Scientific American* 241:113–33.

Daugaard, J. 1981. *Symptoms and signs in occupational disease: A practical guide*.

Copenhagen: Munksgaard. Distributed by Year Book Medical Publishers, Chicago.

Davis, D.L., K. Bridbord and M. Schneiderman. 1981. Estimating cancer causes: Problems in methodology, production and trends. In *Quantification of occupational cancer*, ed. R. Peto and M. Schneiderman, Banbury Report 9:285–316, Cold Spring Harbor, New York: Cold Spring Harbor Laboratory.

———. 1982. Cancer prevention: Assessing causes, exposures and recent trends in mortality for U.S. males, 1968–1978. *Teratogenesis, Carcinogenesis and Mutagenesis* 2(2):105–35.

Dever, G.E. Alan. 1980. *Community Health Analysis: A Holistic Approach*. Germantown, Maryland: Aspen System Corporation.

Doll, R. and R. Peto. 1981. The causes of cancer. *Journal of the National Cancer Institute* 66:1191–1308.

Doull, J.D., C.D. Klassen, and M.O. Amdur, eds. 1980. *Casarett and Doull's Toxicology*. 2d ed. New York: Macmillan.

Effrat, M. 1974. *The Community: Approaches and Applications*. New York: Free Press.

Ehrlich, Paul R. with Anne Ehrlich. 1968. *The Population Bomb: The End of Affluence*. New York: Ballantine Books.

Eifler, C.W., S.S. Stinnett, and P.A. Buffler. 1981. Simple models for community exposure from point sources of pollution. *Environmental Research* 25:139–46.

Epstein, S.S. 1978. *The Politics of Cancer*. San Francisco: Sierra Club Books.

Epstein, S.S., L.O. Brown, and C. Pope. 1982. *Hazardous Waste in America*. San Francisco: Sierra Club Books.

Food Safety Council, Scientific Committee. 1980. *Proposed System for Food Safety Assessment*. Washington, D.C.: Food Safety Council (1725 K Street, NW, Washington, D.C. 20006).

Functional Models of Health Systems. 1971. Chicago: Aldine Atherton.

Gibbons, J.H. 1981. *Assessment of Technologies for Determining Cancer Risks From the Environment*. Washington, D.C.: Office of Technology Assessment.

Gifford, F.A. 1981. Estimating ground-level concentration patterns from isolated air-pollution sources: A brief summary. *Environmental Research* 25:126–38.

Gittelsohn, A.M. 1982. On the distribution of underlying causes of death. *American Journal of Public Health* 72:133–40.

Gloeckler Ries, L.A., Hankey, B.F., and Edwards, B.K., eds. 1990. *Cancer Statistics Review, 1973–1987*. Bethesda, Maryland: National Cancer Institute. NIH Publication No. 90–2789.

Green, L.W. and Anderson, C.L. 1982. *Community Health*. 4th ed. Saint Louis: C.V. Mosby.

Green, L.W., M.W. Kreuter, S.G. Deeds, and K.B. Partridge. 1980. *Health Education Planning: A Diagnostic Approach*. Palo Alto, California: Mayfield.

Griffith, J., R.C. Duncan, W.B. Riggan, and A.C. Pellom. 1989. Cancer mortality in U.S. counties with hazardous waste sites and ground water pollution. *Arch. Environ. Health* 44:69–74.

The Hammond Almanac. 1983. Maplewood, N.J.: Hammond Almanac, Inc.

Hayes, W.J. 1975. *Toxicology of Pesticides*. Baltimore: Williams and Wilkins.

Health System Agency of New York City, 1980. *Environmental and Occupational*

Health Hazards Primary Care Guide. New York: Health Systems Agency.

Hook, E.B. 1981. Human teratogenic and mutagenic markers in monitoring around point sources of pollution. *Environmental Research* 25:178–203.

Howard, R. 1981. One man scoops the experts. *In These Times*, 18–31 March.

Hunter, D. 1978. *The Diseases of Occupations*. 6th ed. London: Hodder and Stoughton.

Infante, P.F. and M.S. Legator. 1980. *Proceedings of a Workshop for Assessing Reproductive Hazards in the Workplace*. Washington, D.C.: Department of Health and Human Services.

Janerich, D.T., A.D. Stark, P. Greenwald, W.S. Burnitt, H.I. Jacobson and J. McCusker. 1981. Increased leukemia, lymphoma and spontaneous abortion in western New York following a flood disaster. *Public Health Report* 96:350–56.

Juchau, M.R. 1981. *The Biochemical Basis of Chemical Teratogens*. New York: Elsevier/North Holland.

Kallen, B. and J. Winberg. 1979. Dealing with suspicions of malformation frequency increase. *Acta Paediatrica Scandinavica* Supplement 275:66–74.

Karstadt, M. and R. Bobal. 1982. Availability of epidemiologic data on humans exposed to animal carcinogens. Chemical uses and production volume. *Teratogenesis, Carcinogenesis and Mutagenesis* 2(2):151–68.

Karstadt, M., R. Bobal, and I.J. Selikoff, 1981. A survey of availability of epidemiological data on humans exposed to animal carcinogens. In *Quantification of Occupational Cancer*, ed. R. Peto and M. Schneiderman, Banbury Report 9:223–42. Cold Spring Harbor, New York: Cold Spring Harbor Laboratory.

Key, Marcus, et al. 1977. *Occupational Diseases: A Guide to Their Recognition*, rev. ed. Washington, D.C.: U.S. Department of Health, Education and Welfare. HEW (NIOSH) publication 77–181

Landrigan, P.J. and E.L. Baker, 1981. Exposure of children to heavy metals from smelters: Epidemiology and toxic consequences. *Environmental Research* 25:204–24.

Landrigan, P.J., K.R. Wilcox, J. Silva, H.E.B. Humphrey, C. Kauffman, and C.W. Heath. 1979. Cohort study of Michigan residents exposed to polybrominated biphenyls: Epidemiologic and immunological findings. *Annals of the New York Academy of Sciences* 320:284–94.

Lebowitz, M.D. 1981. Respiratory indicators. *Environmental Research* 25:225–35.

Legator, M.S. 1979. Chronology of studies regarding toxicity of 1-2-dibromo-3-chloropropane. *Annals of the New York Academy of Sciences* 329:331–38.

Levine, A. 1982. *Love Canal: Science, Politics and People*. Lexington, Mass.: Lexington Books.

Levy, G. 1981. Pharmacokinetics of fetal and neonatal exposure to drugs. *Obstetrics and Gynecology* 58:9–16.

Lippman, M. and R.B. Schlesinger. 1979. *Chemical Contamination in the Human Environment*. New York: Oxford University Press.

Longo, L.D. 1980. Environmental pollution and pregnancy: Risks and uncertainties for the fetus and infant. *American Journal of Obstetrics and Gynecology* 137:162–73.

Lowe, C.U. 1974. From the embryo through adolescence: Special susceptibility and exposure. *Pediatrics* 53:779–81.

Lyon, J.L., M.R. Klauber, W. Graff, and G. Chiu. 1981. Cancer clustering around point sources of pollution: Assessment by a case-control methodology. *Environmental Research* 25:29–34.

Mackarness, R. 1980. *Chemical Victims*. London: Pan Books.

Mason, T.J., J.F. Fraumeni, R. Hoover, and W.J. Blot. 1981. *An Atlas of Mortality from Selected Diseases*. DHEW publication (NIH) 81–2397. Washington, D.C.: U.S. Department of Health, Education, and Welfare: National Cancer Institute, Division of Cancer Cause and Prevention.

Mason, T.J., F.W. McKay, R. Hoover, W.J. Blot, and J.F. Fraumeni. 1975a. *Atlas of Cancer Mortality Among U.S. Nonwhites: 1950–1969*. DHEW publication (NIH) 76–1204. Washington, D.C.: U.S. Department of Health, Education and Welfare.

―――. 1975b. *Atlas of Cancer Mortality for U.S. Counties, 1950–1969*. DHEW publication (NIH) 75–780. Washington, D.C.: U.S. Department of Health, Education and Welfare.

Matanoski, G.M., E. Landau, J. Tonascia, C. Lazar, E.A. Elliott, W. McEnroe, and K. King. 1981. Cancer mortality in an industrial area of Baltimore. *Environmental Research* 25:8–28.

Melton, L.J., D.D. Brian and R.L. Williams. 1980. Urban-rural differential in breast cancer incidence and mortality in Olmsted County, Minnesota, 1935–1974. *International Journal of Epidemiology* 9:155–58.

Meyer, M.B. and J. Tonascia. 1981. Long term effects of prenatal X-ray of human females. 2. Growth and development. *American Journal of Epidemiology* 114:317–26.

Miller, R.W. 1978. The discovery of human teratogens, carcinogens and mutagens: Lessons for the future. In *Chemical Mutagens: Principles and Methods for Their Detection*, vol. 5, ed. A. Hollaender and F. DeSerres. New York: Plenum Press.

National Research Council. 1979. *Biologic Markers in Reproductive Toxicology*. Washington, D.C: National Academy Press.

National Research Council, Committee on Environmental Epidemiology. 1991. *Environmental Epidemiology, Volume 1: Public Health and Hazardous Wastes*. Washington, D.C.: National Academy Press.

National Commission of Community Health Services. 1966. Health Is a Community Affair. Cambridge: Harvard University Press.

Needleman, H.L., A. Schell, D. Bellinger, A. Leviton, and E.N. Allred. 1990. The long-term effects of exposure to low doses of lead in childhood; an 11-year follow-up report. *New England J. Med.* 322:83–88.

Neutra, Raymond Richard. 1990. Reviews and commentary: Counterpoint from a cluster buster. *American Journal of Epidemiology* 132:1–8.

New York Academy of Sciences. 1977. *Cancer and the Worker* (booklet). New York: New York Academy of Sciences (2 East 63rd Street, New York, New York 10021).

Oakley, G.T., Jr. 1975. The use of human abortuses in the search for teratogens. In *Methods for Detection of Environmental Agents That Produce Congenital Defects*, ed. T.H. Shepard, J.R. Miller, and M. Marois, pp. 189–96. New York: American Elsevier.

Ozonoff, David and Leslie I. Boden. 1987. Truth and consequences: Health agency responses to environmental health problems. *Science, Technology and Human Values* 12:70–77.

Paigen, B. 1982. Controversy at Love Canal. *Hastings Center Report*, June, p. 29.

Peters, J.M., S. Preston-Martin, and M.C. Yu. 1981. Brain tumors in children and occupational exposure of parents. *Science* 213:235–38.

Petitti, D.B., G.D. Friedman, and W. Kahn. 1981. Accuracy of information on smoking habits provided on self-administered research questionnaires. *American Journal of Public Health* 71:308–11.

Pickle, L.W., Mason, T.J., N. Howard, R. Hoover, and J.F. Fraumeni. 1987. *Atlas of U.S. Cancer Mortality Among Whites: 1950–1980.* DHHS publication (NIH) 87–2900. Washington, D.C.: U.S. Department of Health and Human Services.

Pless, J.B. and J.R. Miller. 1979. Apparent validity of alternative survey methods. *Journal of Community Health* 5:22–27.

Plunkett, E.R. 1977. *Occupational Diseases: A Syllabus of Signs and Symptoms.* Stamford, Conn.: Barret Book Company.

Proctor, N.H., J.P. Hughes, and M.L. Fischman. 1988. *Chemical Hazards of the Workplace.* 2nd ed. Philadelphia: J.B. Lippincott Company.

Quay, R. and P. Bowman. 1982. *A Toxic Waste Handbook.* Galveston: Galveston County Toxic Waste Task Force.

Rea, W.J., D.W. Peters, R.E. Smiley, R. Edgar, M. Greenberg, and E. Fenyves. 1981. Recurrent environmentally-triggered thrombophlebitis: A five-year follow-up. *Annals of Allergy* 47:338–44.

Rinkus, S.J. and M.S. Legator. 1980. The need for both in vitro and in vivo systems in mutagenicity screening. In *Chemical Mutagens*, ed. F.J. DeSerres and A. Hollaender, 6:365–473. New York: Plenum.

Roberts, D.W. 1982. Tissue burden of toxic pollutants. *Journal of the American Medical Association* 247:2142.

Roberts, H. 1979. *Community Development: Learning in Action.* Toronto: University of Toronto Press.

Rothman, Kenneth. 1990. Keynote presentation: A sobering start for the cluster busters' conference. *American Journal of Epidemiology* 132:S6–S13.

Segal, Edward et al. 1980. *The Toxic Substances Dilemma: A Plan for Citizen Action.* Washington, D.C.: National Wildlife Federation.

Shephard, Roy J. 1982. *The Risks of Passive Smoking.* New York: Oxford University Press.

Siemiatycki, J. 1970. A comparison of mail, telephone, and home interview strategies for household health surveys. *American Journal of Public Health* 69:238–44.

Sierra Club. 1981. *Training Materials on Toxic Substances: Tools for Effective Action, books 1 and 2.* 2d ed. San Francisco: Sierra Club.

Sittig, M. 1980. *Priority Toxic Pollutants: Health Impacts and Allowable Limits.* Park Ridge, New Jersey: Noyes Data Corporation.

———. 1981. *Handbook of Toxic and Hazardous Chemicals.* Park Ridge, New Jersey: Noyes Publications.

Smolensky, J. 1977. *Principles of Community Health, 4th ed.* Philadelphia: W.B. Saunders.

Speth, G. 1980a. *Environmental Quality.* 1980. Washington, D.C. Council on Environmental Quality.

————. 1980b. *Toxic Chemicals and Public Protection*. Washington, D.C.: Toxic Substances Strategy Committee.

Stebbings, J.H. 1981. Epidemiology, public health and health surveillance around point sources of pollution. *Environmental Research* 25:1–7.

Stebbings, J.H. and G.L. Voelz. 1981. Morbidity and mortality in Los Alamos County, New Mexico. 1. Methodological issues and preliminary results. *Environmental Research* 25:86–105.

Stinnett, S.S., P.A. Buffler, and C.W. Eifler. 1981. A case-control method for assessing environmental risks from multiple industrial point sources. *Environmental Research* 25:62–74.

The susceptibility of the fetus and child to chemical pollutants. 1974. Proceedings of a meeting held in June 1973. *Pediatrics* 53, no. 5, part 2.

Suzuki, K. 1980. Special vulnerabilities of the developing nervous system to toxic substances. In *Experimental and Clinical Neurotoxicology*, ed. P.S. Spencer and H.H. Schaumburg. Baltimore: Williams and Wilkins.

Tokuhata, G.K. and M.W. Smith. 1981. History of health studies around nuclear facilities: A methodological consideration. *Environmental Research* 25:75–85.

Trieff, N.M., ed. 1980. *Handbook of Toxic and Hazardous Chemicals*. Ann Arbor, Michigan: Ann Arbor Science Publishers.

United Auto Workers. 1981. *The Case of the Workplace Killers: A Manual for Cancer Detectives on the Job*. Detroit: United Auto Workers.

U.S. Department of Health and Human Services. 1982. *The Health Consequences of Smoking—Cancer: A Report of the Surgeon General*. Washington, D.C.: U.S. Government Printing Office, Publ. no. DHHS (PHS) 82–50179.

————. 1975. *Basic Concepts of Environmental Health* (booklet). Washington, D.C.: National Institute of Environmental Health Sciences, HEW publication (NIH) 77–1254.

————. 1977. *Experiments in Interviewing Techniques*. NCHSR Research Report Series. Washington, D.C.: National Center for Health Services Re search, HEW publication (HRA) 78–3204.

U.S. Department of Labor and Occupational Safety and Health Administration. 1979. *Lost in the Workplace: Is There an Occupational Disease Epidemic?* Washington, D.C.: U.S. Government Printing Office.

U.S. Environmental Protection Agency. 1990. *Toxics in the Community: National and Local Perspectives*. Washington, D.C.: Government Printing Office.

A.C. Upton, T. Kneip, and P. Toniolo. 1989. Public health aspects of toxic chemical disposal sites. *Annual Review Public Health* 10:1–25.

Vainio, H., M. Sorsa, and K. Hemminki, eds. 1981. *Occupational Cancer and Carcinogenesis*. Washington, D.C.: Hemisphere.

Waldbott, G.L. 1978. *Health Effects of Environmental Pollutants*. 2d ed. Saint Louis: C.V. Mosby Company.

We're Tired of Being Guinea Pigs! A Handbook for Citizens on Environmental Health in Appalachia. 1980. New Market, Tenn.: Highlander Research and Education Center.

Wiese, W.H. 1981. Birth Defects in Areas of Uranium Mining. Paper presented at International Conference on Radiation Hazards in Mining. Colorado School of Mines, Golden, Colorado.

Wolff, M.S., H.A. Anderson, and I.J. Selikoff. 1982. Human tissue burdens of halogenated aromatic chemicals in Michigan. *Journal of the American Medical Association* 247:2112–16.

Wynn, M. and A. Wynn. 1981. Historical associations of congenital malformations. *International Journal of Environmental Studies* 17:7–12.

Zdenek, R. 1983. *Management Essentials for Community-based Development Organizations, Neighborhood Ideas*. Vol. 7, no. 9. Washington, D.C.: Civic Action Institute.

INDEX